The
French Revolution
and
the Poor

The
French Revolution
and
the Poor

ALAN FORREST

Basil Blackwell · Oxford

First published in 1981 by
Basil Blackwell Publisher
5 Alfred Street
Oxford OX1 4HB
England

British Library Cataloguing in Publication Data

Forrest, Alan, *b. 1945*
  The French Revolution and the poor.
  1.   France – Social policy   2.   Poor – France –
  History – 18th century
  3.   France – Politics and government – Revolution,
  1789–1799
  I.   Title
  362.5'0944   HN425

ISBN 0-631-10371-6

Printed in Great Britain at
The Camelot Press Ltd, Southampton

Contents

Acknowledgements

The completion of this book in its final form is due in no small measure to the kindness and assistance of a number of friends and colleagues. In its conception it owes much to the inspiration of both Richard Cobb, whose compassionate concern for the lot of *les petites gens* and healthy distrust of the workings of bureaucracies find a willing listener in the present writer, and Olwen Hufton, whose work on the poor of Ancien Regime France has been so influential in rekindling interest in the history of poverty and of charity. In the course of the research I have incurred further debts and obligations, not all of which can be acknowledged in a few brief lines. But I should like to record my thanks to Colin Jones of the University of Exeter for allowing me to make use of his unpublished work on Revolutionary charity and for sharing with me some of his vast expertise on assistance in Montpellier and the Department of the Hérault; to George Sussman for sending me his as yet unpublished articles on wetnursing and the care of children in the eighteenth century; and to Jean-Paul Bertaud of the University of Paris – I for his unstinting help in discussing matters of recruitment for the armies. Through the hospitality of Jonathan Dalby and his intimate knowledge of the archives of the Cantal, I discovered valuable materials on conscription in Aurillac. In Lyon – and a lot of the local evidence in this book is drawn from the great riches of the Department of the Rhône – I owe much to the kindness of Jean-Pierre Gutton of the University of Lyon–II and of the erstwhile archivist of the Rhône, René Lacour. Especially during whistle-stop sojourns in provincial towns, so much is due to the informality and flexibility of local archivists: besides Lyon, I now look back with particular pleasure to illicit late-night reading bouts in such unlikely spots as the *mairie* of Bourges and the Chamber of Commerce in La Rochelle. Here in England, research trips to the British Library over the years have been rendered enjoyable by the warm welcome extended to me while in London by Geraint and Janice Thomas. Finally, I should like to acknowledge the research grants which I received from the British Academy, the Sir Ernest Cassel Educational Trust, and the University of Manchester, which made possible various segments of the research undertaken in the preparation of this book.

Manchester   *Alan Forrest*

Introduction

Revolutionary France set itself very high goals in the field of social policy, and it is by these goals that its record must be judged. If we are to believe the stated aims of its political leaders, the Revolution was aiming at nothing less than the eradication of poverty and the replacement of all private charity by an ambitious system of state welfare. From the outset the government took the bold initiative of establishing a *Comité de Mendicité* to investigate the incidence of deprivation and to suggest remedies that might usefully be adopted. The reports of that committee form one of the main sources for historians of the period, since they were carefully researched and made an honest attempt to quantify the problem. They also made a fundamental assumption that was to be shared by Revolutionary administrations at least until the fall of Robespierre in July 1794 – that any feasible solution to the problem would have to be provided by the state through national legislation and treasury finance. It is the purpose of this book to examine the measures adopted and to assess their impact on the lives of the poor and on the institutions which cared for them.

In part, of course, the Revolution had little choice but to accept a wider responsibility for the poor: the progressive loss of piety in the course of the previous century, the decline in alms-giving in parish churches, and the lack of donations and charitable legacies from the devout all conspired to make the traditional basis of clerical provision increasingly untenable.[1] Already in the last twenty or thirty years of the Ancien Regime, royal governments had found themselves drawn into an unaccustomed and unwelcome role, that of offering succour to local charities threatened with bankruptcy and extinction. Cissie Fairchilds, in her study of charity in Aix-en-Provence, stresses that from around 1760 the traditional, religiously-motivated private charity on which the poor had for so long been dependent had already crumbled into relative decay.

> In France the period from 1760 to 1789 marked the first hesitant steps toward the birth of a modern, secular, state-supported system of public assistance for the poor. The years of financial crisis had revealed the inadequacies of traditional charity, while the shift in mentalities connected with the spread of religious indifference had robbed the problem of poverty of its religious overtones.[2]

As a result Enlightened authors were already advocating strong state intervention, though royal administrations had never been prepared to undertake radical reforms or to accept that poor relief was a normal or proper function of the state. Besides, in the 1780s Louis XVI's governments were in desperate financial straits and were in no condition to assume any additional financial burdens. It was left to the Revolution to take up the mantle of the Enlightenment and to build on the fitful reforms already introduced by its predecessors.

By 1789 there could be no doubt that the existing system of charity had ceased to work even passably well and that the sufferings of the poor had reached intolerable levels. The nature and extent of these sufferings are briefly discussed in the first chapter, which is intended as an introductory conspectus of eighteenth-century poverty to acquaint the reader with the norm that prevailed before the outbreak of Revolution; for a fully-documented study of Ancien Regime poverty he must, however, turn elsewhere, to Olwen Hufton's excellent and sensitive work on *The poor of eighteenth-century France*. This introduction should give an impression of the scale of the problem which the eighteenth century faced, and indicate that, even without the eventuality of political revolution in 1789, some thorough and im- mediate reform of the status quo was imperative. It is not the intention of this book to add its voice to the raucous chorus of those Catholic historians of Revolutionary charity – of whom Lallemand is highly typical[3] – whose primary contention was that the problems of the 1790s resulted from interference by the impious Revolutionaries with the smooth working of the clerical system that had served Frenchmen well for generations. Change was urgent to alleviate existing hardship, and that urgency was only increased in the first months of the Revolution when feudal dues remained unpaid and such charitable giving as remained was killed off by the Civil Constitution of the Clergy. The real question is not whether reform was necessary but whether the specific solutions provided by Revolutionary legislation were either appropriate or effective, whether a nationally-imposed solution could hope to achieve success when poverty was, by its very nature, diffuse and regionalized. The legislators were much better informed of the extent and nature of poverty than their predecessors had been. They understood that there was no single problem of poverty, but rather problems of old age and sickness, of unemployment and industrial injury, of malnutrition and premature death. The poor were categorized, and their needs were dealt with in a torrent of laws and decrees. But how well did these work in practice? Were solutions that suited Paris equally ap- propriate in the Basses-Pyrénées or the Pas-de-Calais? To what extent did the poor reap any real benefit?

These are questions that demand an empirical answer, and the major part of this book attempts to provide such an answer. The time-scale selected, from 1789 through until Year VIII or Year IX, is deliberate, if somewhat arbitrary, in that by the end of that period the great experiments of the Revolutionary years were over and a return was being made to more traditional forms of relief and to traditional sources of finance. The stress on local examples and case-studies is equally deliberate, stemming partly, I suppose, from the fact that my outlook on the Revolution is that of the provincial, distrustful of Parisian panaceas, but mainly from a conviction that it is in the provinces that the real impact of legislation on people's lives must be judged. Paris lay on the politicians' doorstep, and in the sections and the Commune it enjoyed for a large part of the Revolution the means for making its particular in- terests and grievances heard by those in authority. It was very different in Marseille or in Mende, and if departments often exaggerated their deprivations in order to win the ear of the Convention or of the relevant committee, it is none the less in their submissions and in the minutes and correspondence of their hospitals and *bureaux de bienfaisance* that the effects of Revolutionary measures can best be measured. I therefore make no apology for reducing to the bare minimum the space devoted to the laws and decrees themselves, especially since the text of these reforms can be readily obtained elsewhere.[4] Rather, I have concentrated on local records and on reports from departments, both in the F15 series of the *Archives Nationales* and in the departmental and municipal archives of more than a dozen departments. Hospital records proved especially valuable in the case of Lyon, where the Archives of the Hôtel-Dieu have been preserved. And I have turned to numerous local studies of charity or of hospitals in particular towns and departments: often the local approach covers a long period back into the Ancien Regime and has enabled me to understand with greater clarity the context within which the Revolutionary legislators were operating.[5]

One final word of introduction is perhaps called for. The Revolution consistently decried the concept of charity, seeing the government's role as one of intervention to help those members of the community who were unable to stave off poverty by their own efforts. Social legislation and measures of *assistance* lie at the centre of any discussion of government action, the core of state policy towards the poor. But increasingly, as the Revolution progressed, there was another area of government policy which had the most immediate impact on the lives of the poor – the waging of a European war, with its concomitant levies and requisitions. Ordinary Frenchmen who were little affected by the bulk of political reform soon found themselves compelled to serve in the armies, to leave their wives and families, to renounce any hope of acquiring the smallholding that might guarantee their future security, to depend utterly on the government for pay, pensions, and livelihood. Whereas the political wrangles of the Girondins and Jacobins usually left the poor blissfully undisturbed, whereas even the Terror generally passed them by, the war and its constant demands did affect their lives intimately and often tragically. It is for that reason that the impact of the Revolution on the poor cannot reasonably be seen only in terms of welfare legislation, without some analysis of the effects of war on their everyday lives. By Year II the demands of war were being brought home to ordinary families throughout the *hexagone*, to the same sort of people as were the supposed beneficiaries of the government's social reforms. They constitute a fundamental part of the meaning of the Revolution for the several million Frenchmen either categorized as poor or living on the margin of eighteenth-century society.

Notes to the Introduction

1. M. Vovelle, *Piété baroque et déchristianisation: les attitudes devant la mort en Provence au dix-huitième siècle.*

2. C. C. Fairchilds, *Poverty and charity in Aix-en-Provence, 1640–1789*, p. 147.
3. L. Lallemand, *La Révolution et les pauvres.*
4. A. de Watteville, *Législation charitable de 1790 à 1863.*
5. For local studies consulted in the preparation of this book, see the relevant section of the Bibliography. Departmental archives consulted are those of the Bouches-du-Rhône (at Marseille), Cantal (Aurillac), Charente-Maritime (La Rochelle), Cher (Bourges), Haute-Garonne (Toulouse), Gironde (Bordeaux), Isère (Grenoble), Jura (Lons-le-Saunier), Loire (Saint-Etienne), Bas-Rhin (Strasbourg), Rhône (Lyon), Seine (Paris), Seine-Maritime (Rouen), and Haute-Vienne (Limoges).

Note on
the Revolutionary calendar

From about September 1793, as part of the process of dechristianization, the Revolutionary authorities stopped using the Gregorian calendar and replaced it with their own system. This continued in use until well into the Empire. The year was divided into twelve months of thirty days apiece; and the months in turn were divided into three *décades*.

The following concordance gives the equivalent dates in the Revolutionary and Gregorian systems for the Year II:

YEAR II

MONTH	GREGORIAN EQUIVALENT
Vendémiaire	22 September–21 October 1793
Brumaire	22 October–20 November 1793
Frimaire	21 November–20 December 1793
Nivôse	21 December 1793–19 January 1794
Pluviôse	20 January–18 February 1794
Ventôse	19 February–20 March 1794
Germinal	21 March–19 April 1794
Floréal	20 April–19 May 1794
Prairial	20 May–18 June 1794
Messidor	19 June–18 July 1794
Thermidor	19 July–17 August 1794
Fructidor	18 August–16 September 1794

As the year in the Revolutionary system had only three hundred and sixty days, the remaining five days were made up by the simple if rather clumsy expedient of using *jours complémentaires*. Thus, for instance:

20 July 1794   becomes 2 *thermidor* II

19 September 1794   becomes the *troisième jour complémentaire* of the Year II

1 The poor
of eighteenth-century
France

The French Revolution did not create the poor, though it is possible to argue that poverty was exacerbated by a number of its actions and political initiatives. Nor were the poor of the Revolutionary years noticeably very different from their predecessors in the eighteenth century, from the men and women who had suffered deprivation and malnutrition throughout the long years of the Ancien Regime: there is no new and strikingly different social phenomenon, the 'Revolutionary poor', that can be isolated after 1789. It is certainly probable that the lot of the more vulnerable members of society had been growing consistently more precarious in the second half of the century, as Ernest Labrousse has shown, and that price increases were outstripping wage rises while demographic pressures were forcing younger sons and poorer sharecroppers to renounce their ambitions to independent peasant status.[1] But the wider problem of poverty, both as it was experienced by the poor themselves and as it was viewed by the authorities, was one of very long standing. One of the great strengths of Jean-Pierre Gutton's excellent study of the Lyonnais, indeed, lies in precisely that dimension, the dimension of time, for he shows brilliantly the continuity in attitudes, in fears and aspirations, which underlies the whole question of poverty between the mid-sixteenth century and the eve of the Revolution.[2] However brave the intentions of the Revolutionaries may have been, they, too, had to cope with these deeply-entrenched viewpoints, with the traditions of the French countryside. Similarly, no histories of Revolutionary social policy can afford to overlook this longer perspective, and it is for this reason that I intend to start this study not by examining social philosophies or legislative programmes, but by focusing on the poor themselves and on the age-old problems that dominated their everyday existence.

Who were the poor on whom the Revolutionary authorities expended so much care and energy? In statistical terms, as the *Comité de Mendicité* of 1790–1 was to discover only too clearly, there is no easy answer to that question.[3] In part this stems from the lack of accurate statistics held by eighteenth-century governments, including – despite their enthusiasm for census returns – those of the Revolutionary years themselves. Neither local nor national government possessed the manpower or the administrative sophistication necessary to collate such statistics, and in any case work of that kind would have extended far beyond the limited range of activities expected of governments in the Ancien Regime. But in part, too, the vagueness of our information about the poor is a reflection of the imprecise nature of the poor themselves. In an age not equipped with twentieth-century bureaucracies or the guidelines suggested by such as Beveridge or Rowntree, just how could one establish who was and who was not 'poor'? What possible yardstick could contemporaries – or, indeed, historians of the period – apply? Local priests, when asked the number of *pauvres* in their parish, could do little more than make an inspired guess, a guess that would vary markedly according to their own highly subjective concept of poverty. More mathematical, but hardly more accurate, is the rather arbitrary assumption that the capitation rolls can supply a definitive answer, since these assume a permanency and consistency of poverty which takes no account of the uncertainties of everyday life. And yet, as Olwen Hufton has demonstrated, it is precisely to such materials that historians are forced to turn for much of their information.[4] For the ordinary *pauvre* was, only too frequently, mute and apparently passive, accepting his fate with little recorded murmur, leaving none of the letters or memoirs which have allowed other groups in society to stamp their character and their aspirations on historical writings. He surfaced from obscurity only when he broke the law and fell foul of the authorities, or when, sick or broken, he entered the registers of the local hospital or *dépôt de mendicité*. As a consequence, it is always through the eyes of the authorities that we see him, the object of fear and revulsion, concern and the occasional twinge of compassion. Until the recent researches of Professor Hufton and others set out to rescue the poor from this unenviable lot, they were almost invariably presented not as persons in their own right but as the objects of charity and prosecution, the instruments and not the agents of eighteenth-century history.

Definitions of poverty that would satisfy the social scientist are therefore very difficult to apply with any degree of certainty to eighteenth-century France, with the result that the concept of poverty has to remain rather impressionistic. We simply do not know how many Frenchmen and their families could accurately be designated as 'poor' at any one moment, though we do know that the number oscillated fairly violently in accordance with the quality of the harvest and the severity of the winter months. The first systematic attempt to assign exact numbers of *indigents* to the different areas of the country was made by the *Comité de Mendicité* in its fifth report, though the failure of many areas to submit returns made any overall assessment difficult. Nevertheless, the conclusions which the Committee did reach were deeply shocking, suggesting that the rate of misery was as high as one in seven at Soissons, one in six at Montauban, and one in ten at Metz.[5] Even the president of the Committee, La Rochefoucault-Liancourt, was so surprised by these statistics that he was moved to discount them, arguing that local authorities had tended to exaggerate the size of the problem in order to goad the government into action. But more recent research would appear to give new credence to these much-maligned figures, and historians have challenged the eighteenth-century assumption that the poor were in any sense a class apart, isolated from the rest of society. The work of such scholars as Pierre de Saint-Jacob in Burgundy and Jean-Pierre Gutton in the Lyonnais makes it clear that poverty and helplessness could, at least temporarily, afflict a wide spectrum of the local population should good health and employment desert them: far from being a distinct class, the majority of the *indigents* in these regions were ordinary families from the area, well integrated into local society, who were temporarily down on their luck and compelled by the threat of starvation to turn to one of a number of expedients if they were to survive.[6] Olwen Hufton herself, in her earlier work on Bayeux, suggested that as many as one in five of the population was dependent on some form of outdoor relief in order to sustain themselves.[7] And my own work on Bordeaux has led me to believe that in periods of cyclical crisis, even in one of the most prosperous parts in Ancien Regime France, the extent of popular misery cannot have fallen very far short of this figure.[8] Indigence, we may conclude, was a threat that was at any time hanging over the heads of a substantial percentage of Frenchmen, in town and country alike.

In such a society fear was endemic, fear of losing one's independence and the capacity for survival, fear of being deprived of the means of earning even the basic minimum necessary to keep oneself and one's family alive. In practice, that meant the fear of losing one's job, since unemployment was in the majority of cases synonymous with destitution. Most people knew little of luxury or affluence, and even in times of full employment poverty was the norm, a sullen, unending struggle to feed and clothe their families. Unemployment, even of a seasonal or temporary nature, assumed the proportions of a major disaster, tipping the delicately-maintained balance between poverty, which was accepted as unavoidable, and grinding hardship. Contemporaries seem to have been agreed that, in an age before any form of unemployment benefit was ever contemplated, those in work had little to fear; what haunted many of them was the constant spectre of joblessness, of weeks or perhaps months in which the family would receive little or no income or other means of support. In Lyon, one eighteenth-century commentator phrased it with brutal frankness: for the artisan or rural worker, 'il faut qu'il travaille ou qu'il mendie.'[9] What made so many Frenchmen vulnerable in the century before the Revolution was the fact that they could so easily lose the security that a steady job alone could provide. In the countryside, the winter months when there was little demand for farm labour brought a bitter fall in income. And townsmen were no more secure. In many cases the employment pattern of French towns was too inflexible, with a large part of the workforce being dependent on a single industry, whether silk in Lyon or milling in Toulouse, and recessions in these trades could occasion widespread misery.[10] The distinction between town and country was in any case much less crisply drawn than it is today, since many townsmen still lived essentially agricultural lives and urban suburbs, sparse and unplanned, merged incoherently into the hamlets of their hinterland. The relationship between Paris and its countryside has been sensitively investigated by Richard Cobb in one of his books;[11] and similar links could be identified for all France's major cities in the eighteenth century. Urbanization was still in its early stages, and even in cities like Lyon and Bordeaux many families were still dependent on primary production to maintain themselves. In Lyon, for instance, suburbs like Vaise, La Guillotière, Les Brotteaux and the more farflung reaches of the Croix-Rousse were largely given over to small holders, market-gardeners, and carters who took their produce to the city markets. Such men could not but share the vulnerability of other agricultural producers, of the peasants who worked the fields in the villages beyond, in the Lyonnais and the Bresse.

That vulnerability was only increased by the vicissitudes of French climate, which could easily destroy the painstaking efforts of the peasant or agricultural worker in a few savage hours. As François Lebrun has pointed out in his work on rural mentalities in Anjou, the weather could be quite tyrannical in its effects: the peasant wanted plentiful rain in spring and early summer followed by warm sunshine for the harvest and the *vendanges*. A very dry year, like 1719 or 1785, would wipe out the linen crop, which was vital to the survival of many families in the area, whereas late frosts, rightly dreaded by the farming community, attacked the wheat.[12] Frost in winter they had learned to cope with satisfactorily; it was any abnormality in the distribution of the seasons that was wont to bring disaster throughout the locality. Rainy winters, for instance, often resulted in diseased, swollen crops which brought a serious risk of illness and even death to those who ate them; *seigle ergoté* was regarded with an almost superstitious fear in places like the Sologne.[13] The weather could, of course, have even more dramatic effects on a population that was always at its mercy. Lightning could strike with little warning in those intense electric storms so characteristic of the Auvergne and the Midi. At Saint-Martin-de-la-Place in Anjou in 1782, for instance, forks of lightning killed six peasants in a single field.[14] Flooding, too, was commonplace, and we have regular reports of drowning accidents in the swollen streams and rivers on which the people were dependent for transport and for fishing alike. Pont-de-Montvert is a typical riverside commune that was never safe from the danger of floods when the fierce-flowing Tarn burst its banks, as it did, for instance, one August night in 1697. A contemporary diarist, Antoine Velay, recorded the scene for posterity:

> At two in the morning, after it had rained all day, there was such lightning and rain that all the mills of the Pont were carried away, together with six or seven houses, without leaving anything behind.[15]

The serious repercussions of freak weather conditions were beginning to be understood by eighteenth-century governments, and it is no accident that such limited sums of money as were voted by central government for the relief of poverty before the Revolution were often channelled to areas hit by exceptional storms or flooding.[16]

If climatic conditions frequently threatened the people of Ancien Regime France with penury and destitution, so did natural disasters of other kinds. In an age before the introduction of modern crop rotations or the widespread use of fertilizer or drainage techniques – and an appreciation of the primitive state of much of French farming can be readily gleaned from a glance at Arthur Young's description of such areas as the Loire, the Limousin and the Dordogne[17] – the ordinary peasant, scraping a meagre subsistence from the land, could not afford crop failure, and yet that was a regular eventuality. Of course, the various feudal exactions and royal taxes were widely hated throughout the French countryside, and it is true that after 1750 enclosures were driving more and more people off the land or forcing them to sacrifice their independence and become landless labourers. But if there was one fear that haunted the eighteenth-century countryside as that of plague had haunted it in the fourteenth, it was fear of disease and crop failure. The decade before the French Revolution is notable for a number of severe outbreaks of disease which ruined many of the smaller farmers and ended their fragile dreams of self-sufficiency. In many parts of the Midi, for instance, phylloxera ravaged the vineyards, an event that had every bit as serious an impact on the domestic economy of the area as the failure of the wheat crop would have had farther north. Or again, the widespread incidence of foot-and-mouth disease in 1785 caused almost universal disaster in pastoral regions of the country. In Burgundy, like many other parts of the country, the peasants were quite unable to cope with the *épizootie* because of the lack of fodder: the disease spread rapidly from stall to stall, and after one of the most miserable winters on record the local people were reduced to scouring the commons and woodlands for grasses, herbs, twigs and tree-branches to provide clean bedding for their animals. Many, threatened with bankruptcy, had to sell their beasts rather than watch them die, and of course prices at markets in that alarmist winter were miserably low, like the two sous per pound charged for meat at Saulieu.[18] Burgundy was in no way exceptional, and reports from all over France stressed the degree of human suffering that had been caused, especially since, by a cruel irony, grain prices were also low that winter. But the poor of rural France accepted such misfortunes as they accepted indigence itself, as one of the unavoidable facts of everyday life. Hunger was an ever-present reality, which goes far to explain what Poitrineau has called 'l'obsession de la faim' among the population of the countryside.[19] And aid, whether from the king or from the local *parlement*, from the *intendant* or from the product of local charity, was neither adequate nor assured. In the majority of cases the poor had to struggle on without any form of outside assistance.

The devastation caused by such acts of God as fires and floods, disease and harvest failures, was all the greater in that the health of the population was poor and medical care grossly inadequate. The diet of the mass of the people was both meagre and lacking in the nutrients necessary for adequate sustenance, especially since most of the poorer members of society were engaged in long hours of hard manual labour, whether in the fields or in the workshops, docks and markets of the cities. The normal peasant diet can be briefly summarized, consisting primarily of cereals, usually in the form of bread, though often supplemented by various forms of gruel. The basic hot dish of the day was *la soupe*, of which, once again, bread was the staple component, with the result that bread was the basis of every single meal the peasant consumed. It was, of course, variously supplemented, by milk products, by some fruit and vegetables, sometimes by fish, which supplied the bulk of the protein since meat was very rare indeed. Wine or cider would accompany some meals, but even in wine-producing areas the crop was for sale and not primarily for the local people.[20] Beans formed an important element in the diet of many Frenchmen, especially when grain was in short supply; and in large areas of the Auvergne, the very poor had to forsake bread in favour of the cheaper and much-despised chestnuts for a sizeable part of the year.[21] But it is interesting to note that the poor, even when faced by the prospect of starvation, were very conservative in their tastes, and reluctant to contemplate innovation. Attempts by the government and by agricultural improvers to replace grain crops by rice in years of dearth failed to attract the support of the ordinary people, who, even in moments of acute misery, still regarded rice as the source of contagion and disease. In the Auvergne, for instance, the introduction of rice in famine years was greeted with popular anger and outbreaks of rioting.[22] And it is interesting that attempts in the Revolutionary period to alter the traditional tastes of the people by importing rice during periods of shortage were similarly doomed to failure.[23] In matters of food, as in so many other areas, the French people remained deeply inured to accepted ways, and any attempt to disturb these ways was met with suspicion and unrest.

Diet was not, however, the only reason for the poor health and high mortality rate suffered by the poor of eighteenth-century France. For disease was rife, in town and country alike, thanks largely to the indifference of the public authorities in matters of hygiene and sanitation. There were few regulations governing public health, and the people themselves were often lamentably ignorant of even the simplest precautions that could help limit the spread of disease. Piles of offal and pails of animal blood, frequently swarming with flies in hot weather, helped identify butchers' shops; sewers were generally open to the elements; graveyards, fetid with the heavy smell of semi-decomposed flesh, were often placed in the middle of villages and were a major source of epidemics. As Gérard Bouchard has shown in his study of the little village of Sennely-en-Sologne, people seldom died from malnutrition and cold alone, but their constitutions became so weakened as a result that they were vulnerable to every disease and epidemic in the region. The cramped, filthy conditions in which the population lived helped compound the severity of outbreaks. Epidemics of smallpox and pleurisy were major killers in the eighteenth century, as were venereal diseases. But most serious of all in villages like Sennely were violent seasonal outbreaks of fever that attacked a large part of the community: the fevers of 1709, among the most tragic of the century, killed as many as one quarter of the population of the surrounding hamlets.[24] Typhus ravaged parts of inland Brittany throughout the eighteenth century, malaria was deadly in large stretches of the Mediterranean littoral, and throughout France infested lakes, swampy marshes and rivers in spate helped spread various forms of enteric fever.[25] As medicine was still fairly primitive, doctors were seldom able to do much to stem such outbreaks: too often diagnosis was faulty, and many doctors believed that all they could be expected to do was to allow nature to take her course, aided by regular bleedings and *purgations* – among the few treatments on which contemporary medical opinion seems to have been united.[26] Not surprisingly, the degree of faith which ordinary people retained in medical opinion was very low, and doctors were regarded by many with an undisguised sense of fear and foreboding. Hospitals, especially in country districts, were seen less as places where one could be cured than as *mouroirs* where people were taken to die. Traditional superstitions lingered on, so that in many parts of the country almanacs enjoyed a wide circulation, spiritual cures were eagerly embraced, and travelling quacks were given more credence than the village doctor.[27] These super-stitions, among people permanently faced with the imminence and enormity of death, were a sign of the fatalistic sense of helplessness and an essential part of the culture of poverty and deprivation.

Theirs was a culture born of the shared experience of fear, of living on that delicate knife-edge between ordinary poverty and actual destitution. It was a closely-knit society where kinship ties were strong and where the extended family was the first and most natural source of aid when hardship struck. Often, however, one's relatives were as poor as oneself, since wide neighbourhoods would be affected by the same bad harvest or the same hailstorms, and then the desperate family would have to look elsewhere for aid. But at least the village community provided affection and reassurance; there was a permanence and stability about rural society which was further cemented by a long history of common misery and deprivation. It provided a certain moral comfort, a comfort that was notably absent in the dark, lonely garrets of the towns where the urban poor were so often herded, separated from their friends and their families and condemned to face the hardships of everyday life in a strange, hostile environment.[28] The village community may have done something to alleviate the worst effects of grinding poverty, but we should not delude ourselves into believing that it could ever do more. Rural slums were as grim as urban tenements; rural malnutrition could lead to sickness and death as quickly as that incurred in Paris or Lyon.

The death rate, indeed, remained consistently high throughout the eighteenth century, with the weakest and the least resilient to disease the most prone to die off. Able-bodies adults generally survived, except in the most serious epidemics, whereas the very young and the very old were most at risk. In an area like the Sologne, where poverty was ubiquitous, juvenile mortality was especially prevalent. One third of children regularly died in the course of their first year of life; in the commune of Saint-Laurent-des-Eaux, for instance, Bouchard finds that a further 22 per cent died between the ages of one and four, and that if 67.4 per cent of newborn babies were still alive a year later, only 30.6 per cent could expect to reach the age of twenty. Nor did these figures show any signs of improvement in the course of the century. In Sennely, whereas in 1680 53 per cent of the population survived to the age of twenty, by 1779 the percentage reaching adulthood had fallen to 38 per cent.[29] Indeed, a tragic index of the extent of poverty in rural France on the eve of the Revolution is the large number of newborn babies exposed on birth, either because they were illegitimate and unwanted or (more commonly) because their parents simply could not afford to feed and clothe them. Abandonment, in spite of the heartbreak and the sheer risks involved – for if the child were to die the courts could still impose a death sentence – was seen by many people in sternly economic terms, as one of the few practical expedients which they could reasonably take if the rest of the family were to survive. For desperate parents, faced with the unwelcome prospect of an additional mouth to feed, the available alternatives were tragically few. Child-murder was far from being uncommon.[30] Some groups among the poor were even under considerable pressure to get rid of babies lest they become an embarrassment or lead to the loss of their jobs. Domestic servants, for instance, were often dismissed as soon as they became pregnant, which in practice condemned them to a life of penury or to prostitution. As a result, many girls in service felt constrained to conceal their pregnancy for as long as they could, and either to abandon their children at birth or to seek the dangerous aid of the backstreet abortionist.[31]

Short of abandoning his children or passively accepting the inevitability of an early death through chronic malnutrition (invariably and somewhat euphemistically described by contemporary medical reports as 'natural causes'), what exactly could the ordinary Frenchman do in order to stay alive? The expedients available were severely limited, and there were many who failed – young men and women, prematurely aged by the hardships they had endured, who were found dead by neighbours, curled up in roadside ditches or huddling desperately to keep warm in unheated Paris attics. For the rest, the only hope of survival lay in a series of makeshifts, makeshifts which, as Olwen Hufton has felicitously phrased it, formed the very basis of the economy of the poor.[32] If relatives were unable to help, it was unlikely that the state or local charity would be prepared to assume the burden, except in clearly-delineated instances. The very old and sick might be taken into the local *hôpital général* or *hôtel-dieu* if they could prove that they were unable to look after themselves and if they did not have children or other close relatives in the area who could care for them. Those who took to begging or petty crime might also be institutionalized, though it is clear from both the decrees of royal government and the registers of the prisons and *dépôts de mendicité* that the primary intention of the authorities was almost always punitive rather than charitable. Some limited assistance was distributed to the poorest families of the parish by the local *curé*; but again in those areas of the country where need was greatest the product of almsgiving on a Sunday was likely to be sadly inadequate and, even in those instances where the priest supplemented this with a contribution from his own meagre stipend, only a small proportion of the very poor could ever hope to be helped in this way. In towns church assistance was even more scant.[33] Here, as elsewhere, the vast majority of the poor were thrown back on their own resources; the makeshifts had to be of their own making.

Since the nub of their problem was their inability to find work in their own villages, one of the most common responses of the able-bodied poor was to leave in search of employment elsewhere. In farming areas this tended to be a seasonal problem, confined to the months of relative inactivity between the completion of the harvest in September or October and the beginning of the following agricultural year. Migration, therefore, tended also to assume a strictly seasonal pattern, with peasants and rural labourers leaving their cottages and their families during the winter months in search of work elsewhere. Many sought agricultural work in other parts of France, extending the season by moving from harvest to harvest, from grain to flax or grapes, chestnuts or olives; the olive groves, for those fortunate enough to be within reach of the Mediterranean littoral, provided an especially welcome extension to the agricultural year.[34] From the Haute-Auvergne, an area notorious for the poverty of its soil and the harshness of the climate, men and youths would annually trek as far as Italy, Spain, or Portugal in search of manual labour of this kind. [35] Not all, of course, could hope to find employment in agriculture, and among the men of the mountain villages of regions like Savoy and the Massif certain specialisms were already clearly emerging by the middle of the eighteenth century: the Auvergne in particular was widely known as a source of sawyers and builders' labourers, masons and flax-combers, peddlars and second-hand clothes merchants.[36] Such migration, whether seasonal or, as it frequently became, *à temps*, was not without considerable economic importance in an age when French cities were growing rapidly and when manual labour in such industries as building was in high demand. It is no coincidence that in Paris, for instance, jobs in the construction trades should have attracted such an overwhelming preponderence of Creusois and Corréziens, or that, with the passage of time, their migration should have ceased to be purely temporary. But it also aided the economy of the villages they had left behind, villages where a high birth-rate and land hunger had driven men off the land, where the soil was too barren to support the entire population throughout the winter, and where the wages brought back by the men in springtime from their winter labours helped maintain the uncertain balance of the village economy throughout the rest of the year. Without the annual exodus from villages like Saint-Jean-d'Ollières, the extent of suffering in the poorer areas of the Massif would have been infinitely greater.

For those left behind, jobless and without resource, the outlook was much bleaker. And, of course, not everyone could leave: to make the long and arduous journey on foot from one harvest to another, or to the docks and markets of Paris or Bordeaux or Nantes, a man required to be fit and able-bodied, resilient and physically strong. The women and children, the crippled and sickly were compelled to remain at home, along with those men too old to make the journey or to find employment elsewhere. For them, when food and firewood finally ran out, probably in the early spring, there was little alternative to begging if they were to stay alive. Yet begging was unlikely to solve the problems of grinding poverty, especially in the poorer areas, where the number of beggars reached massive proportions and the number of comfortable, well-to-do farmers was correspondingly small.[37] In such cases simple pleading would rarely meet with a charitable response, and the beggar had to have recourse to more devious ploys. The temptations for the desperate were huge, especially if they were young, male and apparently able-bodied, the group least likely to win the compassion of the hard-headed countryman. For the aged, or for women surrounded by a large brood of children, crying piteously by the church door, alms would probably be made available. But others were less fortunate, and the reports of the *maréchaussée* are well stocked with evidence that beggars were not always the humble saintly individuals publicized in Catholic legend. Too often they discovered that human compassion alone would not salvage them from destitution, and they were wont to use threats and physical violence to extract food and money from unwilling householders. Children would be hired out to plaintive mothers in order to evoke unspontaneous sympathy. Wounds would be inflicted and carefully doctored to inspire fear of disease in horrified passers-by. And on dark evenings in the countryside beggars would form themselves into large bands to add extra muscle to their importunate demands. By the later eighteenth century, indeed, the authorities were very awake to the dangers posed by beggars and to the fact that many of them were indistinguishable from thieves and bandits. The *vagabond* was particularly hated throughout the French countryside — the beggar who had left his cottage and his locality behind and had taken to the roads, sleeping rough and wandering from hamlet to hamlet in search of food. Such people, mingling with the regular population of *errants*, those who, like travelling salesmen and *colporteurs*, entertainers and soldiers, were forced to spend long periods away from home on the road, were believed to be capable of all kinds of violence, and local rumour associated them with arson and kidnappings, rape and murder. Yet what was for the wealthy and the authorities a major source of violence and lawlessness, a veritable *fléau social*, was for the poor nothing more alarming than one of the few expedients available to them if they were to avoid starvation.

Poverty, quite clearly, assumed a wide variety of different guises, ranging from the innocent child standing at the door of the village church begging for alms to the hardened criminal like Le Rouge d'Auneau or Le Beau-François of the Bande d'Orgères, which for so long continued to terrorize the exposed highways that criss-crossed the Orléanais and the Beauce.[38] Attitudes to poverty also varied widely. At one extreme was the age-old attitude of the church and of those liberals who were overcome by compassion and moved to insist that it was the duty of those with the necessary resources to come to their aid. At the other was the much harsher view, based on fear and repugnance, that the poor were poor because of their own short-comings, and that for the most part they were indistinguishable from thugs and thieves, pickpockets and prostitutes. As the eighteenth century progressed, it is striking that this second view was gaining more widespread credence, that public attitudes to the poor were hardening as fears of violence and attacks on property became more deeply engrained. The possessing classes were showing noticeably less tolerance towards men and women whom they associated with a seamy, rather degrading lifestyle, men and women who did not and could not share their own ethical code.[39] The French Revolution, which successfully challenged so many of the fundamental political assumptions of eighteenth-century life, showed commendable awareness of the problems posed by poverty and a considerable willingness to translate that awareness into practical social measures. But, equally importantly, it remained a fundamentally middle-class revolution, a revolution moulded and directed by men who shared many of the prejudices and predilections of the social groups to which they belonged. Revolutionary policy towards the poor and indigent could not but reflect the attitudes of the times, the outlook of the lawyers and business interests that were so prominent in every government from the National Assembly in 1789 to the overthrow of the Directory ten years later. The poor might be given civil liberties which they had never previously enjoyed; they might be equal before the law; they might even be granted the right to vote under the Constitution of 1793. But in practice their survival and welfare remained the concern of governments in which they had no representation and over which they could exert little influence. It is to the attitudes and philosophies of Revolutionary governments that we must therefore turn.

Notes to chapter 1

1. E. Labrousse, *La crise de l'économie française à la fin de l'Ancien Régime et au début de la Révolution*.
2. J.-P. Gutton, *La société et les pauvres – l'exemple de la généralité de Lyon, 1534–1789*.
3. C. Bloch and A. Tuetey (editors), *Procès-verbaux et rapports du Comité de Mendicité de la Constituante*.
4. O. Hufton, *The poor of eighteenth-century France, 1750–1789*. This study presents a splendid portrait of the French poor, based very largely on primary materials but also presenting a synthesis of much of the regional social history currently being written on the Ancien Regime in France, of such works as those of Saint-Jacob and Poitrineau, Gutton and Garden. It is a work notable for its sympathy and warmth, and no historian of poverty can fail to be deeply in its debt. The extent of that debt can be seen in this present chapter.
5. C. Bloch and A. Tuetey, *op. cit.*, *Cinquième Rapport du Comité de Mendicité*; A. Mathiez, 'Notes sur l'importance du prolétariat à la veille de la Révolution', pp. 504–5.
6. Modern eighteenth-century social studies are becoming more and more common in France: those specifically referred to here are among the most prominent, J.-P. Gutton, *op. cit.*, and P. de Saint-Jacob, *Les paysans de la Bourgogne du Nord au dernier siècle de l'Ancien Régime*.
7. O. Hufton, *Bayeux in the late eighteenth century*, chapter 5, especially pp. 85–6.
8. A. Forrest, *Society and politics in Revolutionary Bordeaux*, pp. 182–4.
9. Quoted by J.-P. Gutton, *op. cit.*, p. 9.
10. M. F. Buchalet, *L'assistance publique à Toulouse au dix-huitième siècle*, p. 17. Buchalet goes on to point out that the absence of any big industrial concentration other than flour-milling in the Toulouse area may have prevented still greater misery.
11. R. C. Cobb, *Paris and its provinces, 1792–1802*.
12. F. Lebrun, *Les hommes et la mort en Anjou aux dix-septième et dix-huitième siècles*, pp. 127–32.
13. G. Bouchard, *Le village immobile: Sennely-en-Sologne au dix-huitième siècle*, pp. 112–13.
14. F. Lebrun, *op. cit.*, p. 289.
15. P. Higonnet, *Pont-de-Montvert: social structure and politics in a French village, 1700–1914*, p. 1.
16. S. T. McCloy, *Government assistance in eighteenth-century France*, especially pp. 23–39.
17. A Young, *Travels in France*, part 1, pp. 16–39.
18. P. de Saint-Jacob, *op. cit.*, pp. 478–9.
19. A. Poitrineau, *La vie rurale en Basse-Auvergne au dix-huitième siècle*, 1, p. 92.
20. O. Hufton, *The Poor*, pp. 44–8; F. Lebrun, *op. cit.*, pp. 270–2.
21. P. Higonnet, *op. cit.*, p. 48.
22. J. Coiffier, *L'assistance publique dans la généralité de Riom au dix-huitième siècle*, p. 14.
23. A. Forrest, *op. cit.*, p. 194.
24. G. Bouchard, *op. cit.*, pp. 109–14.
25. O. Hufton, *The Poor*, pp. 65–6.
26. F. Lebrun, *op. cit.*, p. 281.

27. *ibid.*, pp. 403–6.
28. For a study of the lot of migrant workers in one of the expanding cities of eighteenth-century France, see my 'The condition of the poor in Revolutionary Bordeaux'.
29. Statistics are taken from G. Bouchard, *op. cit.*, pp. 75–6.
30. An excellent discussion of child-abandonment and child-murder in the French countryside is contained in O. Hufton, *op. cit.*, chapter 12.
31. A most illuminating piece on the *déclarations de grossesse* made by servant-girls in eighteenth-century Lyon, based on the city's police files, is Richard Cobb's essay 'A view on the street: seduction and pregnancy in Revolutionary Lyon', in R. C. Cobb, *A sense of place*, pp. 77–135.
32. O. Hufton, *The Poor*, pp. 69ff.
33. Works on charity and assistance of an institutional kind are quite common, many of them published around the 1890–1914 period, and all lay stress on the inadequacy of the funds available. Prominent among them are such works as C. Bloch, *L'assistance et l'Etat en France à la veille de la Révolution*; C. Paultre, *De la répression de la mendicité et du vagabondage en France sous l'Ancien Régime*; F. Buchalet, *L'assistance publique à Toulouse au dix-huitième siècle*; and H. Chotard, 'L'assistance publique en Auvergne au dix-huitième siecle', *Revue d'Auvergne* 15 (1898). There are many others, often well documented and heavily institutional in their approach to the question. More recently, note should be taken of the work of Y. Bézard on *L'assistance à Versailles sous l'Ancien Régime et pendant la Révolution*. This is not the place to give more than a brief mention to such works; but the chapters on hospitals, poorhouses, *ateliers de charité* and *Enfants Trouvés* in the Revolutionary years will make more substantial reference to them and to the standard of assistance that had been offered earlier in the eighteenth century.
34. On migration patterns, again, the principal source in English must be Olwen Hufton's study, *The Poor*, especially pp. 69–106.
35. A. Poitrineau, *Aspects de l'émigration temporaire et saisonnière en Auvergne à la fin du dix-huitième et au début du dix-neuvième siècle*, p. 15.
36. S. Delaspre, *L'émigration temporaire en Basse-Auvergne au dix-huitième siècle jusqu'à la veille de la Révolution*, especially pp. 26–39.
37. O. Hufton, *The Poor*, pp. 107–27.
38. R. C. Cobb, 'La Bande d'Orgères, 1790–1799', in *Reactions to the French Revolution*, pp. 181–211.
39. O. Hufton, *The Poor*, p. 355.

2 The Revolution and the idea of social obligation

Public attitudes to poverty and charity are deeply engrained and cannot be changed overnight. The Revolution in itself could do very little to alter the basic prejudices of the mass of the French population, and beggars and *vagabonds* remained objects of fear and hatred in rural areas very much as they had been during the previous century. The economic crisis of 1788 and 1789, the famine conditions that cruelly destroyed many peasants' livelihoods, the rash of bread riots in the spring months, and, above all, the terror inspired by rumour during the *Grande Peur* all served to ensure that the threat posed by the poor to those fortunate enough to remain above the bread line would not be overlooked. Popular panic, the prevalence of plot theories, the constant belief that someone – whether aristocrats in 1789 or hoarders five years later – was deliberately trying to starve the people and their families, the role of bakers and stallholders in the demonology of the popular classes, these are constant themes which marked the Revolutionary years as indelibly as they had the Ancien Regime. Outsiders continued to be viewed with the deepest suspicion, whether they were government recruiting-officers and requisition-inspectors or bands of starving peasants from the next department. Fear was present on all sides – fear of the people from the neighbouring village or from across the river, such as the peasants from the Forézien plain felt for the Auvergnats, the men of the mountains whom they depicted in a thousand tales as brutal marauders and arsonists;[1] and fear of people belonging to a different social grouping, the kind of fear which in 1789 persuaded the peasants of Vesoul in Franche-Comté that a simple accident in the course of a village celebration was the start of a deliberate campaign by the nobility to exterminate the Third Estate.[2] Of course it is easy to dismiss such fears with a certain scorn as being nothing more than the figments of a highly excitable popular imagination. Can anyone take seriously, for instance, the idea that the surgeons at the *Ecole de Médecine* in Lyon were kidnapping the children of the poor of the city in order to use them for experiments in vivisection? Yet this notion enjoyed wide credence in Lyon in 1768, where it caused an outburst of angry mob violence.[3] The fear of people 'qui ne sont pas des nôtres' was deeply rooted in the popular imagination and helped to form the social attitudes and prejudices that ran through much of eighteenth-century French society. At this level logic was of little value, for people could not be swayed by reasoned argument: these were fears that would survive, generally intact, the assaults of both the *philosophes* and Revolutionary government.

Similarly, the attitudes of authority, of the state, towards the question of poor relief were already well established before the end of the eighteenth century. As in other Catholic countries, the whole gamut of poor relief and charitable institutions was deemed to fall within the orbit of the church, with the political authorities playing a minimal role in times of disaster. As in Spain and Italy, the care of the poor and the sick was seen in traditional terms as a fundamental part of the role of the church in society, a role which had developed during the Middle Ages and which had been reasserted at the time of the Counter-Reformation.[4] It was, indeed, one of the principal ways in which the medieval church had helped to maintain the fabric of society, stressing the obligation on the rich to give alms to the needy, on the *seigneur* to make provision for the poor on his estates. Charity was thus presented to the devout Catholic in moral as well as in social terms: it was a Christian act that not only helped the recipient but also benefited the generous donor. The church laid great store by this message, pointing out that Christ Himself had not hesitated to humble Himself by washing the feet of the poor and implying that generosity to those in need was a necessary act of self-sacrifice for the Christian who hoped to save his immortal soul. As a result, in the seventeenth and eighteenth centuries charity in France must be seen predominantly in clerical terms.

As there was little formal bureaucracy controlling charitable giving and distribution, the church found itself throughout the Ancien Regime in charge of the everyday organization of relief. Most hospitals were clerical foundations, dating back to pious benefactions of a byegone age and still administered on strict Christian principles. Nursing would be undertaken by one of the great charitable orders like the *soeurs grises*, the administration would be provided by clergymen, while among the highest-paid and most respected figures in the hospital hierarchy would be the spiritual advisers, the almoners who supervised the moral needs of the patients and gave the last rites of the church to the dying.[5] Often, indeed, the very importance of a hospital was a reflection of the role of a former abbey or monastery in the life of the community: to take a single notable instance, it was largely because of a strong Benedictine presence at Aurillac that that town became a great hospital centre for the Auvergne in the seventeenth century.[6] Similarly with outdoor relief, the Catholic church played a predominant part right up until the outbreak of Revolution in 1789. Few communes retained independent funds for the purpose, and generally the main source of relief remained the parish poorbox, the alms of the pious that would be distributed by the priest to those of his flock who had fallen on hard times. As Timothy Tackett has recently demonstrated in his study of the role of the parish priest in the diocese of Gap, the priest was a local *notable* commanding respect and status in the community partly at least because of his control over such vital funds. He knew his parishioners and their family circumstances more intimately than anyone else in the village: he could offer an opinion on the genuineness of their need, and – just as importantly – on their churchgoing and moral standards; and, since promotion was notoriously slow for the eighteenth-century *curé*, he would often know several generations of the same family and be an expert judge of both their standing in the community and the acuteness of their suffering.[7] It was a position which gave him vast influence and power in times of shortage, famine, or family illness. By law he was a member of the governing board of the local *hospice*; and he was largely entrusted with the *greniers d'abondance* which lent the poor reserves of grain during periods of dearth.[8] It was he who advised the local doctor that one of his parishioners was in need of urgent treatment; it was he who recommended admission to hospital in many rural areas; it was he again who made vital decisions as to which of the poor were most worthy of alms and charity. The *bourse des pauvres*, the product of generations of small legacies, would be entrusted to his caring hands.[9] Monasteries and convents also played a prominent part in the distribution of aid, particularly in the highly pious west of France. In a clerical town like Angers, indeed, the church enjoyed a virtual monopoly as an agency of poor relief and charitable works; with its cathedral chapter, its five collegiate churches, its bishop's palace and diocesan administration, and with a number of large monastic foundations in the immediate hinterland, the citizens were dominated by the influence of religion in virtually every walk of life, and in times of dearth the church could be depended upon to come to their aid. Such towns presented an excellent, if highly flattering, shop window for clerical charity and for the cohesion of Ancien Regime society.[10]

But the majority of towns were not like Angers, and with the increasing movement of population in the course of the century and the rapid urbanization that ensued in a number of areas, the contradictions between the incidence of need and of clerical provision became more and more glaring. Already by the seventeenth century population pressure was placing severe strains on voluntary charity, which depended for its success on the retention of small, closely-knit parish communities where the *seigneur* and the richer farmers honoured their Christian responsibilities and where the priest was a sufficiently central figure in local life for him to be able to identify cases of genuine need. Of course there were many such villages still intact at the time of the Revolution, though even they were unable to deal effectively with local disasters like floods or plague or fire. Even in ordinary times such adequacy depended on a delicate balance between wealth and poverty, between generosity and suffering, which was becoming more and more illusory. There were, it is true, regions like the west where urbanization was still in its infancy, where village identity remained strong, and where the provision of legacies and monastic benefactions ensured that the church was still able to cope with the everyday problems of misery. But in much of rural France these conditions did not prevail. The sheer poverty of an area could undermine the effectiveness of voluntary giving. In the Lozère, for example, there were few men of wealth and substantial property who could support the rest of the community in times of suffering, for here the countryside was harsh and unyielding and the standard of living was depressed. Furthermore, it was not an area noted for its piety, and the physical presence of the church was not sufficiently strong to answer the everyday needs of a starving population.[11] More serious still in the eighteenth century was the challenge to Catholic charity posed by the effective dechristianization of large tracts of the country. Voluntarism could hope to provide a solution to the problem of popular misery only in a society where religious belief was deep-seated and where the more prosperous members of the community recognized charitable giving as an integral part of their Christian duty. Yet in the century before the Revolution large areas of the country were witnessing a serious loss of faith, foreshadowing, as Michel Vovelle has shown, the political action of the dechristianization of the Year II.[12] In Provence from around

1720 the old, traditional Christian gestures of the *banquet funèbre* and the legacy to the poor to salve the sins of souls departed had all but disappeared or had been stripped of any religious significance, and Vovelle demonstrates how this had the effect of decimating the sums left to local hospitals and *bureaux de bienfaisance*.[13] Religious observance and ritual were falling away, and with it died an age-old popular association of charity with religious devotion. The very rock on which Ancien Regime poor relief had been constructed was being inexorably chipped away by profound changes in popular culture and the slow decline of popular religious faith.

If the clerical base of charity was under attack in country areas, it was far more vulnerable in the towns and cities. The immigrant worker from the country was, as we have seen, especially liable to suffer short-term deprivation because of illness, injury, or unemployment, and cyclical depression hit hard when there was no vegetable patch to turn to for food. Besides, too many towns were highly dependent on a single industry or economic activity, and when that collapsed – as did silk in Lyon during the twelve years before 1789 – misery reached epidemic proportions. Often the hinterland of the town would also suffer, and artisans, small shopkeepers and workers in the service trades would share the poverty of the unemployed industrial workers. Such was the experience of Carcassonne, where the people were almost wholly dependent for their livelihood on the textile industry, a trade that was notoriously vulnerable to economic slump. In Carcassonne voluntarism predictably proved inadequate to the periodic task of feeding the unemployed, and the recurrent crises reduced large numbers of workers to begging or to the *dépôt de mendicité*.[14] For this the church cannot be freed from all responsibility, as it had visibly failed to keep pace with population movements in the century before the Revolution, preferring to concentrate its resources in areas where it was traditionally powerful and firmly ensconced. Large tracts of expanding cities like Paris and Lyon were cynically abandoned by the church authorities, whose presence in the new *faubourgs* that were thrown up to house the immigrant artisans and labourers was no more than nominal. In Bordeaux, for instance, where three city-centre parishes had fewer than two thousand inhabitants in 1790, the popular suburbs beyond the city walls enjoyed little pastoral care, as *curés* struggled desperately to cope with twenty thousand parishioners apiece: the census return for that year showed that 21,939 people were crammed into the parish of Sainte-Eulalie, 18,593 into Saint-Seurin, and 18,599 into Saint-Rémy, the sprawling quarter that contained many of the boatmen and waterworkers from the port.[15] Circumstances like these made adequate charitable provision quite unthinkable.

The inadequacies of clerical charity in times of crisis and the gross inequalities in its distribution were already leading the impious and the critical to question the church's role in social provision long before 1789. On the intellectual plane, the Enlightenment was producing a new rationalist breed of philosopher who was little inclined to believe that poor relief must necessarily be thirled to the institutional framework of Christianity, especially when Christianity could be seen to be failing in its charitable mission. In bad years of famine, like 1709 throughout much of the country or 1747–8 in Guyenne, that failure was palpable. Writers like Voltaire and

Helvétius were unsparing in their sarcastic attacks on the church, pointing to the cruelly ironic contrasts between the conspicuous wealth of the hierarchy and the miserable plight of the poor. Monks, in particular, were the helpless butt of much Enlightened scorn and were depicted as living lives of parasitic affluence when they were nominally devoted to good works and to a vow of poverty. Voltaire, having posed the rhetorical question of what possible justification a monk could offer for his existence, replied brutally that there was none, that he was as useless as he was unproductive, doing nothing 'except to bind himself by an inviolable oath to be a slave and a fool and to live at the expense of other people'.[16] What made such opinions so powerful was the fact that they were echoed by a wide segment of the ordinary people of France, as, indeed, was demonstrated conclusively in 1789 when the *cahiers de doléances* were finally drawn up. Monks and nuns were lambasted from all sides.[17] The shoemakers of Laval attacked monastic wealth, criticizing the monks – 'ces pieux fainéants' – for their laziness and ostentatious lifestyle, the finery of the abbots and the richness of their retinues. Mendicant orders were just as vitriolically abused, since many members of the Third Estate saw their importunate begging as worsening rather than alleviating the lot of those who were genuinely in need. The artisans of Pont-l'abbé, far from seeing monasteries as a valuable source of charitable aid, bitterly demanded that they be closed down and sold to help offset France's national debt. Such attitudes were formulated not by the Revolution but by years of suffering and personal experience of misery. In the eighteenth century they complemented the views of the *philosophes* and helped to create a new intellectual climate in which clerical control of charity was to be superseded.

The *philosophes* accepted as self-evident that man was at the centre of the universe and was the proper subject for discussion and compassion. The concept of *humanité* was, indeed, quite basic to Enlightened thinking, and it gave rise to a strong element of humanitarianism in the intellectual salons of the day. As Shelby McCloy has argued, the concept was so deeply rooted by the time of Turgot that it had come to assume something of the status of a moral absolute, a value by which all actions and motives must be judged.[18] The Encylopaedists wrote volubly on the idea of the perfectability of man; Helvétius, in *De l'Esprit*, argued that inequalities were not hereditary but were the result of environmental influences, which in turn could be resolved by education; d'Holbach, in his *Système de la Nature*, urged that men's morals would improve if only their physical environment were improved; and, in the most celebrated treatise on education produced in these years, *Emile*, Rousseau sought to show how a child could be educated into a full and uninhibited person without being subjected to the pressures and compulsions of the state. The ordinary people of France, illiterate and reduced to begging by some chance crop failure or hailstorm, were obvious subject-matter for Enlightened discussion, and provincial academies and reading-circles throughout France were treated to long, scholarly papers on the unhappy effects of the environment on the poor.[19] The idea that the evils of the fiscal structure lay at the root of poverty and vagrancy gained a new vogue, and in 1777 the *Académie* of Lyon – one of many to dwell on this theme – devoted its annual competition to the question of whether it was possible to solve the problem of mendicity and what means ought to be adopted.[20] This was a completely new, typically eighteenth-century way of approaching the problem, one that ran counter to the general tenor of the prevailing Catholic teaching. For just as the church taught the virtue of charitable giving, so it accepted the existence of the poor as 'the suffering children of Christ', as unfortunate men and women through whom the more affluent could gain salvation. By the eighteenth century this touching faith in voluntarism and the teachings of Saint Vincent-de-Paul was neither a sufficient remedy nor a satisfactory analysis. The people themselves, frightened by bands of hungry, desperate and importunate beggars, were less and less likely to live up to the church's prescription, while, at the same time, the authors of the Age of Enlightenment were casting serious doubts upon the philosophic validity of its diagnosis.

Perhaps the most telling attack on Catholic ideals of charity, however, centred on the inefficiency rather than the inadequacy of the alms distributed. With the increasing tendency of the Physiocrats and others to view charity as a purely economic activity rather than as one imbued with Christian significance and expectations of salvation, the practical effects of clerical alms-giving came to be more critically scrutinized. It was noted that Catholic charity tended to be indiscriminate, related less to need and suffering than to the duty and conscience of the donor, and the Physiocrats convinced themselves that too much money was being loosely distributed, without adequate controls, in the form of food and clothing. Enlightened authors, supported by the more raucous pamphleteers of the day, noted the increase in the incidence of begging, pointed to the swarms of *vagabonds* around generous centres of clerical charity like abbeys and monasteries, and rushed to the conclusion that the church must bear a large share of responsibility for swelling the numbers of parasites on respectable society.[21] Montesquieu and Voltaire were among the many writers who had hinted that the existing structure of clerical charity did the poor more harm than good; Voltaire, giving no quarter, pointed out that it was in countries like Spain and Italy, where traditional religious charities flourished most freely, that the most wretched poor in Europe were to be found.[22] And in the *Encyclopédie* Turgot claimed that the majority of traditional charities had an effect diametrically different from that intended by those who set them up, since they subsidized laziness, reduced the productive capacity of the country, and raised levels of taxation. In this way, Turgot argued, with that obsessive belief in the virtue of economic production which characterized Physiocratic writers, Christian charities failed in their most basic mission, since they increased the number of families forced to fall back on charity and thus indirectly worsened the sufferings of those already classed among the poor.[23]

From this growing compendium of doubt about the validity of voluntarism there emerged in the half-century before the Revolution the beginnings of a new approach to poverty and assistance. Whereas previously these matters had been adjudged the rightful province of the church and of acts of individual philanthropy, more and more it was felt that the state had a duty to intervene in the free workings of the economy. Again there was a certain dualism in this attitude, reflecting the twin forces of Enlightened thinking and popular fear. Enlightened writers derived from their faith in human perfectability both a strong desire to improve the quality of life and a belief that the lot of the poor was not related to their wickedness or human frailty. They no longer accepted that it was in any way a sin to be poor, but preferred to see poverty as one of the necessary concomitants of economic change. Writing in 1784, Necker reasoned that poverty was, unhappily, 'une des conditions inséparables de l'état de société', a condition to which all who did not inherit either talent or property from their parents were inevitably exposed. And Necker, with the experience of government office behind him and an understanding of the resources available to the treasury, went on to argue that government had a responsibility towards these people, a responsibility which it was duty-bound to honour:

> C'est au gouvernement, interprète et dépositaire de l'harmonie sociale, c'est à lui de faire, pour cette classe nombreuse et déshéritée, tout ce que l'ordre et la justice lui permettent: il doit profiter attentivement de tous les moyens qui lui ont été laissés pour adoucir la rigueur des anciennes conventions et pour tendre une main secourable à ceux qui ont besoin de protection contre les loix elles-mêmes.[24]

This was the standard humanitarian view, the belief that economic wellbeing demanded that some people would languish in misery and that the government would then step in to alleviate their distress. It was not argued that poverty should be abolished or that society should be made less unequal – there is nothing socialistic about Necker's proposals, even if he did go much further than most of his contemporaries in suggesting that the poor and the unemployed had a right to state assistance.[25] Poor relief was generally seen as a palliative, not as a cure. The views of large sections of the liberal nobility and upper bourgeoisie specifically endorsed the need for wide inequalities in society. This analysis was put with great force by the merchants of the Bordeaux waterfront in 1793 when they noted that financial and social inequalities were highly desirable if business and overseas trade were to be allowed to flourish unimpeded, and that to this end they were perfectly prepared to tolerate indigence as 'a sad but necessary consequence' and to contribute towards the cost of poor relief as a debt to be honoured by society.[26]

The move for greater state intervention was not wholly inspired by paternalistic motives. The decline of the Christian view of begging brought in its wake a harsher and, some would say, a more realistic attitude towards *mendiants* and *vagabonds*. The erstwhile children of Jesus had by the middle of the eighteenth century assumed a less beatific countenance and were generally depicted as violent, drunken, and menacing, men and women whose demands should be resisted in the interests of the entire community. Guillaume Le Trosne, in a highly influential tract published in 1764, put the case most cogently for some measure of additional government control.[27] He depicted *mendiants* in the countryside as standing outside civilized society, a breed apart from the community amongst whom they lived, a race that was both indisciplined and dangerous. They inspired fear wherever they went, he explained, with the result that, whereas alms were voluntary in the urban centres, in rural France they became obligatory for everyone who wished his family and his property to remain unscathed. Theirs was 'une rébellion sourde et continuelle', and in fighting it France was engaged in what he saw as an unending civil war: more serious still, he saw it as an increasing problem, since bands of *vagabonds* were daily recruiting new members, which involved a serious drain on the resources of the French countryside, both in produce and in valuable manpower. To counteract this scourge, Le Trosne had no hesitation in demanding harsh penalties for the crime of begging and an active, repressive role for the state. Other pamphleteers and political spokesmen rushed to agree, pointing out that self-help and a sense of sturdy independence ought to be encouraged among the poor and institutionalized charity reduced to a minimum.[28] The widespread element of fear, ever-present in the remote farmsteads of the rural areas, ensured that such an approach evoked a ready and appreciative response, though few pamphleteers of the period were as unconstructively repressive in tone as Le Trosne. His suggested solution was beguilingly simple: he urged that *vagabondage* should be severely punished with the galleys and even the death penalty for persistent offenders, and he asked that the *archers* be introduced into every parish to deal with beggars, and that country people themselves be given, as citizens, powers of arrest.[29]

This change in public opinion was not lost on government circles, and under both Louis XV and Louis XVI there can be observed a distinct rise in the degree of state intervention in the field of poor relief. Disasters like famine and flooding began to prick the public conscience, and the state was impelled to take special emergency measures. When the harvest failed in a particular province, emergency supplies would sometimes be shipped in to prevent mass starvation; or again, a grant might be voted from the treasury to offset the cost of fire damage or of some natural disaster. But, always, it was emphasized that these cases were exceptional; the Ancien Regime always insisted that poor relief was essentially a local matter and that it should therefore be met from local funds, without any intervention from Paris. This was especially true in the *pays d'états*, covering over half the land area of France, where the tradition of government responsibility was minimal. In 1766, for instance, when the olive crop failed disastrously in the Midi and many of the olive trees were permanently damaged, it was the Estates of Provence, not central government, which made a grant towards the cost of relief and replacement.[30] Similarly, in the control of *vagabondage* the state was seen to play a more prominent part in the second half of the eighteenth century. It was, after all, the royal government of the Ancien Regime which first tried to lay down a clear distinction between the *mendiant* and the *vagabond*, a distinction in law between the deserving poor and the able-bodied, between those who were deemed worthy of assistance and those set apart for correction. It was the royal government which, in 1764, gave stern orders to the *maréchaussée* to arrest not only those without fixed abode found wandering on the public highways – the generally-accepted definition of the *vagabond* – but also all those caught begging who were suspected of being without regular source of employment.[31] It was, once again, the royal government, that of Louis XV, which in 1767 established a network of *dépôts de mendicité* in each *généralité*, to which those rounded up on charges of begging for money could be sent. This increase in government activity, like the intellectual clamour for intervention, must not be seen as wholly humanitarian in inspiration, but rather as a result of growing Physiocratic influence in government circles during the 1760s. Plans for poor relief like the one drafted by Bertin's ministry embodied many of the basic ideas of the Physiocrats and aimed at reforms which might increase the wealth and production of the country.[32] Such plans heralded the work of the *Comité de Mendicité* in 1790 and established in broad outline the pattern of state intervention which would be adopted in the Revolutionary years.

The pattern was established, but a coherent and effective social policy was still far from having been attained. Ancien Regime governments always baulked at the idea of more consistent intervention, with the result that initiatives from Paris were little more than somewhat random, staccato responses to crises as they arose. If there were occasional grants of money to blunt the effects of famine, they were rare and quite inadequate to the needs of a society where poverty was the norm and voluntary charity already in decline. If imaginative *intendants* like Turgot at Limoges had established public works to solve localized pockets of mass unemployment, the initiative was his and his alone; there was no standardization, no overall government effort, no research to establish just where the worst incidence of misery was to be located. Similarly, the repressive measures adopted lacked that degree of consistency which could have made them effective. The definition of a *mendiant* and a *vagabond* fluctuated with the zeal of the incumbent Minister of the Interior. The *maréchaussée* were given instructions to declare war on mendicity in their area by arresting all beggars and especially those found roaming the countryside in bands; yet such was the inadequacy of the police budget and so badly undermanned were the local forces that farmers were unable to look to them for protection and the most disruptive of *vagabonds* were generally left free to roam at will.[33] A temporary measure of 1767 to increase the efficiency of the police, by offering them a bounty for every beggar they brought into custody, was hastily withdrawn: it led to both corruption and notorious abuse, with the police arresting the weak, the workless, the genuine *pauvres honteux* who offered no resistance, while leaving the dangerous armed bands in the safety of the hills.[34] Even over dépôts de mendicité, the most important single institutional innovation of the Ancien Regime, there was a sad lack of consistency in government policy. Financing was too frequently left to half-hearted local authorities, and instructions from Paris fluctuated alarmingly. The *dépôt* at Montpellier, for instance, like many others, was opened in accordance with the decree of 1768, closed down in 1775 when government interest seemed to lapse, and reopened under a new ordinance two years later.[35] The treatment of inmates in the *dépôts* was ill-defined by law: in general, first offenders could be released on the word of a sponsor, someone of standing in the community who would command sufficient respect with the *maréchaussée*, whereas the others would be made to serve a three-month sentence, in the course of which they would often be won over to a life of *vagabondage*.[36] Reformers like Montlinot, the administrator in charge of the *dépôt* at Soissons, were given neither adequate funding nor official government encouragement.[37] The overall picture, indeed, was hardly a cheering one. Government intervention was increasing, but in a very haphazard and piecemeal manner and without the bureaucratic infrastructure which alone could make it effective. And the general tone of that intervention was repressive rather than constructive: the aim was clearly to destroy the outward signs of begging and *mendicité* rather than to tackle the economic and social problems of the poor.

The coming of the French Revolution did nothing to reduce the scale of the social problems facing the authorities. 1788 and 1789 were years of serious crop failure throughout large areas of France's grain-producing provinces, and the Revolution added to the food shortage by spreading confusion and bewilderment among the peasantry. Rents, taxes, tithes, and feudal exactions alike often went unpaid as the peasants enthusiastically convinced themselves that the calling of the Estates-General and the storming of the Bastille had coincidentally settled all their longstanding grievances, and sowing and harvesting were seriously disrupted by political meetings and village celebrations, by armed attacks and lurid local scares. Law and order, so essential to the smooth turn-over of the agricultural year, had broken down in many parts of the country, and the grain supply suffered accordingly. Misery and suffering rose apace, as did the numbers of beggars and *vagabonds* who took to the roads once the harvest was in and unemployment loomed. As the Revolution progressed, poverty would remain one of its most urgent problems, with unemployment rampant in many of France's traditional industries and with the widows and dependants of those killed and maimed in the war adding still further to the long roll-call of the needy. The reasons for localized pockets of misery might vary widely: in Lyon it was largely attributable to the grave slump in the fortunes of the silk industry; in Le Havre, where the town's economy was tightly bound to that of the West Indian islands, the insurrection in Santo-Domingo threw ships' carpenters and other tradesmen out of work; in the rural Jura violent hailstorms caused such widespread damage in 1790 and 1791 that some communes reported that their entire harvest had been wiped out and that their farmers were destitute.[38] Military service did help to provide artificial employment for large numbers of the poorer sections of the community, but when men returned from a campaign, like the Bordeaux volunteers marching home from service in the Vendée in 1793, they had no skills to sell and little choice but to join the already swollen ranks of the *indigents*.[39] Uncontrollable inflation following the issue of paper currency added to the financial confusion, made credit almost impossible for the poor to find, and drove even the most basic foodstuffs beyond the grasp of a large section of the working population. The problems for the poor were as stark as at any time in the course of the century: it was still true that the only families who were able to avoid slipping into the *demi-monde* of beggars and *vagabonds* were those where the breadwinner was fortunate enough to find a regular source of employment.

So what, one is entitled to ask, did change? In what ways, if at all, did the Revolution bring help to men and women who had all too often been brushed aside by the public administrations of the Ancien Regime? In practical terms, as the chapters that follow will make clear, the benefits may have been more theoretical than real. The heartrending accounts of human misery which flooded into Paris during the Directory are proof that the legislators of Revolutionary France, however worthy their intentions, were not always successful in translating these intentions into real benefits that could help stem the misery of the poor. In these circumstances it is all too easy to be scathing about their aims and insights.[40] Yet such cynicism would be ill-founded, at least in the early stages of the Revolution, when the deputies to the National Assembly and its immediate successors had a rather naive faith in the power of laws and decrees but were none the less genuinely and very deeply committed to reform. They belonged to that generation which had been most profoundly influenced by the Enlightenment, men who, having been born in the 1750s and 1760s, had been weaned on a literary diet of Rousseau and the Encyclopaedists. Such men found it a source of national humiliation that a large proportion of their fellow-citizens were reduced to begging and to petty crime in order to stay alive. They saw in the very existence of widespread human degradation a challenge to the new and better society which they were seeking to bring into being. Indigence was a constant rebuke to them, an insult to the sacred ideal of *égalité* that was such an essential part of the myth of the Revolution they were directing; in that more equal society work must be the basic right of every Frenchman, not a privilege or a prize to be won or fought over. In the 1770s and 1780s they had discussed these ideas endlessly in the richly-upholstered comfort of Parisian salons and provincial reading-clubs; now, entrusted with power, they saw it as their sacred duty to bring them to fruition. Malouet's proposed law of 3 August 1789, urging the government to accept its responsibilities towards the growing numbers of unemployed, was the precursor of many and an accurate reflection of the new mood of the country.[41]

The Revolutionary years saw poor relief elevated to a new position of importance among the stated priorities of national government, and for the first time there was no question but that this was the rightful province of the state. Under both the Constituent and the Legislative Assemblies, committees of deputies were established on a permanent basis to deal with matters concerning the relief of indigence – the *Comité de Mendicité* from 1790 to 1791, which concentrated on the problems of diagnosis and prescription, and a *Comité des secours* under the Legislative, which was responsible for making assistance payments to the indigent, provisioning hospitals and poorhouses, and processing and answering complaints and petitions. Unlike many of the remedies favoured during the Ancien Regime, this was neither a cosmetic gesture nor an instance of hasty over-reaction by the authorities. The deputies took their new responsibilities very seriously, sifting evidence from their departments and framing laws to deal with what they saw as anomalies and injustices. In a study of the social legislation of the period, Ferdinand Dreyfus notes that the Legislative alone passed fifty-six decrees embodying measures aimed at the easing of poverty.[42] The administration of relief work became increasingly centralized as local authorities, bereft of other, more traditional sources of revenue, became more heavily dependent on the public purse. This was especially so during the Convention, when local initiative was rigorously regulated and all the major spending departments became concentrated on the great committees in Paris. The *Comité des secours publics*, like the other committees of state, established a strongly-centralized executive, which, aided by the new network of departments and districts, attempted to ensure that money was equitably distributed in accordance with the extent of local need. In this regard the Revolution enjoyed the advantage of a bureaucratic structure which had been denied to its predecessors. There was for the first time a chain of command stretching from the committees and ministries in Paris down to the departments, districts and communes, which allowed for a degree of standardization that would have been unthinkable in the Ancien Regime. No longer was the level of relief accorded dependent on such extraneous factors as the average income level of the community, its inclusion in a *pays d'état* or *pays d'élection*, the generosity of the local *seigneur*, or a pious decision in medieval times to found a monastery or an abbey.

Much of the credit for the high priority given to social questions by the early revolutionary administrations must go to the members of the *Comité de Mendicité*, whose energy and enthusiasm were such that the government was constantly kept aware of the special problems and requirements of the poor. The Committee resulted from the debate in the Assembly on 21 January 1790 about how to organize a sub-scription to relieve misery in Paris; yet it emerged with wide-ranging powers of in-vestigation and recommendation and with a responsibility to report to the Assembly its views 'sur les moyens de détruire la mendicité'.[43] In this new guise it was to develop into a formidable pressure-group, urging the Assembly to recognize its obligations to the poor and demanding ambitious schemes of public expenditure. Four commissioners were appointed from the Assembly itself to form the core of the new committee: they included Prieur, the deputy for the Third Estate of Châlons-sur-Marne, and La Rochefoucauld-Liancourt, the nobleman who represented Clermont-en-Beauvaisis and the driving-force behind the establishment of the Com-mittee in the first place.[44] Liancourt was shortly to be appointed chairman, and it was he who, through vigorous reports and agitation, forged the Committee into the openly propagandist body which it became. He was an unrepentant champion of the cause of the poor, relentless in his efforts to build up the reputation and the expertise of his fellow-members and eager to invite established experts in the field of public welfare to join in the deliberations. Boncerf and La Millière were rapidly coopted; so was Montlinot, the director of the *dépôt de mendicité* in Soissons, a well-known advocate of Enlightened reform and the author of some of the most eminent tracts on the whole subject of charity to be published in the last years of the Ancien Regime.[45] Over the next eighteen months the Committee met some seventy times, and the fruits of these meetings – a *Plan du Travail* and seven reports on different aspects of poverty and poor relief – collectively form the basis of the new approach to the question which was to dominate the thinking of the Legislative Assembly and the Conven-tion, especially the Jacobin Convention of the Year II.[46]

The Committee's recommendations were supported by detailed and systematic research into the nature and extent of France's social problems, research which it coordinated by collating the statistics provided by the eighty-five departments. It was an impressive exercise, scientifically conducted by the standards of the day and bearing no resemblance to the casual and often inaccurate figures collected during the Ancien Regime. And even though local administrators anxious to obtain funds for their favourite projects might exaggerate the numbers of their poor or overstate the losses incurred by their hospitals since the Revolution, at least the committees in Paris had at their disposal something approaching a national conspectus of social need. They learned, for instance, of the seasonal problems of the Auvergne which reduced almost every household in towns like Saint-Jean-d'Ollières to misery every winter.[47] They were told of the degree of suffering of the local population in Rodez, where in 1791 one sixth of the people were shown to be in need of immediate assistance and one in nine were *mendiants vagabonds*.[48] And for the larger cities they were provided with even more detailed statistics, collected by the popular sections in 1793 and the Year II to claim their share of government funds for poor relief, so that they knew not only the numbers of *indigents* within the city walls – not the most valuable of information, since often the siting of a hospital or *hôtel-dieu* in a large town would attract beggars from miles around – but also the distribution of these men and women by district and by occupation.[49] Hospitals and poorhouses were obliged to reveal to the committees the most intimate details of their balance-sheets, the numbers of staff they employed, weekly lists of the patients they treated, and the income they had lost since the onset of the Revolution. This storehouse of information was painstakingly sifted and analysed, and it played a major part in helping the *Comité de Mendicité* and its successors to make an equitable distribution of the limited funds available.

The *Comité*'s brief was not simply that of allocating money, even if this was usually its most immediate task. In the longer term the *Comité de Mendicité* was also expected to provide the Assembly with a thorough analysis of the problems of the poor and with suggested remedies. The statistics which it demanded from the departments were similarly not merely entries in an eighteenth-century social security dossier, but the raw material for an ambitious and fairly sophisticated academic exercise, one that was a worthy reflection of the spirit of enquiry that had been born of the Enlightenment. They wanted to know not only the extent of local pockets of misery but also the reasons for them, and communes were invited to explain why they should be suffering particular distress during the Revolutionary years. The answers supplied formed the basis for something approaching a comprehensive social survey of the lot of the French people. Lack of work was the cause most frequently cited: in Evreux in Normandy the decline of spinning was especially blamed, though the local authority added that general labouring jobs were also unobtainable and voluntary charity had dried up completely since 1790.[50] In the Ariège, too, it was lack of job opportunity that was mentioned as being the principal source of indigence, and from Tarascon came a special plea to the Committee to open the local coalmines, which could once again put life into the iron industry in the area.[51] In farming and wine-growing areas the problem of the aged was often referred to, of those workers who had through old age or infirmity outlived their usefulness in the fields and found themselves without any visible means of support. The returns from the District of Cadillac in the Gironde are highly typical: here almost all the *vieillards indigents* were vineyard workers, men who were totally dependent on public charity after a lifetime of hard manual work, a working life which in one case had spanned sixty-four years.[52] Even more common were complaints that the provision of relief locally bore no resemblance to the geographical incidence of suffering. From Tarbes in the Pyrenees, for instance, came a plaintive call for the rationalization of funds, since theirs was an area where income was quite scandalously unequally distributed and where the poor were badly hit by the untoward effects of voluntarism.[53] In all, from tax-rolls and other sources, the Committee was able to build up an informed survey of over half the departments in France, a survey which made a deep impression on the Assembly when it was conveyed to the deputies in 1791. For in fifty-one departments, those which had furnished complete returns, the Committee estimated that the number of *mendiants* was an astonishing 1,928,064 out of a total population of 16,634,466, or almost one in eight of the total.[54]

No such statistics had previously been available, and, even allowing for the customary exaggerations, the rather rough-and-ready methods by which they were collected, and the quite genuine problems of itinerant workers, seasonal harvesters, hawkers and others who must have figured on several different departmental returns, they did provide the authorities with the basis on which to construct a new policy on poor relief. The figures were deeply shocking. They emphasized what historians now appreciate but what was far from being obvious at the time – that the problem of the poor was a general problem affecting a very wide cross-section of the unskilled and semi-skilled workers of France and their dependants, that it could no longer be seen in terms of a narrow class of idle professional *vagabonds*. *Classes dangereuses* there were in France, but they were not a neat, distinct social category, but groups which overlapped with and could often be confused with the *classes laborieuses*. When analysing the causes of poverty in their own areas, most authorities, like the ones that I have cited, discussed economic forces and weather conditions, the problems of joblessness and old age. Very few – in view of the vivid memories of the *Grande Peur*, surprisingly few – delivered self-righteous diatribes about idleness and loose living, and those few that did tended to be in that select group of departments where work was plentiful. In the District of Marseille, for instance, the lot of beggars would seem to have elicited little interest. They pointed out rather acidly that the city census was grossly inaccurate and that it was therefore quite impossible to give an informed estimate of the numbers of *indigents*. And the reasons suggested tend to confirm the District's rather dismissive attitude. The town of La Ciotat blamed mendicity on 'la fainéantise, le jeu, le cabaret', on the failings of the individuals themselves, and Cassis declared bleakly that the problem stemmed from *oisiveté*, that there was work for those who would take it, and that 'il n'y a que l'ordre et la subordination qui puissent ramener au travail les vagabonds sous une inspection sévère.'[55] After the Committee had completed its detailed series of reports on indigence throughout the country, attitudes such as these became much more difficult to sustain.

That is not to say that the Committee ever succeeded in creating a Revolutionary philosophy of social service, a coherent attitude towards the poor that was the product of Revolutionary experience. Indeed, the dualism that characterized the last fifty years of the Ancien Regime was still to be found deeply engrained in the attitudes of the 1790s. Voluntarism, it is true, was largely dead: the Revolutionaries believed that the state had a right to enforce standards on society and, as we have seen, they had evolved the bureaucracy with which to do so. But the question remained: exactly what role was the state expected to play? Were the poor to be regarded as *les enfants naturels de la Patrie* to whom society owed a debt which it was honour-bound to meet, as the humanitarians insisted? Or were they rather *un fléau social*, a scourge on the body politic that must be rooted out in the interests of the nation as a whole? It was the difference between the humanitarian and the punitive approach which was already present before 1789 but which now, with the state ready to take bold new initiatives in social policy, assumed a greater urgency than at any previous time. Both attitudes were represented on the *Comité de Mendicité*, just as both had spokesmen in all the governments of the Revolutionary years.

Quite fundamental to Revolutionary thinking on poverty was the idea that all men had a right to be able to feed and clothe themselves and their families, the notion of *le droit à la subsistance* that was to recur in almost every declaration on the subject. By 1793 the Paris sections were to make the ideal their own, but it had previously been adopted by Revolutionary administrations of widely varying outlooks. It was defined as early as January 1790 by La Rochefoucauld-Liancourt, who argued cogently that the whole concept of charity as understood by contemporaries was wrong-headed and outmoded. Giving, he pointed out, should not be a function of individual contributions by the rich to the less fortunate, whether the product of piety, or genuine compassion, or social condescension. Rather, since poverty was an unpleasant but inevitable by-product of social and economic change, it was incumbent on society as a whole to provide assistance for those unable to fend for themselves. The very connotation of the word 'charity' was offensive, he claimed: aid should be something that a man got as a right, as *bienfaisance*:

> Chaque homme ayant droit à sa subsistance, la société doit pourvoir à la subsistance de tous ceux de ses membres qui pourront en manquer, et cette secourable assistance ne doit pas être regardée comme un bienfait: elle est, sans doute, le besoin d'un coeur sensible et humain, le voeu de tout homme qui n'est pas lui-même dans l'état de pauvreté; devoir qui ne doit pas être avili, ni par le nom, ni par le caractère de l'aumône; enfin, elle est pour la société une dette inviolable et sacrée.[56]

Liancourt took care to note that society as well as the individual *pauvre* must benefit from this new attitude, since he believed that misery was the basic cause of most of the violent crime that was such a scourge in many parts of rural France. And he stressed its political implications, too, believing, as did many of the more reformist members of the Constituent, that destitution could only prolong submissiveness and servitude among the population, a frame of mind incompatible with the new spirit of liberty.[57] For all these reasons it became generally accepted that the removal of this social evil must assume a high priority among the matters to be dealt with by the Revolutionary authorities.

The practical effects of this new and rather idealistic approach were not lost on contemporaries, many of whom were appalled by the thought of vast sums of public money going to subsidize the hated and feared rural beggars. Old attitudes and suspicions died hard: at local level we even find complaints that poor relief in the 1780s had been too laxly administered and that surveillance ought to be stepped up in the interests of both economy and public order.[58] It was commonly held that there could be no panacea for the problems of the poor, and that handing out fixed sums of money to everyone who was unable to make ends meet would both bankrupt the treasury and encourage idleness among large sections of the population. As in the Ancien Regime, it was felt necessary to find some form of words to define those groups to which assistance should legitimately be given without destroying the will to work in the rest of the people. Inevitably such a definition had to be bureaucratic and somewhat arbitrary, one that would serve as a convenient starting-point for further discussion. In its third report, in September 1790, the *Comité de Mendicité* determined that all those whose earnings were so low that they paid less than one day's wages in tax each year were eligible for immediate assistance, and that those paying only two or three days' wages would be able to claim relief should some special misfortune, like an accident or a long and debilitating illness, befall them.[59] The Committee also attempted to make qualitative distinctions among the poor, separating, on the one hand, the aged and the infirm, the blind and the crippled, those who were visibly unable to earn their living, and, on the other, the thieves and vagabonds, the lazy and the drunkards. It was a basic rule with the Committee, and one that found widespread favour in the French provinces with the population at large, that the able-bodied, the *pauvres valides*, should be assisted only through the provision of work; free distribution to them, whether of money or of food, was to be abolished forthwith.[60] Jean-Baptiste Bô, the deputy for the Aveyron, came close to expressing the consensus view among his colleagues in a report to the Convention in the Year II when he stated that it was work that the government ought to guarantee to the able-bodied, not subsistence, since the right they enjoyed was 'le droit à la subsistance *par le travail*'.[61]

The work ethic was very strong in Revolutionary France, reinforced by that stern puritanical outlook that is the hallmark of all revolutions. Were assistance too liberal, it was widely feared that idleness would become respectable and the eagerness of the individual to serve the state would as a consequence be undermined. To the Jacobins, in particular, the interests of the state were paramount, and those who, by making no contribution to the common weal, were breaking faith with the state, were deemed by many to have forfeited their right to some of the privileges of citizenship. Jourdain, from the Ille-et-Vilaine, was one of several deputies under the Directory who argued that Rousseau's concept of a social contract should be applied to the poor, and on that basis idleness, the non-fulfilment of man's obligations to the state, was an offence which should be punished like any other offence.[62] In the same spirit was the view of one of the members from Normandy, Bertrand, who went so far as to say that any man who, by choosing not to work, became a burden on society ought to discover that society owed him nothing in return.[63] It is true that this rather harsh attitude was not universally shared, that some deputies felt that their colleagues were confusing idleness with indigence by attacking only *vagabondage*. After all, as one of them, Baudin, pointed out with some justice, these proposals were discriminating against the poorer members of society, since they were attacking laziness at the lower end of the social scale while turning a blind eye to those more culpable parasites, the idle rich.[64] But all were agreed that *bienfaisance* must never become so lavish as to attract the poor to a life of idleness: the lot of the *pauvre valide* must never be allowed to rival that of the man who worked to earn his living. For this reason the extent of the aid offered to the able-bodied was closely supervised and distinguished from the more generous help afforded to the sick, the old, and the crippled, who could not be expected to turn a hand to hard manual labour.

This rather harsh attitude was reinforced by what many saw as the political implications of begging. For *vagabondage* was not merely a damaging insult to those good citizens who worked solidly and uncomplainingly and contributed to the well-being of France and its Revolution; the repercussions ran deeper than that. It was seen as encouraging crime, and wandering bands of beggars were portrayed as a vile and corrupting nursery breeding bandits and footpads of the kind who, by Year VI and Year VII, were terrorizing the highways of France and interrupting essential communications between Paris and the great provincial centres.[65] Not all these beggars, it was suggested, were driven to pursue that criminal path by misery and the threat of starvation; some, on the contrary, rather enjoyed the excitements of brigandage and found that they could make a reasonable living by persuading the members of the local community to remember their more generous instincts. A local *notaire* in one of the villages of the Dauphiné pointed out in a letter to the Estates-General in 1789 that these people not only posed a threat to public order but also deprived the genuinely needy of the alms on which they were so utterly dependent. They were, he said, a class apart, 'une classe de mendiants qui mendient, non seulement sans besoin, mais encore par avarice et spéculation.'[66] If such people were tolerable under despotism, they were clearly an insufferable blot on the reputation of a regime that had given them liberty. Some deputies even believed, like Chabot, that mendicity was quite natural during the Ancien Regime, a popular protest which frightened kings and their tyrannical ministers into making reluctant concessions.[67] But no such argument could now be seriously mooted in their defence. Indeed, when the activities of *vagabonds* showed no signs of abating, somewhat implausible plot theories began to abound, no doubt strongly coloured by vivid memories of the *Grande Peur* and by the more recent experience of *chouannerie* in Brittany and the Vendée. In Year VIII, for instance, Porcher submitted a paper to the *Conseil des Anciens* which took a particularly hard line on rural crime and argued that there was a strong link between *vagabondage* and the enemies of the Republic, the *chouans*, refractory priests and secret *émigrés*, with the beggars taking messages from one centre of counter-revolution to another in an attempt to overthrow the regime.[68] Chabot, too, took up the cry, denouncing all beggars as the allies of France's enemies abroad and as 'un instrument de contrerévolution' whose avowed aim was nothing less than to destroy the Republic; in his words, 'C'est pour anéantir la République qu'il se livre chaque jour au pillage et aux assassinats.'[69] It is clear that the attitude of such men to the question of mendicity was primarily punitive.

The *Comité de Mendicité* was well aware of the fears and suspicions of the French public: many of its nineteen members had, after all, been protagonists in the debate on charity which had raged through the 1770s and 1780s in the provincial academies and in the pamphlet press. They were not advocating a revolution in social attitudes but were painstakingly attempting to mould the new ideas about poor relief already current in the eighteenth century to the mood and the capability of Revolutionary France. There was an intense practicality about their proposals, a practicality born of the inadequacy of previous reforms as much as of the Physiocratic ideas of wealth and prosperity in which they believed. The probems were well understood: they were analysed, for instance, with as great clarity by the Provincial Assembly in Rouen in 1787 as they were by the Committee three years later.[70] Like that Assembly, the Committee was cost-conscious, it believed that the provision of adequate work would contribute most to the welfare of the *pauvres valides*, it was suspicious of the utility and high cost of small hospitals and of unnecessary institutionalization, and it inherently favoured *secours à domicile* as a more economical, less socially disruptive means of aid in periods of short-term crisis.[71] The Committee was in so many ways representative of the enlightened opinion of the second half of the eighteenth century.

What distinguished its members from the men who had been advocating reform during the previous twenty or thirty years was the degree of influence which they were able to bring to bear. They were a full committee of an Assembly eager to listen to reformist ideas. They had in Liancourt a spokesman and propagandist of the very highest calibre, indefatigable in pursuing his proposed reforms and in pressing them on both deputies and hospital administrators. Not least, they could point with a new urgency to the needs of the poor, for, as the following chapters will show, some of the earliest Revolutionary measures in other fields had the effect of attacking the independent funds enjoyed by hospitals and charities and thus rendering them even more ineffective unless the state stepped in to fill the breach. Suspicion of the church and its political influence added further support to the Committee's belief that in future the main provider for the poor and needy, the main agency to provide funds in cases of hardship should be the state, since the state alone could ensure an equitable distribution of resources. Increasingly the Committee became a pressure group against clerical charity, against voluntarism, in favour of a kind of welfare state in which Revolutionary France would assume responsibility for the sick, the disabled, and the destitute. Poor relief would no longer be a form of charity but a basic human right, a debt owed by the nation to its citizens. It is a reflection of the Committee's persuasiveness and of the humanitarian ethos of the early years of the Revolution that these ideas were accepted and that a series of laws attempted to translate them into reality between 1790 and the fall of the Montagne in July 1794. Hospitals funded by central government funds, a rational and comprehensive system of state pensions, public works schemes for the unemployed, and guaranteed care for abandoned children, all these were essential parts of an overall scheme of *assistance*, paid for out of taxation and applied equally across the length and breadth of the country. It was a noble ideal, and Revolutionary governments looked to their new, centralist administrative system to put it into effect. Under the Jacobins it became a matter of faith; to the Thermidorians it was a hopelessly expensive and unrealistic dream which placed anticlerical ideology and mindless egalitarianism above the needs of the poor themselves and starved the service of money. Yet, whatever its shortcomings, it was a most imaginative experiment in public welfare provision, which illustrates the idealistic enthusiasm of the early years of the French Revolution.

Notes to chapter 2

1. C. Lucas, *The structure of the Terror*, chapter 1; also 'Auvergnats and Foréziens pendant la mission du conventionnel Javogues', in *Gilbert Romme et son temps*, p. 131.
2. G. Lefebvre, *La Grande Peur de 1789*, pp. 110–12.
3. A.D. Rhône, C6, *Police, 1739–89*, report to the *chancelier* about a riot in Lyon, 28 November 1768.
4. The role of the church in charitable works in early modern Europe has been widely discussed elsewhere, notably by J.-P. Gutton in his *La société et les pauvres en Europe (16e–18e siècles)*. For France see the same author's thesis on *La société et les pauvres: l'exemple de la généralité de Lyon, 1534–1789*, and part 2 of Olwen Hufton's *The poor of eighteenth-century France, 1750–1789*.
5. The importance of the religious presence in the life of Ancien Regime hospitals is clear from their archives and minute-books: as examples one could cite the *hôtel-dieu* in Lyon and the *Hôpital Saint-André* in Bordeaux. Many local monographs on hospitals during the second half of the eighteenth century illustrate the same pervasive clerical influence. See, for instance, B. Bellande, *L'ancien Hôpital-Général d'Issoire*; M. Fortin, *La charité et l'assistance publique à Montbéliard sous l'Ancien Régime*; L. Merle, *L'Hôpital du Saint-Esprit de Niort, 1665–1790*; or H. Desgranges, *Hospitaliers d'autrefois: l'Hôpital Général de Paris, 1656–1790*.
6. M. Quétin, 'L'hôpital d'Aurillac de 1649 à la Révolution'.
7. P. Loupès, 'Le clergé paroissial du diocèse de Bordeaux d'après la grande enquête de 1772'.
8. T. Tackett, *Priest and parish in eighteenth-century France*, p. 157.
9. P. Loupès, 'L'assistance paroissiale aux pauvres malades dans le diocèse de Bordeaux au dix-huitième siècle'.
10. J. McManners, *French ecclesiastical society under the Ancien Regime: a study of Angers in the eighteenth century*, chapter 1.
11. A.N., F¹⁵1861, letter from the Department of the Lozère at Mende, 4 April 1793.
12. M. Vovelle, *Religion et révolution: la déchristianisation de l'an II*.
13. M. Vovelle, *Piété baroque et déchristianisation en Provence au dix-huitième siècle*, pp. 230ff.
14. A.N. F¹⁵138, *mémoire* (undated) of Louis XVI's reign from the *dépôt* at Carcassonne.
15. A. Forrest, *Society and politics in Revolutionary Bordeaux*, pp. 10–11.
16. Quoted in J. McManners, *The French Revolution and the church*, p. 9.
17. The examples that follow are drawn from P. Goubert and M. Denis (editors), *1789: Les Français ont la parole*, pp. 175–81.
18. S. T. McCloy, *The humanitarian movement in eighteenth-century France*, pp. 1–4.
19. See, for instance, P. Barrière, 'Les académies et la vie intellectuelle dans la société méridionale au dix-huitième siècle'.
20. J.-P. Gutton, *La société et les pauvres: l'exemple de la généralité de Lyon, 1534–1789*, pp. 425–9.
21. O. Hufton, *The poor of eighteenth-century France*, p. 194.

22. Voltaire, *Lettres philosophiques* 20.

23. Turgot, article on 'Fondations' in the *Encyclopédie*.

24. J. Necker, *De l'administration des finances de la France* (1784), III, pp. 160–1.

25. H. Grange, *Les idées de Necker*, pp. 185–6.

26. A.D. Gironde, 12L3, Section 5 (Simoneau), minute of 10 May 1793.

27. G. le Trosne, *Mémoire sur les vagabonds et sur les mendiants*.

28. Du Pont de Nemours, *Idées sur les secours à donner aux pauvres malades dans une grande ville* (1786), p. 16.

29. G. le Trosne, *op. cit.*, pp. 63–8.

30. O. Hufton, *op. cit.*, p. 180.

31. A.D. Seine-Inférieure, C2284, royal declaration of 3 August 1764.

32. C. Bloch, *L'assistance et l'état en France à la veille de la Révolution*, pp. 157ff.

33. O. Hufton, *op. cit.*, p. 222.

34. De Ballainvilliers, *Mémoire sur le Languedoc – hôpitaux* (MS. Montpellier, 1788), p. 246.

35. *ibid.*, p. 243.

36. J.-C. Gorjy, *Mémoire sur les dépôts de mendicité*, pp. 3–4.

37. De Montlinot, *Etat actuel du Dépôt de Soissons*, pp. 1–4.

38. A.D. Jura, L861, reports to the Department on the effects of natural disasters, 1790–91; Arch. Mun. Le Havre, F²8, report of 13 March 1790.

39. A.D. Gironde, 4L133, decree of the Department, 6 August 1793.

40. L. Lallemand, *La Révolution et les pauvres* is a good instance of this scathing approach.

41. *Le Moniteur*, 32–3, *séance* of 3 August 1789, speech by Malouet.

42. F. Dreyfus, *L'assistance sous la Législative et la Convention, 1791–1795*, p. 16.

43. C. Bloch and A. Tuetey (editors), *Procès-verbaux et rapports du Comité de Mendicité de la Constituante, 1790–91*, p. ix.

44. F. Dreyfus, *La Rochefoucauld-Liancourt, un philanthrope d'autrefois*.

45. Among his most influential writings were three pamphlets which drew on his experience in Soissons: his speech on *Les moyens de détruire la mendicité dans la ville de Soissons*; a pamphlet on the *Etat actuel du Dépôt de Soissons, précédé d'un essai sur la mendicité*; and his *Observations sur les enfants trouvés de la généralité de Soissons*.

46. C. Bloch and A. Tuetey, *op. cit.*, part 2.

47. A. Poitrineau, 'Aspects de l'émigration temporaire et saisonnière en Auvergne à la fin du dix-huitième et au début du dix-neuvième siècle', p. 37.

48. A.N., F¹⁶967, *Tableaux de population et de mendicité*, return for Rodez (Aveyron), 1791.

49. A.N., F¹⁶968, *Tableaux de population et de mendicité*, returns for Paris; Arch. Mun. Bordeaux, L66, L67, *Secours aux indigents*, distribution lists for poor relief funds among the sections of the city.

50. A.N., F¹⁶966, *Tableaux de population et de mendicité*, return for Evreux (Eure).

51. A.N., F¹⁶966, *Tableaux de population et de mendicité*, return for Tarascon (Ariège).

52. A.D. Gironde, 7L97, District of Cadillac, return on *vieillards indigents*, 5 prairial II.

53. A.N., F¹⁵1861, return from the Department of Hautes-Pyrénées, 1791.

54. A.N., F¹⁵1861, report entitled 'Etat de population et de mendicité' submitted to the *Comité de Mendicité*, 1791.

55. A.N., F¹⁶967, *Tableaux de population et de mendicité*, return for the District of Marseille (Bouches-du-Rhône).

56. De Liancourt, 'Plan de travail du Comité pour l'extinction de la mendicité', dated 21 January 1790, in C. Bloch and A. Tuetey (editors), *Procès-verbaux et rapports du Comité de Mendicité de la Constituante, 1790–91*, p. 311.

57. *ibid.*, p. 315.
58. Arch. Chambre de Commerce de La Rochelle, carton 1, dossier 15, *Mémoire de la part des administrateurs de l'Hôpital de La Rochelle*, presented to the Chamber of Commerce (undated).
59. C. Bloch and A. Tuetey, *op. cit.*, p. 379.
60. *ibid.*, pp. 377–8.
61. A.N., AD.XIV⁹, Jean-Baptiste Bô (Aveyron), *Rapport et projet de décret à la Convention*, Year II.
62. A.N., AD.I⁸⁸, report of Jourdain (Ille-et-Vilaine), 4 *vendémiaire* VIII.
63. A.N., AD.I⁸⁸, report of Bertrand (Calvados), 1 *germinal* VII.
64. A.N., AD.I⁸⁸, report of Baudin (Ardennes), 6ième *jour complémentaire* VII.
65. A.N., AD.XIV⁹, report of Bô, *op. cit.*
66. A.N., F⁷3035, letter from a *notaire* in Gap to the president of the Estates-General, 18 December 1789.
67. A.N., AD.I⁸⁸, report of Chabot (Allier), undated.
68. A.N., AD.I⁸⁸, report of Porcher (Indre), 11 *vendémiaire* VIII.
69. A.N., AD.I⁸⁸, report of Chabot, *op. cit.*, p. 2.
70. A.D. Seine-Inférieure, C2111, *Procès-verbal des séances de l'Assemblée Provinciale de la généralité de Rouen* for 1787.
71. C. Bloch and A. Tuetey, *op. cit.*, reports of the *Comité de Mendicité*, *passim*.

3   The Revolution
and French hospitals I
From the *Comité de Mendicité* to
Jacobin centralism

If the social attitudes of the Revolutionary leadership seem reasonably lucid, the practical consequences of these attitudes can be appreciated only at the local level. Social theories were frequently formulated in the vaguest of terms, which made them difficult to apply in a country where the existing framework of charitable provision had been built, falteringly and piecemeal, over the centuries. In the ten short years of the Revolutionary period there was a limit to the extent to which the authorities could alter the habits of centuries, and it is clear that many of the changes effected were less than radical acts of surgery on the firmly-established infrastructure of the social services. Nowhere was this more patently true than in the field of hospital provision. For hospitals, particularly in urban France, had become the focal point of Ancien Regime charity, the single institution in many towns and *bourgs* that cared for the poor and the sick, and the natural object of legacies and benefactions from the leading figures in the local community. They were administered by worthy representatives of the local establishment, both the aristocracy and members of the bourgeoisie, who saw their service as a good deed to the general public and who in consequence might expect to bask in the grateful esteem of their fellow-citizens. Many hospitals were Catholic charitable foundations which had been developed from humble medieval beginnings, institutions which had grown in a highly random way and which had begun to be subjected to a degree of rationalization only in the course of the eighteenth century. By the outbreak of the Revolution such rationalization was starting to bear fruit, smaller *hospices* were being amalgamated, and every major urban centre was generally equipped with an *hôpital général* capable of dealing with routine illnesses and caring for the aged of their area. In the diocese of Bordeaux, for instance, there were by 1789 seven *hôtels-dieu*, varying in size and in efficiency, ranging from the Hôpital Saint-André in Bordeaux itself, which could care for some four hundred patients, to the little cottage-hospital at Saint-Macaire, which could tend no more than half a dozen at any one time.[1] This structure was to remain largely unaltered throughout the Revolutionary years.

So, too, was the purpose to which the hospitals were put. As in the Ancien Regime, they served both the poor and the aged, those who, whether through dire penury or through the lack of able-bodied relatives to look after them, had no option but to seek the shelter provided by an institution. In the eyes of the majority of

Frenchmen, indeed, admission to hospital was a fate that inspired dismay and terror, since hospitals were seen as simple *mouroirs*, buildings where the afflicted and the unfortunate were taken to die. This applied especially to the old, tired out by hard manual labour and without the wherewithal to keep themselves alive: they had no alternative to the poorhouse or the *hôtel-dieu*. The *intendant* of Poitiers phrased it very succinctly in 1684 when he painted a stark picture of the fragility of the rural economy, adding that in his region 'les artisans sont si pauvres qu'il faut les mettre à l'hôpital dès qu'ils cessent de travailler'.[2] The Revolution did little to change such attitudes, deeply embedded as they were in the demonology of the poor. Hospitals remained places of refuge for the lower classes of society, shunned by men and women of even modest means. The register of admissions to the *hôtel-dieu* of Lyon, one of the largest general hospitals in the country, bears eloquent testimony to this, listing, almost monotonously, the names of silkworkers and domestic servants, bleach-workers and starch-makers – the standard occupations of the labouring classes and the poorer artisanal groups in Lyon society.[3] In their report of November 1790 on the running of the hospital, the administrators of the *hôtel-dieu* in Saint-Etienne went so far as to state that the number of patients was closely regulated by the general economic climate in the town, given that Saint-Etienne was a community of some forty thousand people, 'dont le plus grand nombre sont des artisans et journaliers qui n'ont d'autre ressource que leur travail et qui dans la moindre maladie sont forcés d'avoir recours à l'hôtel-dieu'.[4] It follows that the standard of hospital services during the Revolutionary years was a matter of the utmost consequence to the poorer and more vulnerable members of French society.

Or at least it was of the utmost consequence unless the Revolution could come up with a viable alternative to hospital care for a substantial proportion of the *pauvres* in need of some kind of assistance. The very fact that hospitals smacked of deprivation and were so grimly associated in the public mind with death and abandonment made them a rather unsuitable basis on which to construct the whole system of Revolutionary *bienfaisance*, and their overwhelmingly urban setting made them inappropriate for the care of the people of large areas of rural France. In the first stages of the Revolution, the period which was overshadowed in terms of social policy by the exhaustive researches of the *Comité de mendicité*, hospitals and their functions became the object of increasingly critical scrutiny. Were they an efficient way to guarantee society against indigence and disease? Were they not wasteful of resources, imposing needless institutionalization at great expense when a relatively small short-term grant or pension might tide a family over a period of temporary distress? How far should they be allowed to retain fiscal and other privileges which had their roots in the same feudal law which the Revolution was attacking in other spheres? These questions were never far from the minds of the *Comité* and of the legislators who read its reports.[5] There was no necessary assumption in these years that the central role of the hospital or *hôtel-dieu* in the structure of relief must be continued, and the aim of political leaders was less to guarantee the status of the hospitals than to place them within the more generalized framework of an integrated welfare programme. Pensions and short-term benefits for the poor – *assistance à domicile* – were to complement the role of institutionalized charity, and many revolutionaries preferred informal relief, pointing out that it was both less expensive to the state and less socially disruptive for the community. Hence, for much of the Revolutionary period – and certainly up to the fall of the Montagnards in *thermidor* of Year II – we must attempt to assess the overall effectiveness of social policy rather than concentrate narrowly on the fate of a few major institutions. In this and the following chapters, the lot of hospitals and relief schemes, public workshops and the *Enfants Trouvés*, will each be examined in turn as the major component parts in the Revolution's dream of a total state-financed welfare scheme. After *thermidor* this ambitious concept was to come close to collapse, and the hospitals, as the most stable, permanent element in the entire structure, were to assume once again much of their traditional predominance.

The most important and immediate effects of the Revolution on the hospital service were undoubtedly financial. For in the eighteenth century their income came from widely diverse sources, not all of which were looked upon with total equanimity by the legislators of the National Assen.bly and the Convention. In the main that income was of four kinds: the product of rents paid by tenant-farmers for the lands which they worked; the produce of lands exploited directly by the hospital; feudal exactions; and a wide variety of charitable trusts, legacies, benefactions, and collections. There were, of course, huge variations from area to area and from hospital to hospital. In the Gironde, for instance, income from rents seems to have played a slightly more important part than that from feudal exactions, but each was significant, constituting about one third of the total revenue.[6] In contrast, the principal hospital in Toulouse, the Hôpital Général de la Grave, received little from such sources: it had made a large money payment to the royal exchequer back in 1765, with the result that its lands were largely sold off and it depended almost totally for current income on an annual pension of sixty thousand livres which it received from the crown.[7] Many of France's hospitals were substantial landowners, their possessions varying widely in yield and stretching over very scattered areas. The *hôtel-dieu* at Sens, for example, received an annual income of 8,600 livres from properties spread across twenty communes, ranging from meadows at Courtois and vineyards in Paron to woodland at Villeperrot and good arable land at Jouy: the hospital can be seen as a highly imaginative and successful rural entrepreneur.[8] In an industrial area such as Saint-Etienne, hospital administrators might hope to reap for themselves some of the new-found wealth of their region; in that case we find that revenue came not only from land, wood, and the rents from houses in the town, but also from more speculative ventures like coalmines and a stone quarry.[9] Hospitals, in short, behaved very much like other landowners in exploiting their possessions to maximum advantage.

They were not, however, entirely dependent on lands and *rentes*, for, as we have seen, the spirit of charitable giving remained fairly strong in the eighteenth century, lubricated by the active encouragement of the church hierarchy. And though the Revolution tended to despise this approach, seeing in it a form of paternalism and a cruel insult to the principle of equality, it remains true that in the years up to 1790 it had a very important role to play in funding hospitals and making good the growing deficits that many of their treasurers were being forced to report. Smaller hospitals, enjoying longstanding influence in their immediate localities, often benefited disproportionately from legacies and charitable gifts, especially in the south where feudalism was less deeply engrained and large landowning less widespread. In the Hérault, for instance, Colin Jones has noted that only a very small fraction of hospital income, possibly around 5 per cent, was derived from property, in striking contrast to many of the great civic hospitals of the north, which could be counted among the leading landowners of their region.[10] In 1791 the expenditure of the little Hôpital Saint-James in Libourne amounted to some 9,494 livres, whereas the income from all forms of property and *rentes* totalled only 5,408 livres: the difference, over four thousand livres, had to be covered from the product of alms and voluntary donations.[11] Less fortunate *hospices* had already been forced to close before the end of the Ancien Regime. Indeed, if the survey of hospital incomes undertaken by the *Comité de Mendicité* proves anything – its value is somewhat undermined by an understandable tendency on the part of treasurers to make polemical use of them and by the very fragmentary response that was achieved[12] – it is that there were such glaring discrepancies in the eighteenth century between income and requirement. Some of the most generously endowed hospitals had embarrassingly few demands upon them. It was this imbalance, the highly inequitable distribution of resources, which so offended the rationalist spirit of the Revolution and encouraged the deputies to seek a more ordered system of financing. That quest occupied the attention of all governments between 1790 and 1794, as they moved progressively towards the ideal of an equitable system of distribution by the state that was the dream of La Rochefoucauld-Liancourt.

Yet much of the disintegration of the former finances of the hospitals resulted not from deliberate innovation but from the impact of economic recession. Harvests failed badly in the late 1780s and early 1790s, with a dire effect on the price of basic staples. The non-payment of taxes and the collapse of the luxury trades had serious effects on the economic infrastructure, and this was aggravated by the involvement of France in the Revolutionary Wars after 1792. Above all, the country suffered an almost permanent monetary crisis in the 1790s, especially after the government decided to launch a paper currency, the *assignat*, backed by sales of national lands. The result was a quite frightening level of inflation, which could be contained only by the severe application of the general *maximum* and the use of economic terror in 1793 and the Year II. Hospitals' costs spiralled alarmingly, even before the disastrous attempts of the Thermidorians and the Directory to steer France back to a free market economy. It was not only food that rose giddily in price: so, too, did the cost of labour, of the maintenance work that had to be done on hospital buildings if the fabric were to be maintained. In Paris a day's work by a stonemason rose from 2 livres 10 sous in June 1792 to five livres in *messidor* II, and that of a joiner from 2 livres 15 sous to six livres over the same period, while the materials they used rose in price apace.[13] It is little wonder that essential repairs remained undone. For the government failed to take account of this level of inflation when budgeting for hospitals; they made allowance only for current expenditure and ignored the very considerable arrears which piled up in the majority of hospitals;[14] and only belatedly and rather begrudgingly did they accept that harm was being done to the hospitals' finances by other strands of Revolutionary policy. Nowhere was this more evident than in the field of charitable giving. For many of those most able to give were rich and aristocratic, the very people for whom the Revolution spelt exile, emigration, economic ruin, and possibly even death. The waves of emigration that started with the storming of the Bastille deprived the French hospital service of much-needed revenues. Equally, as with poor relief, much of the charitable giving to hospitals was inspired by religious piety, an impulse that dried up almost completely after the Revolution broke with the Catholic church in 1790. And potential donors were only further discouraged when Revolutionary administrators insisted on alienating existing legacies and using the moneys for their own purposes. At the Incurables in Paris, for instance, beds in the gift of the parish clergy were arbitrarily assumed by the state;[15] while the authorities at Agen, desperate for additional revenue, rather callously used private legacies to meet everyday running costs at the local hospital.[16] Such actions did little to encourage the rich and the pious to perpetuate the long tradition of voluntary charity.

More deliberate was the Revolution's attack on feudal and seigneurial rights, which, from the outset, figured among the principal social and political aims of the National Assembly. The attack was not, of course, aimed specifically at hospitals and charitable foundations, though in practice little was done to exclude them from the financial effects of legislation intended principally to curb the old aristocracy and the church. Laws cannot discriminate too finely, and in the eyes of the law many of France's hospitals, with their extensive holdings of land and urban real estate, were feudal overlords like any other, dependent to an unacceptable degree on the benefits of the seigneurial system. These benefits could be very substantial. The accounts of the Hôpital Saint-André in Bordeaux for 1790 indicate, for instance, that the total income from feudal dues of various kinds – tithes, *cens* and *lods et ventes* were the most lucrative – amounted to 51,436 livres, a very important element in its total income of 131,667 livres and a sum that was sorely missed once such revenues were abolished during the general dismantling of feudalism in the early 1790s.[17] It is true that the government realized the sufferings which they risked causing and that they did sometimes exclude hospitals from the full financial impact of their legislation. In April 1790, for example, it was decreed that hospitals could provisionally continue to manage their property and collect tithes.[18] Equally, in October 1790 hospitals were momentarily excluded from specific legislation on what constituted *biens nationaux*: they could in the short term continue to own, farm, and lease out agricultural lands.[19] In 1791 another law allowed them to continue to collect income from their properties, but only for one further year, until 1 January 1792 when such revenues were to be stopped.[20] All these were minor concessions which delayed the full effects of anti-feudal legislation, but in no sense did they mean that hospitals would be treated by the Revolution in any more generous way than any other feudal *seigneur*.

The degree to which anti-feudal reform attacked the finance of individual hospitals varied dramatically from place to place. In the Midi, the losses were arguably less significant than in the rolling agricultural lands of the north and the Paris basin. But everywhere the reforms did serve to increase the insecurity and the dependence of hospitals at the very moment when they were most vulnerable, when, through emigration, the decline in charity, the poor harvest returns and the general reluctance to pay taxes in large areas of the country, hospital revenues were being severely cut back. If the figures provided by the *Comité de Mendicité* are to be believed, then, for the 1,438 hospitals which bothered to submit reports, total income fell from 20,874,665 livres in 1788 to 13,987,778 livres in 1790.[21] The abolition of tithes was widely resented, since it was argued with some justice that the hospital service was exactly the sort of charitable use which alone could justify their continued imposition, and in some hospitals, like Saint-Alexis in Limoges, the contribution of tithes was considerable, constituting something like one sixth of the total revenue.[22] Even more serious was the effect of the abolition of the tithe on some small country hospitals where there was little wealth in the local community and few alternative sources of income: at Gaillac in the Tarn, for instance, the local cottage-hospital, Saint-André, claimed that tithes had formed over half its regular running expenses.[23] Another major form of income for many hospitals and charities in the Ancien Regime was the welter of local taxes and *octrois* which survived largely intact until their abolition in 1791. The *octrois*, the toll duties exacted by most municipal authorities in the eighteenth century, were often used for charitable purposes, and hospitals had been among the main beneficiaries. In Hérault it was their abolition, far more than that of feudal *rentes*, which caused real suffering: in the case of one hospital, Saint-Charles at Sette, income from *octrois* had amounted to 40 per cent of its total resources.[24] In big cities, too, the *octroi* had often been a valuable source of funds. In Lyon, for instance, the *hôtel-dieu* had enjoyed a steady income from the *droits d'entrée* imposed on all shipments of wine into the city, both by road and by river: in 1790, the last year in which these dues were collected, the product of the eight tollgates came to nearly sixteen thousand livres[25] – a very useful form of revenue, even if, as the Charité was forced to admit in 1790, most of it came indirectly from the poor themselves, the very social groups whom the hospital was intended to aid.[26] Other, less spectacular local sources of income were also lost. Many hospitals, like those at Marseille, had benefited under the Ancien Regime from the moneys raised through the imposition of fines by the courts, a concession which, like so many others, was withdrawn in 1790.[27] Others again had enjoyed a monopoly right over the supply of meat during Lent – a small matter, to be sure, but one which deeply affected the hospital service throughout France and might raise anything from 23,602 livres in an average year, as for Saint-André in Bordeaux, to the 148 livres which went to the tiny *hôtel-dieu* at Feurs in the Loire.[28] For it was such sources of income as these, the results of local benefactions and long-standing traditions, which had saved many French hospitals from bankruptcy in the years up to the Revolution.

The overall effect of these various changes was to annul much of the independent income enjoyed by eighteenth-century hospitals. Treasurer after treasurer complained to the *Comité de Mendicité* that they had suffered such deprivations as to make the maintenance of existing standards, inadequate as these might be, quite unthinkable. One example will serve to illustrate the plight of hospitals throughout France. In January 1793 the treasurer of the *hôpital général* in Limoges produced figures to show the full effects of the new law code on his annual budget: their income from lands had fallen by three thousand livres; tithes had been annulled in their entirety; *cens, lods et ventes* and other feudal exactions had likewise been cancelled; alms and collections from the churches of the parish had totally dried up; they no longer levied a due on burials in the town; and the sums owed to them by the local clergy had been written off. In all, the hospital reckoned that losses totalled around eleven thousand livres, with only the income from rents left unscathed.[29] No treasurer could face such losses with equanimity, the more so as inflation was gathering pace and the essential requirements of the service were placing still further demands on their overstretched finances. It is true that the imposition of the *maximum* gave hospitals, as it gave ordinary individuals, some meagre respite from this pressure, but already in September 1793, on the eve of the Maximum Law, the position of many hospitals was desperate. To feed their patients and provide for their most urgent needs was becoming well nigh impossible, since there were a number of everyday consumer goods which hospitals simply could not do without. One Marseille treasurer pointed out with some bitterness that these staple items were the very goods on which price rises had been most flagrant: the cost of bread had already doubled, he protested, while vegetables, oil, firewood, straw, and soap had all increased in price fivefold.[30] Yet at the same time hospital incomes were often actually falling, with the result that for many bankruptcy and even closure seemed unavoidable.

Of course the deputies had no desire to see the hospital service disintegrate, whatever their views of the role that it should play in the care of the old and the sick. What the *Comité de Mendicité* proposed was that funds lost through the modernization of feudal society and the decline of local charity should be replaced by block grants from the central treasury, rationally shared out to reflect the level of need and the numbers of patients. Access to hospital care should be equally available to all Frenchmen irrespective of where they happened to live. The money to pay for the service would come out of central taxation, and sums of several million livres were voted every year from 1791 for hospital management and paid to departments on the basis of their population levels for reallocation to the various hospitals in their territory.[31] The theory was unquestionably sound, since only by central government taking responsibility for the management of some two thousand hospitals could they be made to serve the welfare state which the Revolution was committed to establish. But between theory and practice stretched a widening chasm with every year that passed. The millions voted in Paris might give the appearance of solving the problem, but too often the sums allocated were based on the previous year's expenses, now being overtaken by inflation and by the loss of independent revenue. From 1 January 1791 hospitals lost another of their Ancien Regime privileges when they were obliged to pay tax on their lands and buildings.[32] Increasingly hospital administrators found their allocations arriving hopelessly late, with the result that their creditors began to lose patience and their debts mounted rapidly. The root of the problem was not any lack of good intentions on the part of the ministers in Paris, but the almost permanent bankruptcy of the state treasury, denuded of tax revenue and increasingly harassed by the costs of war and of political revolution at home. Hospitals were only one priority among many, and they therefore found themselves having to compete with the costs of equipping men for the armies, the costs of pensions to widows and orphans, the burdens of requisitioning, and a host of other emergency expenses, in their quest for scarce government funds. Unavoidably there was suffering. Patients got less to eat as the Revolution progressed: in *floréal* II the Committee of Public Safety solemnly decreed that the meat ration in Paris hospitals should be restricted to sixteen ounces every ten days, and by Year III even the basic bread ration was being cut.[33] There were periods during Year II in Bordeaux when meat was totally unavailable at the city's markets, and at such moments patients were even deprived of the *bouillon* which was deemed essential for building up their strength and aiding their recovery.[34] In the Jacobin period, there were shortages and suffering in many hospitals, but price controls and tight requisitioning powers kept the most essential supplies trickling through to their hard-pressed administrations. It was when these controls were removed, when the centralized bureaucracy of the Jacobin months was finally dismantled, that the hospitals' real problems began.

For the Jacobins left to their successors a hospital service stripped of its independent resources and closely tied to the will and the prosperity of the state. *Secours publics* had been moulded into a section of central government in which the hospitals were expected to respond to a defined area of need. Under the Constituent and Legislative Assemblies, while feudal income had been abolished, *octrois* lifted and new taxes imposed, the hospitals had nevertheless been allowed to retain control of their own lands and farm them or lease them out. For many hospitals this was their last source of truly independent income, the last to which they could turn when grants from Paris failed to arrive. By the law of 23 *messidor* II the government removed this last resource, declaring that hospitals' lands and properties were henceforth to be considered *biens nationaux* and were to be put up for sale in exactly the same way as lands confiscated from *émigré* nobles or from the clergy.[35] The Jacobins' motives were mixed: on the one hand, they saw it as an excellent opportunity to bring those centres of Ancien Regime privilege fully and finally within their welfare state, but on the other – and much more immediately – they needed the money that would be raised by the sales for other purposes, most notably for the waging of war. At this level the exercise was little more than a hasty and opportunistic liquidation of assets to raise revenue. Its impact on individual hospitals varied widely, whatever conservative historians like Lallemand may claim in their denunciation of this decree.[36] Indeed, at the other extreme de Watteville could even allege that it had no impact whatever, since it was never carried out, being prorogued in Year III and finally annulled two years later.[37] The truth, as so often in these matters, is nothing like as clearcut as either of these protagonists would suggest. Where local administrators acted promptly and efficiently, or where political pressures were brought to bear strongly upon them, sales could be made very promptly, often in the most unfavourable market conditions since vast estates were coming on to the market and the prices they fetched were correspondingly low. The *hospice civil* at Tarbes, for instance, obliged by selling off nine plots of farmland, both arable fields and meadows, on the instructions of the Convention.[38] Other hospitals, like that at Saint-Etienne, were compelled to sell lands and buildings that were an integral part of the hospital itself, again for sums of money that were soon spent on immediate running costs.[39] The impact of the law was very uneven, since many hospitals derived their income from sources other than land and could not be affected, and since the prorogation of the decree after *thermidor* salvaged the property of the laggardly or the cunning from instant disposal. Doubtless there were isolated cases where the sale of hospital property could be seen as beneficial, like that of the *hôtel-dieu* in Lyon which finally got permission to dispose of some waste land it owned at Les Brotteaux on the other bank of the Rhône.[40] But much more commonly these sales were forced, against the better judgement of *économes* who viewed the lands as a last buffer against insolvency and who understood only too well that what was under attack was the last vestige of their economic independence. Chabot, the deputy for the Allier, acknowledged as much in Year IX when, looking back over the Revolutionary years, he condemned the law of 23 *messidor* II as the cause of much later suffering and emphasized that the real interests of the hospitals had been sacrificed to the immediate financial needs of the local authorities.[41]

It is perhaps surprising in these circumstances that the majority of hospitals survived the financial upheaval of these years. A few, it is true, were forced to close down by the new financial stringencies they encountered: one such was the Hospice des Pauvres Passants which the city of Lyon had maintained in La Guillotière, the sprawling and somewhat seedy suburb which had developed on the other side of the Rhône. For over a century the *hospice* had served the needs of the sick and the needy in a suburb where poverty was endemic and injury and disease legion; but in 1790 Lyon's seigneurial rights over La Guillotière were abolished and the *faubourg* became part of the Department of the Isère, a known refuge across the river for thieves and highway robbers, pimps and murderers, since it lay beyond the jurisdiction of the Lyon police. When economies had to be made, therefore, it is hardly surprising that the Lyonnais should have reconsidered their responsibilities to the poor of 'La Guille', especially in the light of the new bureaucratic divisions that ensued from departmentalization. And so in February 1791 the municipal council resolved to withdraw the annual grant of 900 livres which it had previously made to the *hospice*, to close it down, and to sell off its lands and buildings to the highest bidder on the open market.[42] Fortunately, relatively few charitable institutions were so brutally axed, though widespread economies had to be made throughout the hospital service. Indeed, where closures did take effect, they were often planned moves to increase efficiency and centralize available resources. Some Ancien Regime foundations were exceptionally difficult to justify in financial terms. At Saint-Mandé, for instance, the *hospice* was housed in vast buildings on a forty-acre site, requiring the services of twenty-three former nuns as nursing sisters and fifteen cooks, cleaners and other domestics; yet it cared for only ten infirm old ladies. The local council at Saint-Mandé was outraged by the size of the hospital's deficit (around 15,000 livres by the end of 1793) and by what it saw as an obviously uneconomic use of resources, and it argued strongly in Year II that it should be closed down, that 'une telle monstruosité' be terminated without delay.[43] The case for rationalization was overwhelming, as it was in the Bouches-du-Rhône in Year IV, when it was suggested with some vestige of realism that Aix did not need to have eight separate hospitals to care for its five hundred patients, and that two of the institutions in Arles could reasonably be closed.[44] But the number of hospitals that were forced to close as a simple consequence of the loss of their independent income was very small indeed.

Money was, however, desperately scarce and, as their plight became more serious, many hospitals were reduced to stop-gap measures, hastily-devised expedients to raise funds and keep their creditors at bay. The hospital at Besançon, overcrowded with wounded soldiers from the eastern front, appealed to the Convention in the Year II to be given permission to harvest its wine crop, even though the hospital vineyards, its most treasured possession, had just been nationalized.[45] Lyon's *hospice général* showed other forms of business acumen in its bid for solvency, and in Year II it found itself denounced to the municipal council for raising money by charging visitors a fee when they came to visit sick friends and relatives and by reserving a number of rooms in the hospital for paying patients. Both practices were deemed to be anti-egalitarian and were suppressed by the Jacobin authority.[46] Less provocative and much more lucrative was the solution found at Saint-Etienne, where the local hospital increased quite dramatically the level of rents it charged for those farms which still remained in its possession. Overall, its income from agricultural lands rose from 3,070 francs to 15,160 francs, almost a five-fold rise, and in one extreme case Jean Magaud found that the cost of his lease at La Côte had been pushed up a staggering twelve-fold, from 600 francs to 7,600 francs.[47] Heartless such measures may appear; yet they were the very minimum demanded if patients were still to be adequately fed and cared for.

They were made all the more necessary by the fact that many hospitals were faced with the parallel problem of rising numbers of patients at the very time when their income was being eroded. Reports from many different parts of the country show that, as the Revolution progressed, overcrowding became almost as serious a threat to patients' welfare as the shortages of money and materials throughout the medical service. In the last years of the Ancien Regime overcrowded wards and overworked staff were already commonplace, but the problems of that period were made to appear insignificant when compared to the situation in many establishments in the later 1790s. At Saint-André in Bordeaux, a hospital of 260 beds, the numbers admitted rose steadily through the Revolutionary years. In 1791 the average number in the hospital at any one time was 440, by 1792 it had exceeded 500, and by the Year VIII the figure was 607, all tended by twenty-three nurses who tried to perform their duties adequately under conditions of impossible pressure. At one period during that year, indeed, there were as many as 850 sick and wounded patients crammed into the hospital's rooms and corridors.[48] For this dramatic rise in the demands made on medical facilities the war must bear a heavy responsibility. Among civilians, many of the able-bodied and the young were absent from their homes to fight on the frontiers, with the result that the old and the frail, less able to depend on friends and relatives for succour, had often no recourse but the local *hospice* when they were no longer able to care for themselves. But the biggest strain on resources came from the military, as wounded and diseased soldiers from the war-front descended on civilian hospitals in quest of medical attention. And since the sums paid by way of compensation for the expenses incurred invariably arrived months late and failed to cover the fast-rising costs of treatment, administrators and treasurers were entitled to see the use of their establishments by the army and the navy as yet another unwelcome burden on their overstrained finances.[49]

It was not only the finances of the Ancien Regime hospital service that were seriously undermined by the French Revolution, however: so, too, was the staffing of the hospitals, the nursing staff and the administrators alike coming under the vigilant scrutiny of the Revolutionary authorities. Administrators were deemed to be a particular threat to the moral and political fibre of France: they were, after all, caring for ordinary people at one of those moments in their lives when they were most vulnerable, when they were ill, often with incurable diseases, and when, by the very fact of being in hospital, they were frightened and more than usually impressionable. The administrators, by controlling the regulation and financing of hospitals, especially in such politically-delicate matters as the religious ministering that should be provided for the sick, were placed in a very powerful position of trust; given that before 1789 the majority of them were drawn from the upper echelons of local society, it was a position which, in Jacobin eyes at least, they would be only too ready to abuse. As late as 1791, for instance, the new administrators chosen for the Hôpital Saint-Jacques in Toulouse constituted a small clique of the most prominent professional men in the city, some so well known locally that their very names would be sure to inspire confidence in Toulouse society; and of those whose occupations were listed, it is interesting that commerce and the law were predominant among them, including as they did five merchants, two former prosecutors, and five other members of the legal fraternity.[50] Such men were proud of their status in the community, and they conformed naturally to the values of their social peers. The hospitals, one could rest assured, would reflect these values and would be managed with due regard to economy, and, above all, to religion and a known standard of morality. Religion, the Revolutionaries noted with a marked distaste, continued to play a prominent part in the everyday routine of hospital life. The almoner was a valued and respected member of the permanent staff, and, as a report of 1790 on the Charité in Paris makes clear, the patients were subjected to various forms of religious observance from the moment they entered the doors of the building:

Aussitôt que les malades sont couchés on leur propose de se composer. On dit au moins deux messes par jour dans les salles. Presque tous les malades peuvent l'entendre. Indépendamment de la messe, un religieux fait la prière soir et matin dans chaque salle, et à midi une lecture spirituelle.[51]

As the Revolution developed, the tensions inherent in French society were given free rein, and hospital administrators were among those who found themselves under fierce attack. In some cases, it is true, there were serious considerations of economy and efficiency which led to the centralization of services and the closure of some of the smaller institutions. But often the motives for removing hospital administrators were more avowedly political, with the incoming local authorities eternally suspicious of those who had served the reactionary regimes that had preceded them. Very occasionally there was a whiff of scandal when the new authorities demanded that hospital accounts be audited and, with such a large part of their revenues coming from the public purse, the demand for public accountability was naturally widespread. The town of l'Arbresle in the Rhône reported to the District authorities in 1792 that it was unable to gain access to the hospital records or to obtain the information it required to write the statutory report on its maintenance and financial position – circumstances which led them to suspect the director of the hospital of peculation.[52] But such judicial proceedings are comparatively rare, and accusations were more commonly of a political rather than a criminal nature. At Nogent, for instance, the board of the local hospital was subjected to intense political scrutiny in Year VI; at Evreux the president of the hospital board, a former noble, was dismissed for his allegedly counter-revolutionary attitudes; and at Auxonne, despite certain qualms on the part of the local authority, one of the administrators was removed from his post because he had the misfortune to be related to an *émigré*.[53] The municipal council at Lyon was perfectly within its rights in terms of the law when it replaced all the administrators of the city's main hospitals in 1791; indeed, it could argue that it was doing no more than what patriotism and civic consciousness demanded. Yet the men they were dismissing had all given years of faithful service to the city and had, as a token of their concern for alleviating human misery, made considerable interest-free loans to the institutions on which they served, for which they were in no way reimbursed by the new authorities.[54] Gratitude, after all, played little part in Revolutionary decision-taking. And the administrators were frequently prey to petty jealousies and personal squabbling. At Montbrison in the Year II, the deputy on mission to the Loire, Claude Javogues, used the excuse of financial mismanagement to suppress the revolutionary administration of the Hôpital des Pauvres, a body only recently established by such worthy Jacobins as Maignet and Couthon, and to reappoint the former administrators to their old jobs. Some mismanagement there may have been; but, given Javogues' bellicose temperament and partisan spirit, it is far more probable that the administrators were merely another of the many victims of the inter-community wrangling that marked the history of the Revolution in the department.[55]

Priests and nuns were even more at risk than were administrators, especially after the full onslaught of dechristianization in 1793. Every hospital under the Ancien Regime employed one or more priests as almoners to minister to the sick, counsel anxious relatives, and bring comfort to the dying; they, more than anyone else, provided what there was of pastoral care in the eighteenth-century hospital service. In Revolutionary eyes, however, their role was much more insidious: they were apostles of reaction, playing on people's fears to woo them and their families away from the Revolutionary cause to the support of *émigrés* and refractories. To the dedicated dechristianizer, every almoner assumed the devillish guise of a recruiting-officer for the Vendeans, sowing the seeds of disaffection in the distracted minds of the politically naive and innocent. Envy only added to the intensity of the hatred that was reserved for the almoners, for they were among the most highly-paid personnel in most hospitals and enjoyed valuable side-benefits. At the Hôpital Saint-André in Bordeaux, for instance, a large general hospital which suffered serious staff shortages in other fields, there were only four doctors and two *chirurgiens* to care for the physical needs of the sick; yet there were three almoners employed to look after their spiritual needs, each enjoying a salary of four hundred livres per year with free board and lodging – a very comfortable remuneration by the standards of the day, especially, as the mischievous were wont to comment, for men who had presumably taken a vow of poverty.[56] Popular opinion was vocal in many parts of France in demanding that such an abuse be ended forthwith, and finally found expression in a decree of 26 August 1792 ordering that all almoners who ought to have left France as refractories should be forced to do so without delay. Reports from various parts of the country indicated the enthusiasm that greeted the promulgation of this law. In Beaune the sacking of the priests in the old medieval hospital was accompanied by outbursts of public jubilation.[57] And in Toulouse the local council did not even wait for the new law to be formally passed, but dismissed the almoners somewhat cavalierly on its own initiative, without even referring the matter to Paris for guidance.[58]

Where priests and almoners were often chased from the hospitals amidst considerable public enthusiasm, the *soeurs grises*, the nuns who devoted themselves to the physical care of the sick and wounded, were treated with far greater respect and circumspection. For the nuns were not disliked by the generality of Frenchmen. They were seen to devote themselves to reducing the suffering of their patients, and their painstaking labours were, not unnaturally, deeply appreciated by people who viewed the prospect of admission to hospital with fear and foreboding. The work they did was neither easy nor pleasant, in a world of dank wards and ill-ventilated operating-rooms, of contagious disease and gangrenous wounds, where anaesthetics were unknown and the treatment prescribed often horribly primitive. As the nurses at the *hôtel-dieu* in Paris pointed out in an address to the National Assembly in 1791, their dedication sprang from their holy vows and these alone could explain the thirteen hundred years of service which their order had given to the sick, driving them to risk their own lives in times of pestilence and condemning them to long hours in fetid wards among the groans and wails of the dying.[59] What is more, the fact that they had taken a vow of poverty meant that they gave their services to the hospitals at derisorily low rates, which by 1789 could not meet even their most basic needs; it is interesting that at the onset of the Revolution many hospitals gave some thought to these rates of pay for the first time in decades, realizing, like the *hôtel-dieu* in Lyon, that the social climate had changed and that the sisters were no longer so likely to be the daughters of wealthy and aristocratic families as they had been in previous generations. Yet, even after long deliberations, the salary agreed upon – an annual honorarium of nine livres, with the guarantee of a fortnight's holiday – shows to what extent the Revolution's social provision remained dependent on the attitudes of the medieval church to the care of the sick and the poor.[60] When in 1790, with the Civil Constitution of the Clergy, the Revolution broke with Rome, the price that had to be paid in the social sphere was to be a very heavy one indeed.

For this reason the Revolutionary authorities were at great pains not to antagonize the nursing orders, treating them, at least until the Jacobins came to power in the summer of 1793, with the greatest caution. The Civil Constitution specifically excluded them from the oath of obedience to the state that was imposed on other religious orders; the law of 17 April 1791 extended this requirement to all concerned in education and public instruction, and though certain local councils – as at Le Havre – tried to argue that this stipulation included nurses, the government was quick to countermand them;[61] only in October 1793 did the Convention finally accept that this concession was irrational and insist that the *soeurs grises*, like all other public servants, be brought within the terms of the Civil Constitution. Only the most immoderate dechristianizers applauded this decision, though many were critical of certain aspects of the nuns' social and political behaviour. At Saint-Brieuc in Brittany, for instance, the sisters' communal life-style had come under attack, and the municipality had expressed the view that, in spite of the practical difficulties involved, it would be preferable to split up the communities and ask the nuns to take lodgings in town.[62] Or again in Toulouse, there were allegations that the nuns in the Hôpital Saint-Jacques were guilty of discrimination in their treatment of patients, neglecting those who were well disposed towards the Revolution and lavishing attention on those of Catholic and counter-revolutionary sympathies.[63] But in general there would appear to have been little overt malice towards the nuns in the French provinces, a fitting tribute to the work which they had carried out over the years.

Even before the Jacobin *coup*, however, the old assumptions had largely disappeared and the quiet tenor of hospital life had been irreversibly broken. For in the eyes of many of the nurses the Revolution itself was anti-Christ: had not its leaders been condemned by the Pope, and was it not intent on attacking the most basic freedoms of the Catholic church? In an age of inflation, their poor wages had become a major source of grievance, particularly as the lands and *rentes* owned by their order were not infrequently being taken over by the government or the local authority without compensation. In Toulouse, for example, a house owned by the order and used to provide accommodation for fourteen nuns was arbitrarily taken into municipal ownership and the rents payable to the order just as arbitrarily suppressed.[64] More important still for the future of their order was the fact that the *soeurs grises* were forbidden to train novices, as the Assembly had decreed that it was illegal to impose such unnatural vows on young girls. In 1791 the sisters working in the *hôtel-dieu* in Paris pointed out to the Assembly just what such legislation implied in terms of the general welfare of the hospital. At full strength, they said, it had been staffed by 105 nurses and 64 novices, but already they were being forced to do the same work with a severely reduced complement of 64 nuns and only eleven novices; soon, unless the law was reversed, the supply of novices would dry up altogether and with it all hopes of future recruitment.[65] The expulsion and frequent imprisonment of the almoners appeared to prove what many of them already suspected, that there was no real place for religion in the Revolutionary social order. So for many of the nuns the decree of 26 August 1792 merely confirmed their worst fears: in Bordeaux, the sisters who served in Saint-André responded to this final provocation by refusing to work and threatening to leave the hospital altogether, a prospect which the local authorities in the southwest viewed with understandable apprehension. The sisters, indeed, won their point, as the district council, in a desperate bid to restore calm and avoid unnecessary suffering, rushed to order the almoners' immediate release.[66] But good relations between the nuns and the Revolutionary authorities could never again be restored.

Relations were finally severed completely by the Jacobin legislation on hospitals, which declared that the job of nursing should be performed by the laity and which resulted in those nuns who were refractory in terms of the Civil Constitution being imprisoned as well as dismissed. This was, it is clear, a purely political decision, taken without reference to the requirements of the sick and the aged. For, despite the undoubted patriotism of many local authorities, their welcome for this particular piece of legislation was carefully muted. Some boldly claimed that the dismissal of the nuns would make little real difference to the standard of the care provided: in the previous January, for example, a petition signed by a large number of citizens in Limoges had demanded that exactly such a measure be taken, pointing out that the nuns were not, as they seemed to believe, indispensable, and that good, virtuous women were queuing up to do this work and would bring to it a zeal which the politicians in Paris were not entitled to ignore.[67] But once such a drastic step had actually been taken, realism was soon to replace such wildly optimistic responses. At Bazas in the Gironde the authorities reluctantly agreed to carry out their obligations in replacing the nuns, but the three women whom they found to assume their tasks proved sadly inadequate, and the municipality could scarcely conceal its pleasure when, in *pluviôse* Year II, several of the nuns agreed to take the civil oath and resume their charge.[68] At La Réole the two nurses whom they were able to recruit were, typically, totally lacking in any experience of hospital work, having been employed previously as a seamstress and a textile-worker.[69] When the Dames de Saint-Thomas were dismissed at Le Havre and gaoled by the authorities, even the Jacobin town council drew attention to the pressing needs of the hospital and expressed regret that 'cette mesure extraordinaire' had been deemed necessary.[70] And when in the Year III, as occurred all over France, the nuns were eventually released from prison, it is no way surprising to find that many of them signed the oath of allegiance to the more malleable Thermidorian authorities and were at once reintegrated into the nursing service.[71] It is clear that hospitals and government alike had made no contingency plans for caring for patients during those desperate weeks that followed the arrest of the nursing orders: it is one case where the poor and the sick were made to suffer by the dictates of political orthodoxy.

These sufferings, despite all the good intentions of politicians and administrators, were very real. The new civilian personnel frequently lacked the skill and the experience that were so necessary at a time when the war was placing ever-heavier demands on the hospital service. And they were not infrequently motivated less by a desire to staunch human misery than by sheer necessity, by the quest for money to rescue their own family economy in hard times. Their attitudes, therefore, often appeared to be bluntly mercenary: by Year III nurses in hospitals all over France were submitting demands for higher pay, again placing an added burden on the already overstrained budgets of local authorities. It is perhaps significant that it was on exactly such financial grounds that the administrators of hospitals like those at Limoges had rejected earlier demands for the laicization of their staff: such a move, they rightly saw, would be to the disadvantage of their institutions and would put them still further at the mercy of the public purse and government diktat.[72] In the event, the effects of the loss of their nursing staff were to be even more deepseated than was generally realized in 1793. The administration at Le Havre protested in vain that there were now no nurses capable of performing such fundamental tasks as registering patients and indenting for supplies, including urgently-needed medicines.[73] They were recognizing at the time what many others came to appreciate only later. In dismissing the nursing sisters, the Revolution showed an intolerance that was actually harmful to its hospital services. It is an instance of dogma, in this case anticlericalism, assuming precedence over any consideration for the patients' welfare.

Yet it would be naive to conclude that there were no real benefits derived from the fresh attitudes and the administrative reorganization which the Revolution entailed. On the contrary, very positive gains were made during these years, gains which stemmed from the new enthusiasm in government circles for social justice and *bienfaisance*. Despite the financial problems, new buildings were opened and existing hospitals extended: indeed, in this regard dechristianization served the hospitals well, as the closure of abbeys and monasteries placed at the disposal of the state many large, solid buildings of exactly the kind that were ideally suited to conversion. There can have been few towns that did not have ambitious plans of this kind, and administrators purred with evident satisfaction as they uncovered their favourite schemes to the public gaze. Dumont, the civil engineer employed by the municipality of Limoges, was typical of such men, committed to a plan that would have extended the *hôtel-dieu* into the adjacent church and monastery: he described at some length the overcrowding and the dank, unhealthy environment in the existing buildings, especially bad for the many children who were housed there – 'la plupart y contractent une couleur livide et une maladie des yeux' – and held out the prospect of a new Jerusalem at a bargain price.[74] In Libourne it was convincingly demonstrated that the transfer of the town's hospital to buildings previously used as a convent by the Récollets would not only improve the facilities offered to patients and staff but would actually make a profit for the local authority, since the sale of the old site would raise twice the sum required to cover the cost of conversion.[75] Money, of course, was not the only or even the main element in many of the decisions that were taken: in the Revolutionary years humanity and compassion figured prominently in the discussions of administrators and politicians alike. And they were helped by national measures aimed at eradicating the worst abuses and health hazards in the old system. The siting of the main abattoirs at the *hôtel-dieu* in Paris, for example, had for generations posed a serious threat to public health. Cows, calves, and sheep slaughtered for consumption in Paris were taken there, and there had been constant complaints - especially during Lent, when the *hôtel-dieu* had a monopoly of all slaughtering in the city — about the heat and the smell of rancid meat in the wards, the swarms of insects in the summer months, the exclusion of sunlight from some of the rooms in the hospital. During the Revolution such complaints were listened to with sympathy and interest, it was recognized that the abattoirs did create 'une corruption dangereuse' for the patients at the *hôtel-dieu*, and finally, in *floréal* II, the Committee of Public Safety ordered that they be replaced by four new slaughterhouses, to be sited elsewhere in the city.[76] It is a small example, perhaps, but one symptomatic of the new, rather paternalistic interest of central government in matters of social concern.

A good example of this new, more open-minded approach can be seen in the Revolution's provision for a group shunned and discarded by eighteenth-century society, the insane. Before the Revolution they had been seen even by relatively enlightened families as a source of shame and of nuisance, best locked up in secure institutions and virtually abandoned to their *folie* without much pretence of medical attention.[77] At best they might be sent to the local hospital or *dépôt de mendicité* to share their lives with the sick, the frail, prisoners and prostitutes, beggars and *vagabonds*. In contrast the Revolutionary authorities seemed eager to understand the nature of madness and to listen to medical opinion: they were even on occasion prepared to put finance into the care of the insane in the belief that their madness might eventually be cured. In Lyon, for instance, the old *hospice* at the Couvent des Picpus was abandoned by the order in 1790 and the building deserted — a building with sixteen bedrooms, a high boundary wall, and a small, secluded central courtyard, ideal for some form of *enclos*. Bravely, in view of the hostility of public opinion and the *frisson* of horror which the very mention of madness created in the community, the Department decided to assume direct responsibility for the care of mental illness and went ahead with the conversion of the convent into a hospital for the insane of both sexes.[78] And at Charenton in the outskirts of Paris the authorities allowed Pinel, a specialist in psychiatric problems and one of the few men of his time to seek to treat and cure the insane, to experiment with his novel methods and offer patients something more than simple custody. Pinel believed that they should be treated as human beings and not as chained animals; he isolated them from other human contact and banned the sightseers who had previously flocked to the hospital; he abolished corporal punishment and relied on two less primitive penalties, the straitjacket and periods of solitary confinement; and, above all, he experimented in the use of hydrotherapy to help overcome their mental disorders. His was a moral treatment as much as a medical one; but he did believe that through his regime some form of cure could be found.[79] Under Pinel the lunatic asylum assumed a shape and purpose that distinguished it from the hopelessness of an eighteenth-century prison.

It was not only the insane who benefited from the new, more progressive attitudes of the Revolution to different aspects of care and medical attention. Minority interests of various kinds were listened to with sympathy and funds made available to a whole range of novel projects that could be shown to help the underprivileged. Considerable improvements were made to the Paris hospital that cared for the blind, the Quinze-vingts in the Faubourg Saint-Antoine, and to the institute for the deaf-and-dumb, the Sourds-muets. In dealing with such problems, authorities would occasionally pool their resources, especially where only small groups of patients were involved: in their provision for the deaf-and-dumb and for the blind the Districts of Lyon, Lyon-campagnes and Villefranche-sur-Saône willingly cooperated among themselves, thus demonstrating one of the benefits of the reorganization of local government in 1790.[80] Even individual citizens with promising ideas for particular areas of charitable provision might hope to obtain a sympathetic hearing. In Bordeaux Jean Saint-Sernin led a vigorous campaign, begun in 1790, to establish a suitable school for deaf-and-dumb children, since the existing church school was badly organized and had fallen into almost total disrepair. Saint-Sernin himself founded a small school for these deprived children, offering them specially-tailored instruction and attempting to cope with their little-understood educational needs. To their credit, the members of the Convention were impressed both by his achievement and by his request for a regular government grant so that the children of poor parents could benefit from his teaching: a decree of 12 May 1793 established that the school should henceforth be considered to be 'under the special protection of the nation', and it made an annual payment of 16,000 livres to Saint-Sernin so that he could carry on his work.[81] Such decisions were not isolated exceptions. Rather they show that there were areas in which Revolutionary government, for all its faceless centralism and dogmatic insistence on orthodoxy, could be both flexible and generous. The much-vaunted humanitarianism of Revolutionary social policy was not an empty sham, though the impact of government intervention remained severely circumscribed even at the height of Jacobin *étatisme*.

Notes to chapter 3

1. P. Loupès, 'L'hôpital Saint-André de Bordeaux au dix-huitième siècle'.
2. J.-P. Gutton, *La société et les pauvres*, p. 9.
3. Arch. Hôtel-Dieu Lyon, F.HD·227, register of patients for 1793.
4. A.D. Loire, 844L, *Tableau de la maison d'Hôtel-Dieu de Saint-Etienne*, 28 November 1790.
5. C. Bloch and A. Tuetey (editors), *Procès-verbaux et rapports du Comité de Mendicité de la Constituante*.
6. *ibid.*, pp. 564–5.
7. A.D. Haute-Garonne, L4066, letter from the *Comité de Mendicité*, 23 August 1791.
8. A.N., F¹⁵436, *Revenus des hôpitaux avant la Révolution*, case of *hôtel-dieu* of Sens (Yonne).
9. Arch. Mun. Saint-Etienne, 3Q249, *Etat de revenus et de dépenses de l'hospice de Saint-Etienne*, Year VIII.

10. C. Jones, *Poverty, vagrancy and society in the Montpellier region, 1740–1815*, p. 296; see also the table of incomes for 1764 admitted by 957 hospitals in their returns to the *Comité de Mendicité*, in C. Bloch and A. Tuetey, *op. cit.*, pp. 564ff.

11. A.D. Gironde, 10L101, District de Libourne, accounts of hospitals for 1791.

12. C. Bloch and A. Tuetey, *op. cit.*, pp. 564ff.

13. A. Tuetey, *L'assistance publique à Paris pendant la Révolution: documents inédits*, III, pp. 256–7.

14. *ibid.*, p. 5.

15. *ibid.*, pp. 218–19.

16. A.N., AD.XIV.[8], decree of 9 *ventôse* X concerning a legacy of 1785 to the hospitals of Agen (Lot-et-Garonne).

17. A.D. Gironde, 11L31, Bordeaux-Intra-Muros, *Etat général des hospices de Bordeaux, prairial* V.

18. A. de Watteville, *Législation charitable*, I, p. 1.

19. *ibid.*, p. 3.

20. *ibid.*, p. 8.

21. C. Bloch and A. Tuetey, *op. cit.*, pp. 568–9, appendix 1.

22. A.D. Haute-Vienne, L373, list of losses sustained by Hôpital-général Saint-Alexis in Limoges, 8 January 1793.

23. A.N., F[15]260, letter from administration of Hospice Saint-André, Gaillac (Tarn), 17 January 1791.

24. C. Jones, *op. cit.*, pp. 282–3.

25. Arch. Hôtel-Dieu de Lyon, E.[HD.] 1694, 1722, 1750, 1777, 1805, 1816, 1843, 1870, and 1894, *Recettes des droits d'entrées sur les vins pour l'année 1790*. The figures of tax raised at the various *octroi* gates are shown in table 1.

Table 1

	livres	sols	deniers
Porte Saint-Just	647	0	1
Porte Sainte-Sébastien	113	3	0
Porte de Vaise	3,216	4	9
Porte Saint-Georges	1,572	13	6
Porte du Rhône	244	2	7
Porte de l'Isle Mogniat	4,422	15	4
Port du Temple	1,874	10	1
Port de l'Abondance	3,672	0	5
Port Saint-Clair	198	11	3
	15,941	1	0

26. A.D. Rhône, 1L1137, *Rapport sur la Charité*, 1790.

27. Arch. Mun. Marseille, Q[3]1, *Etat des amendes envoyées par la Municipalité à l'Hôtel-Dieu, 2 juillet 1790–28 janvier 1791*; MS., n.d.

28. A.D. Gironde, 11L31, Bordeaux-Intra-Muros, *op. cit.*; A.D. Loire, 843L, *mémoire on the*

suppression of feudal dues and its effect on the *hôtel-dieu* in Feurs, 17 March 1791.

29. A.D. Haute-Vienne, L373, list of losses suffered by the Hôpital-Général Saint-Alexis in Limoges, 8 January 1793.

30. Arch. Mun. Marseille, $Q^3$2, *mémoire* by the Maison de Refuge Saint-Joseph in Marseille, 2 September 1793.

31. A. de Watteville, *op. cit.*, pp. 9ff.

32. *ibid.*, pp. 1–3.

33. A. Tuetey, *op. cit.*, III, pp. 72, 423–4. The decrees cited are those of 2 *floréal* II and 1 *germinal* III.

34. Arch. Mun. Bordeaux, 18/25, Tustet, *Tableau des évènements qui ont eu lieu à Bordeaux depuis la Révolution de Quatre-vingt-neuf jusqu'à ce jour*, p. 37.

35. A. de Watteville, *op. cit.*, pp. 32–4.

36. L. Lallemand, *La Révolution et les pauvres*.

37. A. de Watteville, *op. cit.*, p. 32n.

38. A.N., F^{15}294, letter from *hospice civil* of Tarbes, 7 *pluviôse* V.

39. A.D. Loire, 846L, petition from the administration of the hospital of the District of Saint-Etienne, *prairial* III.

40. A.D. Rhône, 1L1144, documents relating to the sale of lands belonging to the *hôtel-dieu* at les Brotteaux, 1793.

41. A.N., AD.XIV.[7], report of Chabot (deputy for the Allier), 1 *ventôse* IX.

42. A.D. Rhône, 1L1167, letter from *Conseil Municipal* of Lyon to the *recteurs* of the *hôtel-dieu*, 12 February 1791.

43. A.N., F^{15}258, letters from *Conseil Municipal* of Saint-Mandé, dated 3 *ventôse* II and 24 *pluviôse* II.

44. A.D. Bouches-du-Rhône, 1L1240, letter to the Department from the Minister of the Interior, 22 *nivôse* IV.

45. A.N., F^{15}1862, letter from the District of Besançon (Doubs) to the *Commission des secours*, 13 *fructidor* II.

46. A.D. Rhône, 1L1150, register of the *Conseil Municipal* of Commune-affranchie (Lyon), 8 *ventôse* II.

47. A.D. Loire, 844L, *Etat des baux du prix desquels les fermiers et locataires des immeubles des hospices civils de Saint-Etienne demandent la réduction*, 25 *thermidor* VII.

48. A.D. Gironde, 4L133, Hôpital Saint-André, report of 1792; 11L27, *Précis sur les hospices de la Commune de Bordeaux*, 10 *vendémiaire* VIII.

49. For a full discussion of the role of civilian hospitals in the care of French soldiers and seamen during the Revolutionary years, see below, chapter 4, pp. 66–71.

50. A.D. Haute-Garonne, L4066, list of administrators of the *hôtel-dieu* (Hospice Saint-Jacques) in Toulouse, 1791.

51. A.N., F^{15}1861, report on hospitals and poor relief in Paris, sent to Jussieu in May 1790.

52. A.D. Rhône, 3L179, District de Lyon-campagnes, letter from the administration of the *hospice* in l'Arbresle, 23 May 1792.

53. A.N., F^{15}129, reports from Nogent (Eure-et-Loire), dated 17 *nivôse* VI; from Evreux (Eure), dated *germinal* VI; and from Auxonne (Côte d'Or), dated 4 *thermidor* VII.

54. A.N., AD.XIV.[7], de Branges, *Rapport sur la pétition des ci-devant trésorier et administrateurs de l'Hospice-Général de N.D.-du-Pont-de-Rhône et grand Hôtel-Dieu de Lyon*, p. 2.

55. A.D. Loire, 845bis L, decree of Javogues on the hospital at Montbrison, 23 *pluviôse* II; see also C. Lucas, *The Structure of the Terror*, *passim*.

56. A.D. Gironde, 4L133, Hôpital Saint-André, *mémoire* on staffing written during 1792.

57. A.N., F^{15}129, report on action by the Department of the Côte d'Or in dismissing the priests attached to the hospital at Beaune, 19 December 1791.

58. A.D. Haute-Garonne, L4066, letter to the Minister of the Interior on the lot of the almoners at the Hôtel-Dieu Saint-Jacques in Toulouse, 1792.

59. Arch. Assistance Publique, NS 72, *Adresse aux membres de l'Assemblée Nationale par les religieuses hospitalières de l'Hôtel-Dieu de Paris* (1791).

60. Arch. Hôtel-Dieu de Lyon, E.$^{HD.}$18, minute of the *bureau* of the *hôtel-dieu* for 13 December 1789.

61. Arch. Mun. Le Havre, Q17, documents concerning the law and the nurses in the municipal hospital, 1791–3.

62. A.N., F^{15}129, report from Saint-Brieuc (Côtes-du-Nord), 16 October 1792.

63. Arch. Mun. Toulouse, 3Q5, denunciation of the sisters at the Hôpital Saint-Jacques in Toulouse, an V.

64. A.N., F^{15}130, letter from the Department of Haute-Garonne, 3 May 1792.

65. A.N., AD.XIV.^{8}, *Adresse à Messieurs de l'Assemblée Nationale par les religieuses hospitalières de l'Hôtel-Dieu de Paris*, 1791.

66. A.D. Gironde, 4L7, District of Bordeaux, minutes of 24 April 1793.

67. A.D. Haute-Vienne, L373, petition from the citizens of Limoges, dated 27 January 1793.

68. Arch. Mun. Bazas, BB2, *registre* 7, minutes of 14 *ventôse* II and 18 *messidor* II.

69. A.D. Gironde, 8L70, District of La Réole, *mémoire* of *ventôse* III on the state of the hospital in La Réole.

70. Arch. Mun. Le Havre, Q17, *Conseil Municipal du Havre*, minute of 9 *germinal* II.

71. J. Adher, *Recueil de documents sur l'assistance publique dans le district de Toulouse de 1789 à 1800*, p. 85n.; also decree of deputies-on-mission Mallarmé and Bouillerot, quoted by Adher (6 *vendémiaire* III).

72. A.D. Haute-Vienne, L373, reply of hospital administration to petition of 27 January 1793.

73. Arch. Mun. Le Havre, Q17, letter from the administration of the city hospital, 10 *germinal* II.

74. A.D. Haute-Vienne, L373, *Observations de l'Ingénieur des ponts et chaussées sur la nécessité d'augmenter le logement de l'Hôtel-Dieu de Limoges, et de rendre cette habitation plus salubre*, 18 February 1793.

75. A.D. Gironde, 10L101, District of Libourne, letter to the Department of the Gironde from the hospital administrators of Libourne, n.d.

76. A. Tuetey, *op. cit.*, III, pp. 146–9.

77. C. Jones, *Social aspects of the treatment of madness in the Paris region, 1789–1800*, pp. 1–5.

78. A.D. Rhône, 1L1162, minute of 15 September 1790 setting up the hospital at Les Fontaines.

79. C. Jones, *Social aspects*, pp. 35ff.

80. A.D. Rhône, 1L1163, 1164, administration of *dépôts* for the blind and for *sourds-muets*.

81. Arch. Mun. Bordeaux, Q17, *Ecole des Sourds et Muets, 1790 – an VIII*, decree of 12 May 1793.

4 The Revolution and French hospitals II The collapse of the Revolutionary ideal

Only if this study were to be closed at *thermidor* – a quite arbitrary and rather whimsical approach – would it be possible to defend the view that Revolutionary policy towards hospitals had achieved any substantial degree of success. For however disappointing the results, there was an undeniable logic about the early plans for centralized charitable provision and state welfarism. The humanitarian impulse of the period had led to new and worthwhile creations, especially for groups among the poor and the sick who had been previously neglected. Above all, other areas of *bienfaisance*, notably pension schemes and informal, extra-institutional relief, had received the lion's share of attention and a substantial proportion of the funding, with the result that the hospitals had been relegated to a rather less central role than they had enjoyed during the Ancien Regime. But even in 1794 it would be difficult to push this case too far. The delays in making payments were already serious and were having deleterious effects on the standard of the services offered; the new demands being made on hospitals were often out of proportion to the resources provided; and, as we have seen, there were widespread staffing problems in large measure the result of other aspects of Revolutionary policy. Control over inflation during the period of the Terror was admittedly a major benefit, but already administrators and treasurers were protesting about the shortages they had to bear and – often unrealistically – were conjuring up roseate images of a previous golden age when their finances had been relatively unfettered and when shortages on the scale they were now experiencing had been virtually unknown. In fact, most of them had little reason to sing the praises of the Ancien Regime, which had already accustomed them to hardship and sacrifice. Both the major Lyon hospitals, for instance, had grown used to severe shortages in the decades before the Revolution. In 1779 the *hôtel-dieu* had had to turn to the king for help, which he had provided in the form of a fixed annual grant out of the moneys raised by the city's *octrois*; and four years later both the *hôtel-dieu* and the *hôpital général* in Lyon were being ordered by the crown to auction off the buildings they owned in a bid to raise the cash they needed to repay their outstanding debts.[1] Equally, it must not be forgotten that administrators were more than a little given to exaggeration. They always tended to lay extra emphasis on what they imagined the government ought to know: in 1764, for example, when asked to supply Paris with an accurate statement of their revenues, they had shrewdly underplayed their real income, judging, no doubt accurately, that total frankness would only lead to higher taxation.[2] In a highly-centralized government like France of the Year II it was even more important to phrase one's submissions in such a way as to please or impress the ministries in Paris. A hospital administrator in need of extra funding from the *Comité des secours* knew that it was no more than his duty to describe the plight of his hospital in the most searing terms, and that anything else would be coldly ignored or taken as a sign of relative affluence.

Under the Jacobin Convention conditions had worsened, but at least the government remained committed to a clear ideal, that of social provision by the state for all those who were unable to sustain themselves and their families; and it seemed prepared to assume that responsibility at the highest level. Under the Thermidorians and the Directory any such firm commitment disappeared as the government struggled desperately from one crisis to another. With their belief in reducing the extent of state intervention in the running of services, the overall aims once so crisply enunciated by the *Comité de Mendicité* now became increasingly blurred and indistinct. The economic backcloth did not help to strengthen the government's commitment to poor relief, since the years after 1794 were marked by harvest failures and bread shortages, industrial recession and quite horrendous levels of inflation once the *maximum* was removed. They were years of general misery for large sections of the population, years of insecurity which tested to the full the efficacy of the free market. The sense of uncertainty and lack of direction caused by administrative breakdown only added to the scale of the problem, while the terrible winter of 1795 made the lack of firewood almost as serious a deprivation as the shortage of grain for bread.[3] It was hardly an auspicious period in which to reduce the extent of state support for the hospital service.

Yet that was precisely what the Thermidorians proceeded to do. Beset by economic problems and the mounting costs of war, and liberated from any feeling of commitment to Jacobin *étatisme*, they sought to reduce state involvement in areas where it had recently and, they argued, unnecessarily been increased. Their principal target was that most Jacobin of laws, the law of 23 *messidor* II, which had nationalized hospital properties and effectively made hospitals totally dependent on the state. The new regime, believing in free enterprise, made it a matter of faith to restore decision-taking and financial responsibility to local administrators, which was, after all, exactly what they had been demanding for several months. No time was lost. A decree of 2 *brumaire* IV took immediate action in suspending the Jacobin law, ordering that sales be temporarily halted and that the individual hospitals should be allowed, until such time as permanent legislation was passed, to enjoy the fruits of their possessions.[4] That legislation was not long delayed. On 16 *vendémiaire* V the Jacobin initiative was finally overturned when the Convention ordered that hospitals should continue to own and lease their lands and derive income from them. Commissions of five members were to be established in each commune to administer the hospitals in their area and to be responsible to the municipal councils, which were to draw up lists of lands sold off as a result of the law of 23 *brumaire*: the government, for its part, undertook that where such sales had already been carried out, *biens nationaux*

of equal value to the lands alienated would be given to the hospitals so that their independent income could be guaranteed.[5] This represents a complete reversal of aims,
in part ideologically inspired, but in part, too, a response to the drying-up of
traditional sources of charity which had so markedly accompanied the nationalization campaign. Hospitals' independent income had in many instances slumped to
quite minimal levels during the Jacobin period; and the new government, without its
predecessor's contempt for individual acts of charity, saw this in simple bookkeeping
terms as a needless loss of valuable revenue.[6] Much more than the Jacobins, the
regimes which replaced them sought to cut back on social expenditure and save what
they deemed to be a very considerable burden on the national treasury. They also
made what seemed to them an unobjectionable assumption that, left to their own
devices, the hospitals would solve the extreme financial problems of the previous few
years and emerge stronger and financially more secure.

They were to be sadly disappointed, since for many hospitals the law of 16
vendémiaire V was far from being the panacea which the government hoped for. In
the first place, there was no compensation for the losses which they had incurred
during the period from Year II to Year IV, a long period of deprivation for many institutions which were already running up substantial debts even before the
nationalization of their property. Smaller hospitals in particular lacked cash flow,
and their economic base had been so seriously attacked that they found recovery very
difficult.[7] Secondly, and more fundamentally, the new legislation proved highly dis-
criminatory in the kind of property which it handed back: it dealt with hospital lands
and buildings, but not with *rentes*, which were still regarded as seigneurial exactions
and were consequently not restored. Especially in the southern half of France, as we
have seen, these constituted a high proportion of hospital properties, and there the law
of 16 *vendémiaire* brought few benefits. Montbrison in the Loire is a case in point, a
hospital with little landed property which had been stripped of some 52,000 livres in
rentes constituées by anti-feudal legislation: the interest from these *rentes*, amounting to
7,000 livres per year, was not covered by the law and the hospital suffered very real
misery as a result.[8] Similarly, the little cottage-hospital of Maurs (Cantal) argued
that, the new law notwithstanding, it had lost almost all its capital through abolitions
and forced sales;[9] and the hospital at Tarbes (Hautes-Pyrénées) clamoured for further
concessions, insisting that, there, too, the law had little effect since it had not repealed
the 1791 measures which abolished feudalism. The hospital could be restored to
financial viability, declared the Department, only 'dans la supposition que le décret
portant abolition des fiefs et autres redevances féodales seroit rapporté', which was,
by common consent, a most unlikely eventuality.[10] Hence, a measure which would
supposedly solve the financial embarrassments of hospitals often had sadly deleterious
results. Expectations were encouraged to rise much too high, and the government,
bolstered in the belief that all hospitals had had their independent revenues restored,
became convinced that further complaints and alleged shortfalls were a matter for
local officials and treasurers to solve. A rather damaging insouciance crept into
relations between central government and local hospital administrators.

Even those institutions which had owned lands and buildings and had obediently sold them off during the Jacobin months – the very ones which the law of 16 *vendémiaire* most clearly covered – frequently discovered that their financial problems were only beginning. Only rarely could they quickly and smoothly resume the properties that had been put up for sale, and then generally where the lands were unproductive and buyers had not been found. The lucky hospitals were those which had, through ruse or simple lethargy, not got round to offering their *biens nationaux* for sale, and they by definition tended to be among the least impoverished, since desperate treasurers had often rushed to realize their assets to pay urgent running costs. More often the lands had new owners, and the hospitals could only wait for the government to fulfil its promise to replace them with other properties in the locality which produced the same income.[11] This sounded fair and reasonable, but, as a solution on a national scale, it begged many questions. Often suitable alternative estates and buildings were not obligingly on the market at the required time; and endless squabbling could ensue over the value of proposed substitutes. The Department of Cantal pointed out that a solution which seemed excellent on paper was illusory in practice, since many hospital estates no longer existed, having been parcelled out in small lots by the *régie des domaines* during its period of stewardship.[12] Frequently, all that the hospital received in Year IV or Year V was a promise that lands would be found, whereas their real need was for short-term advances of money to deal with urgent crises. At Douai they even lacked the money for essential drugs, such was the draining, enervating effect on their resources of two years of continuous shortage.[13] In such cases the hope rather tenuously held out by the law of 16 *vendémiaire* provided little sustenance: in the first year of the law's enactment, indeed, only two hospitals out of more than two thousand in France received any payment.[14] More typical was the case of the Hospice d'Humanité in Amiens, which complained in Year VI that lands it had owned to the value of nearly 734,000 francs had been sold off and an annual income of 36,691 francs lost without any compensation from the state.[15] As late as Year VIII there were frequent angry allegations that, for all the importance attached to the new law, all that had been provided was empty promises.[16]

One reason for the relative ineffectiveness of such legislation lies in the confusing web of bureaucracy which it created. The Jacobin law ordering the nationalization of hospital property had set the tone for this, sending out model answer forms to local *hospices* and demanding detailed information on acreages and incomes, information which the hospital administrators, accustomed to a more leisurely approach, often failed to provide. The result had too often been a long and tiresome correspondence with Paris and a concomitant delay in issuing payments.[17] The Directory, perhaps predictably, learned nothing from this confusion and proceeded to impose even more crushing bureaucratic norms of its own. Before an institution could hope to redeem its alienated properties, a lengthy bureaucratic ritual had first to be completed. Hospitals were rebuked for their vagueness in referring to fields and woodland without more precise details of income and acreage: information had to be provided on the extent of alienations, with an exact statement of the properties once owned, an exact statement of those still held, and an exact indication of the dates of any sales.[18] They were further thwarted by the confusing bureaucratic duplication insisted upon by the government. At Condom in the Gers no lands were replaced for a period of three years during which letters passed back and forth to Paris and additional information was requested: the *Conseil des Cinq Cents* even insisted in Year VIII that the hospital despatch to them information already supplied to the Ministry of the Interior before their application could be filed.[19] Delays of this kind were frustrating, time-consuming, and harmful, since patients suffered and died while bemused hospital administrators searched despairingly in their archives and mounds of unread memoranda piled up on ministry desks in Paris. Submissions often took a fortnight or more to prepare, during which untold misery was left untreated; and it angered hard-working local officials in towns like Metz that the reasons for that misery were not such as could be accepted as sad inevitability, but stemmed from the loss of letters, from the reduplication of dossiers, from general bureaucratic incompetence and a pettifogging obsession with form-filling.[20] That, as much as any loss of idealism, lay at the heart of many of the failings of the social policy of the Directory.

The problem was not assisted by the administrative responsibilities created by the law of 16 *vendémiaire* itself. For the Directory replaced the old hospital administrators, many of whom had served faithfully for long years and who guaranteed a valuable continuity, with commissions of five members, responsible to the elected members of the local municipalities. The idea behind the change was clear enough – the avoidance of tight local oligarchies and some degree of democratic control. But the actual effects of this measure were much less clear, causing still further confusion and administrative reduplication. For in fact these commissions soon became vested with total administrative power, dealing with lands and properties, ordering maintenance programmes, auditing the finances, and taking over the entire internal regime of the hospitals. The result was predictable, in that in many areas constant bickering and burning resentments on the part of the existing local authorities undermined the smooth running of the institutions to whose welfare they were supposed to be devoting their energies, with jealousies and bad blood severely impeding efficient administration. Decisions were held up for months at a time and puerile, time-wasting debates deliberately prevented much-needed initiative.[21] Indeed, when a supervisory role was given to sub-prefects in Year VIII, the change was interpreted as a significant improvement which would restore some semblance of order after the confusion of the previous five years.[22] Administrative reforms under the Directory had few friends. The old, loyal, committed *directeur* or *économe* had been forced to give way to a commission of men whose skills were often limited and who were seldom so singleminded in their concern for the hospital that they devoted more than a fraction of their time to its problems. The resultant confusion only underlined and exaggerated the slow, maddeningly inefficient way in which hospital business was conducted.

Slowness and obstructionism also characterized the government's cash payments to hospitals in the years of the Directory. Especially between Year III and Year V the demands of war were overwhelming, and the government, struggling to pay massive military bills against a backcloth of harvest failures and economic stagnation, was in no hurry to meet its obligations to hospitals. The flow of money from Paris, always liable to serious delay, now dried up into a spasmodic trickle, particularly after the law of 16 *vendémiaire* seemed to relieve central government of its clear responsibility in this area. Grants often arrived months in arrears;[23] usually they were calculated on the unrealistic basis of the level of expenditure incurred in the previous *trimestre*;[24] and sometimes the sums received had been arbitrarily cut back on the unanswerable grounds that the funds simply were not available in the coffers of the *Commission des secours publics*.[25] Whereas the hospitals expected the government to continue to make regular payments and to service their rapidly rising debts, Paris was increasingly reluctant to commit state funds to the purpose and hid behind the new economic freedoms which the hospitals enjoyed. Writing to one hospital in Dunkirk in Year V, for instance, an official in the Ministry of the Interior spelt out his department's new hard line on subventions, reminding the hospital of its independent revenues and making it clear that the grain currently being forwarded would not be provided again, that 'c'était le dernier secours de cette nature qu'il étoit possible de lui accorder'.[26] By Year VI straight cash grants had almost entirely ceased for general running costs, even though the tribulations of local hospitals and *dépôts* had changed very little. When the hospitals of the Gironde were rash enough to petition for money from Paris, they, in common with their counterparts in other departments, received short shrift: the only concession which the government would make was to offer to return their tax contributions for the previous year. But that was a cynical offer, glibly indifferent to the department's plight, since Paris was well aware that the hospitals were in such financial straits that their taxes had never been paid in the first place.[27]

Illusory benefits from the ending of nationalization, the withdrawal of the state grants on which hospitals had come to depend, and long bureaucratic delays in making payments of any kind – all these changes spelt economic disaster for France's hospital service in the Directory period. And if these problems were all worrying local treasurers, they were compounded by the impact of inflation, an inflation which had been a constant threat since the initial issue of paper money but which reached frightening proportions only after the lifting of the General Maximum and the return to the economics of the market. All main areas of hospital expenditure – labour, drugs, foodstuffs, firewood – were highly susceptible to the ravages of inflation, and any attempt to balance their books had to be abandoned. Between *brumaire* IV and *vendémiaire* V, for example, the collective deficit of the seven hospitals in Bordeaux soared to over ten million livres in *assignats*.[28] The fact that former sources of income, many of them paid in specie or in kind, had been forfeited was now felt especially cruelly, since virtually all income came in the form of rapidly depreciating paper currency. Even where farms were leased out, it was rare for a hospital to reap the benefits in produce, since it was clearly in the interests of the peasant or tenant-farmer to pay in *assignats*. Not for nothing did many contemporaries view inflation as the most important single cause of the 'grand délabrement' in which hospitals found themselves.[29]

Various expedients were tried in the late 1790s to overcome the permanent deficit of the hospital service, for it had soon become starkly obvious that the return of their confiscated lands was not going, at a stroke, to provide a solution to the problem. But these were almost always desperate, local measures which did little to reduce the level of debt, while the new liability of hospitals to state taxation more than offset the income obtained. Radical steps like the selling off of property to realize assets were frowned upon by the authorities, which saw these as extensions of the previous experiment of *biens nationaux*, and special permission had to be sought from Paris. Hence in most cases the most immediate means of raising short-term capital was ruled out.[30] As a result, *économes* were increasingly obliged to return to their former sources of revenue and to move yet further away from the idealistic stance adopted in Year II. In some cases the embarrassing gaps between the arrival of funds from Paris had to be covered by loans from the administrators themselves, or from the wealthier members of the local community.[31] At Auxerre in Year VII, for instance, the hospital admitted ruefully that it had been thrown back on private charity to an extent worthy of the Ancien Regime in order to tide it over a period of misery, and that to avoid closure it had been necessary to appeal to the conscience of the more prosperous of the town's citizenry:

> Remuer les entrailles du riche, recueillir jusqu'au denier de la veuve, voilà ce que nous nous efforçons de faire.[32]

In bigger cities, hospitals benefited after Year V from another source of revenue which smacked of a stopgap measure – the levy authorized on the sale of all tickets to theatres and other types of *spectacle* to aid all forms of *bienfaisance*, of which one quarter at least was specifically assigned to the hospitals.[33] It was a sort of general entertainments tax for the benefit of the poor: at Lyon's *Grand Théâtre* it raised nearly thirty thousand francs in each of the years in which it was in force,[34] and much smaller sums were gleaned from other theatres in the city, from dances and concerts, firework displays and horse races.[35] But it could not be a real substitute for assured funding on a regular basis, and its weakness was fully exposed in Year VIII when payments finally dried up.[36] In Paris, by way of contrast, the levy must be seen as something of a success, since the city could boast over twenty theatres as well as numerous *bals* and *fêtes publiques*. There the *taxe* was still being scrupulously collected in Year VIII and Year IX, bringing in a regular income of around ten thousand francs each *décade*.[37] But Paris, of course, was not France, and this tax was notoriously uneven in the benefits it conferred.

It was the lack of certainty in these years which hurt the hospitals most, the fact that they could never with any assurance plan for the weeks and months ahead. It is true that government moneys were not always withheld, though they were generally very late; and after the rundown of the ambitious plans for a *Livre de Bienfaisance Nationale*, more funds may even have been assigned to hospitals.[38] But what was really needed was a source of income on which they could rely, and that was something which the Directory never succeeded in providing. The *étatisme* of Year II had been reversed, greater freedom was allowed to local initiative, but the practical effects of these changes remained piecemeal and inadequate. The measure which more than any other restored to the hospitals a more solid financial base was the law of 5 *ventôse* VIII, which ordered that local councils should help finance their hospitals by establishing *octrois de bienfaisance* on foodstuffs entering their communes – in effect a return to the system of levies and tolls which had been abandoned by the Revolution in its more idealistic phase as being random and inequitable.[39] Initial response to the reintroduction of such tolls was far from favourable. Many councils, burdened with immediate debts, saw it as a lengthy, bureaucratically cumbersome way to raise the revenue, and stressed the uncertain yield of any tax that was dependent on the level of trade.[40] Local instances could be cited to support their qualms: in Year IX, for example, four fifths of the *octroi* was lost at Quimper because of very high grain prices which destroyed the grain trade in the region, with the result that the *hospice général* suffered new extremes of distress.[41] But during the Consulate and the early years of the Empire, French hospitals were to find their revenues restored to some sort of stability after years of uncertainty, and, as Colin Jones has shown for the Department of Hérault, it was principally the restoration of the *octrois* – the law of 5 *ventôse* VIII supplemented by a further circular on 21 *germinal* XII – that was responsible.[42] The experimentation with state welfare and the chaos that followed were finally reversed under Napoleon, and financial initiative was once again left to local administrators and treasurers using largely local sources of revenue, though under the ultimate supervision of the sub-prefect as the representative of central authority.

The financial confusion of the Directory had serious implications for the hospitals and their patients. Repairs to the fabric of buildings remained undone and physical dilapidation threatened many hospitals, which could in turn increase the risk of disease and death among the inmates. At Valenciennes, for instance, the roof of the *hospice civil* was leaking so badly by Year VI and the general state of disrepair was so serious that the doctors working in the hospital felt constrained to warn the authorities of possible repercussions. The atmosphere was permanently humid and dank and health was suffering, with the result that every ten days or so five or six of the patients had to be sent to another, more salubrious building if their recovery was not to be endangered. Besides, outbreaks of fever were common and especially difficult to control; the doctors added, in some despair, that the humidity had become a positive encouragement to fever, which spread inexorably from ward to ward.[43] If capital improvements could not be undertaken for want of funds, so the debts of hospitals mounted and bills from creditors and suppliers were left unpaid. Some treasurers overcame the lack of grain on the open market by borrowing from military stores, but that loophole could be used only for a limited period before repayments were demanded and further supplies were refused.[44] More commonly, they relied on the patience and public conscience of their suppliers. One Bordeaux wine merchant was still petitioning in Year VI to be paid for twelve and a half barrels of Médoc which he had supplied to the city's Hôpital Saint-André three years before, adding, more in hope than expectation, that he would like some account to be taken of the collapse of the currency in the period between sale and payment.[45] He could possibly afford to shoulder the cost of one bad debt, but often the unpaid bills were to small artisans and shopkeepers who had done some service for the hospital and who required immediate reimbursement. The Evêché in Paris in Year III is a case in point: there bills were piling up from a host of small suppliers, from carters and soapmerchants, from an *orfèvre* who had completed some work in the hospital's pharmacy and from the widow who did the hospital's laundry.[46] All Paris hospitals were getting a bad name for unpaid accounts during these years, and they were constantly aware of the serious effects that could result from a loss of creditworthiness in their local communities. For their credit was all that saved many hospitals from closure in this troubled period. With payments from the commission in Paris perennially late, they were suffering a double disadvantage: on the one hand, they had to pay higher prices than those people who could advance money to wholesalers and had no opportunity to shop around for the most advantageous terms, while on the other they lived in constant fear of forfeiting their credibility and trust.[47]

Opinion at the time was unanimous in remonstrating with the authorities about the condition into which the hospital service was allowed to decay after 1795. As treasurers struggled against creditors and government to keep their patients tended, it was inevitable that the patients should be the ones to suffer. Food had never been lavish in Revolutionary hospitals, consisting of a base of bread, vegetables, *graisse*, some meat and wine; but as income fell away, so their purchases became determined by price rather than nutritional value, till by Year V meat and *bouillon* were often just fond memories. Even that most basic of staples, bread, could not always be relied upon. At Versailles in Year V, the hospital protested that it had only three days' supply of grain in its granaries, largely on account of the long delay in paying out sums already approved by the government.[48] Increasingly, grain was unobtainable on the open market, and hospitals had to resort to whatever pressures they could exercise to ensure that they obtained their share of the country's dwindling stocks. Some used the local military magazines, as we have seen, though this was of uncertain legality; others tried to assume for their own needs the supplies which had previously been distributed to the poor in their homes once that much-needed form of *assistance à domicile* stumbled to an end in Year VI.[49] In many hospitals there were no drugs to treat patients and their entire function was put at risk: at Dieuze in the Meurthe, a town where large numbers of injured and sick soldiers came to be treated, the municipal council could list twenty-six essential drugs that were impossible to obtain and without which any hope of cure would have to be abandoned.[50] Bedlinen, too, was unavailable, and existing stocks dwindled fast. The *hôpital général* in Lyon, for example, complained in Year III that it now had fewer than two pairs of sheets for each bed, that sheets were constantly being worn out by frequent washing, and that they had no money for replacements. In such circumstances, the administration protested, it was quite impossible to ensure that patients were kept in conditions of even the most basic cleanliness.[51] Across the city at the *hôtel-dieu*, nightclothes for the sick had long been in such short supply that the hospital reserved the right to confiscate for its own use the clothing worn by patients who died.[52] These problems only grew worse during the acute deprivations of the Directory.

The spartan conditions of these years are eloquently described in some of the thousands of petitions which assailed the *Commission des secours publics*, and even if allowance is made for the customary hyperbole inherent in Revolutionary rhetoric, the picture which they paint is a bleak one indeed. From Bourges in Year VI, a hospital without funds and with debts totalling 455,000 francs, came a blunt, clinical statement of the austerity which it was compelled to demand: the regime had now become 'infiniment sévère', with bread the only form of food consumed, yet soon they would be faced with a clear choice between buying even that most fundamental foodstuff and paying the creditors who were hammering at their door.[53] In all parts of the country treasurers were forced to make the most cheeseparing savings in an attempt to stave off bankruptcy. At Cadillac (Gironde), almost shamefacedly, the administration admitted that it was taking money from the seven patients able to pay even a small *pension* for their food, but was using that money to maintain the whole hospital population of forty-five.[54] The commissioner representing the civil hospitals in Toulouse expressed in Year VI with an admirable crispness the complaints of his counterparts throughout the land:

> Les maux des hospices vont croissant chaque jour. Encore une décade et il ne sera plus possible d'y porter remède . . . . Les greniers sont absolument vides, plus d'huile, plus de graisse, plus de sel, plus du vin, plus du bois à brûler, aucune espèce de toile ni d'étoffe pour le vêtement, absolument aucune espèce d'approvisionnement. La pharmacie manque de toutes les drogues et médicaments, le payement des employés surveillants et domestiques suspendus depuis plus de huit mois; enfin, ces deux maisons manquent de tout, et la commission est réduite aux abois.[55]

In some hospitals it was noted, with a wry feeling for the irony implicit in the situation, that the priests and nuns who till 1793 were the very backbone of the service were by 1795 beginning to present themselves, sick and broken and penniless, as patients, to become a further burden on the hospitals' contracting resources.[56] Overall, the picture was a most depressing one, one heavy with the musty smell of neglect and decay. Even some committed revolutionaries began to have doubts about the success of their social policies towards hospitals: in Year V, in a report to the Convention on the state of the service, Trotyanne noted rather plaintively that standards had fallen noticeably since 1789 and went on to depict the Ancien Regime's record in this field in exaggeratedly complimentary terms.[57] Like many of his fellow-countrymen, he was prepared to make what at the time seemed a quite monstrous admission – that much of the legislation passed by the various assemblies in Paris had remained inoperative at local level and must now be adjudged to have failed.

Jacobin welfare schemes had effectively underpinned French hospitals and prevented closures; but the Thermidorian and Directorial regimes, providing no safety-net, presided over a severe reduction in the size of the hospital service. The expressed fears of treasurers, that they might be forced to close their doors, often turned out to be real enough by the end of the decade. Hospitals simply did not have adequate resources to fulfil all the functions expected of them, as supplies and care became increasingly depleted. By Year V the Cantal was no longer issuing threats of what would happen in the future: at Saint-Flour patients were being turned away, old people and infants were being forced by sheer nakedness to remain constantly inside the dank, fetid buildings, and babies were dying for want of medical attention.[58] In Dijon a man whose state pension was months in arrears risked being sent home to die;[59] in the Dordogne one hospital was turning away old, sick people 'n'ayant même pas la force d'aller mendier leur subsistance'.[60] Even large hospitals in major towns feared for their continued existence, though in practice it was the smaller country hospitals, less visible and often less able to make their views known, which actually closed down. In the Hérault, Colin Jones has calculated that nineteen of the department's forty-three hospitals, the majority of them small and catering for only a few patients, were forced to close, temporarily or for good, between Year III and the turn of the century. And some of those which remained, in the words of a prefectoral inquiry of *messidor* VIII, were transformed into little more than 'des établissements de bienfaisance pour secours à domicile'.[61] Every department told its own story of closures and abandonments in these years. The local hospital at Tarare in the Rhône was virtually abandoned by Year VI, receiving no new patients and offering succour only to two *vieilles filles*, and it was turned, rather appropriately, into a barracks for the local *gendarmerie*.[62] There were even instances where institutions that had been opened during the first, optimistic phase of Revolutionary enthusiasm were shut down before the end of the decade. In Agen, for example, where a separate building for children had been opened in the early 1790s, the Directory ordered in Year VI that all patients should again be treated in a single establishment, on the grounds that a town of ten thousand people could not justify the expense of more than one hospital.[63]

Financial constraints were by far the most serious threat to French hospitals after 1795 and dominated all discussion of social provision. But again hospitals found themselves affected, socially and economically, by the implications of other aspects of government policy. Staffing, so gravely threatened by Jacobin anticlericalism, ceased to be a problem of great moment, inasmuch as the new regime, while nominally anticlerical and in dispute with Rome, in practice showed none of the venom which its predecessor had reserved for the nursing orders. The same *soeurs grises* whose requests for pensions had been so summarily rejected in Year II on the grounds that they were refractories had little trouble in obtaining them a year later. Public attitudes had changed, and the mood was now one of sympathy and understanding, especially since many of the former nurses were in dire straits of poverty.[64] Besides, the lay *citoyennes* who had taken over their work were seldom as dedicated, and even as late as Year VII and Year VIII reports on the state of care from various parts of the country were still invoking the lack of adequate staffing as a major failing of the system. Increasingly, therefore, hospitals which had given in to Jacobin demands in Year II and had divested themselves of the services of non-juring nuns – and many smaller country hospitals had simply ignored these pressures – set about reinstating the sisters to what many Frenchmen saw as their natural role in the wards. At Blangy in the Seine-Inférieure they were invited to return in Year VIII by a grateful local population, which noted that, even after their dismissal, they had continued to visit the wards and take an interest in the sick. The Minister approved, observing that it was 'le voeu unanime des habitants' that they should return.[65] Where staff shortages occurred, it was increasingly to the nuns that hospitals turned, especially to fill positions of responsibility. For there were no other candidates with the skills and experience required for the post of *économe* or *pharmacien*: it is interesting that in the Vosges in Year III there is already a preponderance of ex-nuns in senior positions in local hospitals.[66] Gradually the disruption caused to hospital staffing was eased and greater continuity assured, although of the *soeurs* recalled many were ageing and no young blood was entering the nursing orders. By Napoleon's time the majority of French hospitals were slowly recovering from the effects of dechristianization, and it is interesting to find an Imperial decree of 1807 permitting those nuns who cared for the sick of Aix-en-Provence to return undisturbed to their former life-style and take up residence in a convent in the city.[67]

The period from Year II to Year IV was also that when the French war effort was at its peak and when the impact of that war on the hospital service was maximized. The needs of the army were huge, especially in areas close to frontiers, and their own field ambulances and hospitals behind the front line soon proved hopelessly inadequate. No group was given higher priority than sick and wounded soldiers, since Jacobins and Thermidorians alike made the war effort their very first consideration, and emergency beds had to be found, often at very short notice, to care for the troops.[68] In general, three complementary approaches to the problem were adopted. First, the state could build or designate special military hospitals for the use of the army alone, but that could be a very expensive measure, particularly as the intensity of the war increased. In February 1793, for instance, four million livres were specially earmarked for such provision, and that was only one of many such allocations.[69] Secondly, a proportion of the beds in ordinary civilian hospitals could be set aside for soldiers injured in action, a cheaper solution and one which often had the advantage of providing care for the sick nearer to the place where the troops were billeted. Or, thirdly, where the strain on hospital resources became unbearable, it was even permitted that wounded soldiers whose homes were less than sixty miles away could return to their own families to be tended and cared for.[70]

Special military hospitals, frequently former monastic buildings hastily converted for the use of the army in 1792 and 1793, were often ill-suited to the task and were the subject of numerous complaints from both staff and patients. In Mâcon, for instance, the former abbey of the Carmelites, one such conversion, was visited by inspectors in Year II, who promptly declared that the buildings were 'insalubrious, inconvenient, and cramped', able to hold no more than three hundred patients at any one time and forcing the authorities to break the hygiene regulations by making them sleep two to a bed. The report urged that, to improve the state of public health in the hospital, certain categories of infectious patients should be moved out forthwith to Villefranche-sur-Saône, while the wounded could be better cared for at the civilian hospital in Mâcon.[71] Not all military hospitals were so grossly inadequate: indeed, they were in some respects highly privileged institutions, benefiting from grants and concessions denied to their civil counterparts. Just as vital supplies could be commandeered for the army, so they could be requisitioned to serve the needs of military patients. In Year II, for instance, a succession of *commissaires des guerres* attached to the army in Italy requisitioned the utensils and bedlinen they required for the hospital at Aix-en-Provence from monasteries and seminaries in the area; a shortage of beds in *messidor* of the same year, resulting in sick soldiers having to sleep on mattresses on the floors, was solved when a nearby convent was ordered to transfer its stock of beds to the hospital and place them at the disposal of the men.[72] Shortages often became desperate, and both clerical and *émigré* property was sequestrated for hospital use, the items demanded including such diverse commodities as jugs and basins and cauldrons – all seized from leading *émigré* nobles in the district around Aix – and a variety of everyday consumer-goods such as coal and charcoal, straw and candles, vinegar and olive oil.[73] When times were hard, the needs of military hospitals were given the very highest priority.

A typical military hospital of the Revolutionary years was that at Limoges, which served soldiers from a very wide catchment area, stretching across the Eure, Loiret, Saône, Deux-Sèvres and Nièvre, besides occasional men from the Charentes and from Paris. Not being immediately adjacent to a war zone, it treated a wide range of ordinary ailments as well as wounds inflicted in battle: in three months of the Year IV, for instance, the hospital treated 222 patients for diverse complaints from open wounds to fevers, from eye troubles to venereal diseases. And, perhaps significantly in an age when hospitals were rightly regarded with fear and suspicion by the general public, they lost only one patient in that three-month spell, despite the fact that many of the sick were seriously ill and spent more than two months in hospital.[74] It is not difficult to understand why the military authorities favoured such institutions over the admission of soldiers to ordinary civilian wards. Hion, the *commissaire-ordonnateur* of the 19th Military Division, argued cogently in *frimaire* II that committing troops to civilian hospitals was a false economy. For in military hospitals diet was stringently controlled, visits from friends and relatives prohibited, and the patient's life style closely regulated. They were, he suggested, more efficient, as was proved by the relatively low loss of life. In contrast, the soldier in the civilian hospital could eat what he chose, leave the hospital grounds almost at will, and, while convalescing, lead an idle and debauched life in town. Hion's central argument was the need for a soldier, even when sick or wounded, to remain subject to rigid military discipline, and in military hospitals alone did that regime pertain. The soldier remained a soldier, stripping off his uniform on admission and getting it back when he was cured and ready to rejoin his battalion. In this way alone, he concluded, could malingering be avoided and the safety of the Republic be guaranteed.[75]

If, however, the army looked on these institutions with considerable favour, the community at large continued to see them as a real and highly unwelcome source of contagion. Nowhere was this fear more deeply rooted than in Dijon, a city well endowed with military establishments since it boasted not only two military hospitals (Cérutti in the town centre and Jean-Jacques Rousseau beyond the city walls) but also a *dépôt* for deserters from the French armies and three *dépôts* for prisoners-of-war. In the Year II, when a particularly virulent epidemic threatened to decimate the patients in Dijon's hospitals, public alarm was at its peak and a member of the Convention, Bernard, was sent down from Paris to make a thorough investigation. His findings indicated that the alarm was not totally without foundation.[76] He reported that the fever currently scything through the wards of the hospitals had its origin not in the hospitals themselves but in the *dépôts*, from which a number of prisoners had been transferred for treatment. The prisons were unhealthy, overcrowded warrens: the air was cold and fetid, there was little sanitation and a total absence of latrines, and prisoners were simply heaped on top of one another with little fresh air to breathe and the very minimum of medical attention. Men had been found dead in this dank and squalid environment, and those transferred to the hospitals were already diseased and dying when they were moved. With patients sleeping two to a bed in all the city's hospitals, it was only to be expected that the fever would find a ready breeding-ground. Such a drastic situation required a drastic remedy, and Bernard, to his credit, urged immediate measures to prevent the further spread of the disease and to stop the armies from losing still more men. Fevered patients were to be separated from the others and moved into an isolation hospital established outside the city; patients were to be shaved to prevent the spread of vermin; and prisoners-of-war and deserters were to be compelled to give service as hospital orderlies to ease the tasks incumbent on medical and nursing staff. More important still, Bernard insisted that the authorities adopt a more responsible attitude towards the prisoners in the *dépôts*, changing their straw every ten days, assuring some regular medical attention, and policing the buildings in a more orderly and disciplined manner. Above all, the numbers herded together in dank dungeons like Saint-Julien were to be reduced immediately in the interests of public health and public confidence. All men, even deserters, must enjoy some human rights, argued Bernard, the more urgently since only by guaranteeing them could the perfectly natural suspicions of the local community be effectively laid to rest.

A large proportion of sick and wounded soldiers, however, were treated not by the army but by local civilian hospitals. In part this stemmed from the government's failure to provide adequate military establishments, a failure that became more glaring as the scale of war increased. A city the size of Lyon, for instance, had no such provision after 1793.[77] But there were also good reasons for directing the sick to a local hospital rather than to one that might be many miles distant: it saved the soldier a long and uncomfortable journey on foot to get the treatment he required, a journey that often aggravated his injury and might render him unfit for further service; it cut down the costs to the army of such *congés militaires*: and it reduced the scope for desertion and malingering.[78] To balance hospital budgets it was accepted that the army would reimburse them for the treatment they provided, and scales of daily payment were agreed upon which, in theory at least, offset the full costs involved. With rampant inflation and serious delays in making these payments, however, complaints were legion. In April 1793 the management of the hospital at Carpentras protested that, although the cost of treatment was some 35 sous per man for each day spent in the hospital — and that without taking account of laundry and medical supplies — the army was paying only twenty sous by way of reimbursement.[79] Indeed, the argument raged on throughout the decade, and the sums paid oscillated wildly. At the *hôtel-dieu* in Lyon, care had been free before 1782, when fees were first introduced; until 1790 the rate was fixed at 15 sols, then in September 1790 it rose to 17 sols, in 1793 to 20 sols, and in the Year II to 35 sols; but in *fructidor* IV the sum paid had been reduced to 30 sols, and in *nivôse* V it was further cut to only 20.[80] Yet throughout this period the hospital could complain that the state was failing to honour its debts and that this failure was leaving the administrators of the *hôtel-dieu* in a quite intolerable financial crisis.[81] Even more seriously, the real sufferers were the ordinary people of Lyon, who were being deprived of the medical attention to which they were entitled.

In many areas it was not only the threat of bankruptcy which was harming the efficiency of hospitals; it was also the sheer scale of the invasion by wounded servicemen in need of attention which dramatically cut the number of beds available for others. Of 885 patients at the *hôpital général* in Limoges in *messidor* III, for example, 142 were soldiers.[82] Even the Hôpital Saint-Jacques in Aix, an institution intended primarily for the care of abandoned children, was housing 150 troops by the Year II, and the administrators could make the quite reasonable point that it had become for all practical purposes a military hospital which should therefore be granted the privileges which that status conferred.[83] Since soldiers were often in need of protracted treatment, they not infrequently occupied hospital beds for long periods and still further disrupted the normal routine of a local general hospital. The figures of military admissions to the old *hôtel-dieu* in Lyon (table 2) show graphically how severe was the increase in pressure on limited resources resulting from the requirements of the military.[84]

Table 2

Year	Number of soldiers admitted	Number of days in hospital	Number of soldiers who died
An II	4,360	88,669	272
An III	2,298	58,695	319
An IV	4,720	86,153	126
An V	3,568	73,436	130
An VI	3,726	85,713	85
An VII	6,279	118,790	169
An VIII	7,592	161,978	528
	32,543	673,434	1,629

Not surprisingly, the rest of the community suffered. In the words of the administrators of the *hôtel-dieu* in Troyes, 'La quantité de soldats dont l'hôpital . . . est encombré . . . ne laisse plus de place pour y recevoir les pauvres malades de la ville.'[85] They could scarcely have made their point more brutally.

It is true that hospitals agreeing to care for troops could hope to reap some benefits from their magnanimity. The payments for *journées* of soldiers and sailors might be late and insufficient, but at least they stood a marginally better chance of being honoured than did general bills for civilian treatment. Besides, hospitals treating soldiers could take advantage of some of the privileges accorded to *hôpitaux militaires* but generally denied to civilian institutions – they could, quite legally, take grain from army magazines in lieu of payment[86] and commandeer linen from clerical establishments.[87] Disillusionment, however, soon set in, especially once the spread of the war front in Italy led to a steady stream of troops using hospital facilities. Then there were constant complaints of shortages of linen and of a serious distortion of the uses for which the hospitals were intended. There was increasing frustration when payments authorized by the ministry in Paris never reached the hospitals in question. Anger erupted that hospital beds needed by the local community were being occupied by soldiers who were not really ill but were simply malingering.[88] Above all, it was frequently felt that the service supplied by the hospital was being deliberately run down in order to assuage the needs of the military. At Gray in the Haute-Saône two of the three wards were made over for military use, with the result that all local patients had to be tended in a single ward, a total distortion of its original function and one deeply resented by doctors and staff.[89] At Neufbrisack in the Haut-Rhin the remedy imposed was even more drastic, for the town found itself deprived of a civilian hospital altogether in deference to the needs of the soldiers. The commune, protesting at this imposition, gave vent to strong local feeling that the people of the town had been robbed of something that was in a very real sense theirs: 'Les pauvres de cette commune', wrote the mayor, 'sont propriétaires d'une grande hospice [*sic*], mais depuis longtemps ils n'ont plus pu l'occuper.'[90] Their sense of ownership, of property, was clearly outraged. And even where wards and buildings were not alienated, their use often became confused or indiscriminate, as soldiers were mixed with abandoned children and as hospitals built to treat the sick and aged suddenly had to deal with *scrofuleux* and *vénériens*.[91]

The degree to which hospital services declined was further aggravated by the disruptive behaviour of many of the troops during their stay there as patients. For many of the men it was their first experience for many months of that freedom which came with the release from military discipline, and not all of them were equipped to use it responsibly. Reports flowed in from all sides bitterly criticizing the conduct of the soldiers and demanding that the army take immediate measures to control them. The police in Paris, for instance, complained that they were creating a serious nuisance in the streets of the capital at night, getting drunk, accosting strangers, falling asleep in doorways, fighting among themselves, refusing to pay for drinks they consumed in local bars, and generally taking advantage of the wounds they had received to justify inexcusable conduct that was leading many of them to spend the night in the cells.[92] In Bordeaux two grenadiers from a local battalion caused similar outrage when they were discovered in the arms of prostitutes on the very night of their release from hospital after treatment for syphilis.[93] Such licence undermined the regular routine on which the smooth running of any hospital depended. In Lyon it was pointed out with some bitterness that soldiers being treated for venereal diseases – always the group which gave the authorities most trouble – would frequently get up out of bed and leave the hospital without permission to enjoy a night on the town – debauched behaviour which, it was noted, had a detrimental effect on their prospective recovery.[94] And the *hôtel-dieu* in that same city was so outraged by their activities that it closed down the special ward for venereal patients sent from the army and insisted, as a measure of discipline, that they be mixed in with beggars and other civilian sufferers. Even while they were undergoing cures for their affliction, these men had been accustomed to go out into the hospital courtyard at night, where local prostitutes would be waiting for them; and women passing on their way to visit relatives in other parts of the hospital had been accosted and jeered at.[95] Life in military wards was dominated by drunkenness and horseplay, gambling and indiscipline, while vandalism and wanton destruction were commonplace. At the Hôtel-Dieu Saint-Eloi in Montpellier patients even developed their own hospital ceremonials, welcoming newcomers by drenching them in pailfuls of water as they were admitted.[96] It is clear that in many hospitals where soldiers were treated their presence had an increasingly deleterious effect on the morale of staff and civilian patients alike.

The presence of large numbers of troops and the alienation of hospitals for army use added to the tribulations of the old and the sick during the Revolution. But the tribulations were already there, the end-product of a decade of vaccillating social policy. The economic base of French hospitals had never been strong and was already being severely dented by the slow decline of piety and charity during the eighteenth century. That base was wrenched out by the *Comité de Mendicité* and the Jacobin Convention, each in turn committed to a policy of state welfare and dreaming of a more equitable France where all would have equal access to hospital care. Their dream was shattered by the war and by competing priorities long before the Ninth of Thermidor; it was subsequently destroyed by the new economic aims of the Thermidorians and the Directory, and French hospitals suffered grievously as a result. But at least, for the most part, they survived. They had a physical, structural existence which was more difficult to kill off than the purely financial transactions which constitute the essence of poor relief and *bienfaisance à domicile*. For that very reason they proved more durable, despite the insistence of many reformers at the time that it was on outdoor relief, the payment of temporary grants and pensions to specific categories of the poor, that Revolutionary social policy ought to be concentrated.

Notes to chapter 4

1. A.D. Rhône, C162, *mémoires* of 28 November 1782 and 19 July 1785.
2. C. Bloch and A. Tuetey (editors), *Procès-verbaux et rapports du Comité de Mendicité de la Constituante*, pp. 564–5.

3. For a study of the inflation and the economic insecurity of these years, see R. C. Cobb, *The police and the people*; and A. Mathiez, *La vie chère et le mouvement social sous la Terreur*.
4. A. de Watteville, *Législation charitable*, I, p. 40.
5. *ibid.*, p. 41.
6. A.D. Rhône, 1L1145, Hôtel-Dieu de Lyon, *comptabilité*, 1792–an II.
7. A.N., F[15]264, letter from Department of Gers to Ministry of Interior, 25 *nivôse* IV.
8. A.N., F[15]440, petition from Canton of Montbrison (Loire), 9 *frimaire* V.
9. A.N., F[15]308, letter from Department of Cantal, 28 *frimaire* VI.
10. A.N., F[15]294, letter from Department of Hautes-Pyrénées, 7 *pluviôse* V.
11. Law of 16 *vendémiaire* V, clause 6, in A. de Watteville, *op. cit.*, p. 41.
12. A.N., F[15]280, letter from *président* of Department of Cantal to Minister of Interior, 26 *prairial* V.
13. A.N., F[15]267, letter from administrators of hospital at Douai, 11 *brumaire* IV.
14. A.N., AD.XIV.[8], report of J.-A. Delacoste, 5 *frimaire* VI.
15. A.N., AD.XIV.[8], discussion by the *Conseil des Anciens* of a petition from the hospitals of Amiens (Somme), Year VI.
16. A.N., F[15]433, letter from the *hospices civils* of Béziers, 9 *pluviôse* VIII.
17. A.N., F[15]444, report on the working of the law of 23 *messidor* II.
18. A.N., F[15]308, letter from Department of Calvados to Minister of Interior on the hospital at Honfleur, 27 *fructidor* VI.
19. A.N., F[15]373, letter from Minister of Interior to deputies from the Department of Gers, 27 *brumaire* VIII.
20. A.N., F[15]266, letter from Department of Moselle to Minister of Interior, 28 *brumaire* V.
21. A.N., F[15]103, letter from Pius on hospital administration, *fructidor* VI.
22. A.N., F[15]104, report entitled 'Situation des hôpitaux au premier nivôse an VIII'.
23. A.N., F[15]268, letter from *maire* and *officiers municipaux* of Gray (Haute-Saône), 29 *vendémiaire* IV.
24. A.N., F[15]252, letter from commune of Perreux (Loire) to Minister of Interior, 20 *ventôse* IV.
25. C. Jones, *Poverty, vagrancy and society*, p. 315.
26. A.N., F[15]291, letter from the *chef de la 6ième Division des bureaux du Ministre de l'Intérieur* to the commune of Dunkirk, 4 *pluviôse* V.
27. A.N., F[15]312, letter from the *Commission Administrative de Bordeaux* to Minister of Interior, 13 *floréal* VI.
28. A.D. Gironde, 11L27, *Etat général des dettes passives des hospices du canton de Bordeaux* (Bordeaux, an VIII).
29. A.N., F[15]267, *mémoire* on the state of the hospital at Douai, 1 *germinal* IV.
30. A.N., F[15]249, letter from municipal council of Moissac (Lot) to Minister of Interior, 19 *germinal* VI.
31. A.N., F[15]283, letter from Department of Gers on the funding of the *hôpital civil* at Auch for Years II, III, and IV (18 *messidor* V).
32. A.N., F[15]382, report from Auxerre (Yonne), 1 *fructidor* VII.
33. A.D. Rhône, 1L1176, 'Bureau de Bienfaisance – gestion et comptabilité, an III–an VIII': receipts of the *caisse des indigents* in Lyon.
34. A.D. Rhône, 1L1178, receipts from the *Grand Théâtre* of Lyon, an V–an VII.
35. A.D. Rhône, 1L1177, law of 7 *frimaire* V.
36. A.N., F[15]377, report on the 'situation des hospices de Lyon', 8 *nivôse* VIII.

37. A.N., F¹⁵104, 'Droit pour les spectacles', monthly accounts.
38. C. Jones, *op. cit.*, p. 318.
39. A. de Watteville, *op. cit.*, pp. 67–8.
40. A.N., F¹⁵382, report of the *commission administrative des hospices* in Caen, 2 *messidor* IX.
41. A.N., F¹⁵384, report from *hospice civil* at Quimper (Finistère), 6 *germinal* IX.
42. A. de Watteville, *op. cit.*, p. 107; C. Jones, *op. cit.*, pp. 360–6.
43. A.N., F¹⁵440, letter from *officiers de santé* at the *hospice civil* in Valenciennes, 16 *prairial* VI.
44. A.N., F¹⁵274, letter from *hospice général* of Rouen to Minister of Interior, 18 *ventôse* IV.
45. A.N., F¹⁵312, letter from Martineau to *commission administrative* of the Hôpital Saint-André in Bordeaux, 25 *ventôse* VI.
46. A.N., F¹⁵259, bills made out to the *hôpitaux civils* of the Seine, Year III.
47. A.N., F¹⁵260, letter from hospital at Niort (Deux-Sèvres), 12 *fructidor* III.
48. A.N., F¹⁵303, letter from Department of Seine-et-Oise to Minister of Interior, 1 *thermidor* V.
49. A.N., F¹⁵312, petition from the hospitals of Bordeaux, 7 *vendémiaire* VI.
50. A.N., F¹⁵266, letter from municipal council of Dieuze (Meurthe), 21 *thermidor* II.
51. A.D. Rhône, 1L257, *Hospice Général des Malades de Lyon*, minute of 9 *vendémiaire* III.
52. Arch. H.-D. de Lyon, E.HD. 18, minute of 31 March 1790.
53. A.N., F¹⁵250, letter from *hôpital général* in Bourges (Cher) to Minister of Interior, 5 *pluviôse* IV.
54. A.N., F¹⁵283, letter from hospital of Cadillac (Gironde) to Municipal Council, 6 *messidor* V.
55. Arch. Mun. Toulouse, 3Q2, letter from the *Commission administrative des hospices civils de la commune de Toulouse* to the Municipal Council, 16 *pluviôse* VI.
56. A.D. Haute-Vienne, L373, 'Etat des prêtres et religieuses qui sont domiciliés à l'Hospice Civil de la commune de Limoges au 12 vendémiaire VIII' (MS.).
57. A.N., AD.XIV.⁷, report by Trotyanne on French hospitals, 13 *thermidor* V.
58. A.N., F¹⁵308, letters from the *commissaire* to hospitals in Saint-Flour, 5 *brumaire* V and 30 *floréal* V.
59. A.N., F¹⁵310, petition from Barbeck, *pensionnaire* in the *hospice civil* in Dijon, 5 *frimaire* VI.
60. A.N., F¹⁵310, 'Tableau de l'état où se trouvent les hospices du département de la Dordogne', description of the *hospice* in Montignac, 13 *brumaire* VI.
61. C. Jones, *op. cit.*, p. 320.
62. A.N., F¹⁵312, report from Tarare (Rhône), 4 *fructidor* VI.
63. A.N., F¹⁵316, letter from Department of Lot-et-Garonne, 28 *brumaire* VI.
64. A.N., F¹⁵249, correspondence between District of Trévoux (Ain) and the *Commission des secours publics*, *vendémiaire* III.
65. A.N., F¹⁵382, letter from *commissaire du gouvernement* in Blangy (Seine-Inférieure) to Minister of Interior, 23 *nivôse* VIII.
66. A.N., F¹⁵260, staff lists for *hospices* at Epinal and Mirecourt (Vosges) in Year III.
67. A.N., AD.XIV.⁸, Imperial decree on the *soeurs grises* of Aix, 23 April 1807.
68. Throughout the Revolution the very highest priority was given to the supply and care of the armies, often to the detriment of other government aims. see below, chapter 8.
69. A.D. Rhône, 1L901, *Hôpitaux militaires*, instructions and circulars, decree of 3 February 1793.
70. A.N. Bouches-du-Rhône, L785, *Hôpitaux militaries*, decree of 6 *messidor* II.
71. A.D. Rhône, 1L221, report on conditions in military hospital at Mâcon, 1 *pluviôse* II.

72. A.D. Bouches-du-Rhône, L785, requisitions for hospital at Aix-en-Provence, Year II.

73. A.D. Bouches-du-Rhône, L785, requisitions for hospital at Aix-en-Provence, 25 June 1793 and 2 *nivôse* III.

74. A.D. Haute-Vienne, L375, *hôpital militaire* at Limoges, report sent to military authorities, 9 *vendémiaire* V.

75. A. D. Rhône, 1L221, report of Hion on the need for a military hospital in Lyon, 6 *frimaire* II.

76. A.D. Rhône, 1L221, report of Bernard on the epidemic raging at Dijon, 6 *ventôse* II.

77. Arch. Hôtel-Dieu de Lyon, E.$^{HD.}$ 1618, minute of 15 December 1793 (25 *frimaire* II) noting the decree transferring all responsibility to civilian hospitals.

78. A.D. Bouches-du-Rhône, L451, decree of Committee of Public Safety, 5 *fructidor* III.

79. A.D. Bouches-du-Rhône, L451, letter from the *commissaire-ordonnateur* at the War Ministry in Paris to the department, 12 April 1793.

80. Arch. Hôtel-Dieu de Lyon, E.$^{HD.}$ 1613, *mémoire* on cost of soldiers' treatment in the hospital, Year VIII.

81. Arch. Hôtel-Dieu de Lyon, E.$^{HD.}$ 1613, letter to Minister of the Interior of *ventôse* V.

82. A.D. Haute-Vienne, L373, register of the *hôpital-général* of Limoges, 5 *messidor* III.

83. A.D. Bouches-du-Rhône, L858, Hôpital Saint-Jacques, note by the *recteurs* in Year II.

84. Arch. Hôtel-Dieu de Lyon, E$^{HD.}$ 1613, *Etat des militaires malades*, report of Year VIII.

85. A.N., F^{15}129, letter from administration of the *hôtel-dieu* in Troyes, 5 October 1792.

86. A.N., F^{15}308, minute of Department of Cantal, 6 *prairial* V.

87. A.N., F^{15}276, minute of Department of Haute-Vienne, 11 *thermidor* III.

88. A.N., F^{15}261, reports from the hospitals of Bourg-en-Bresse (Ain), 22 *nivôse* IV and 20 *pluviôse* IV.

89. A.N., F^{15}268, letter from *hospice* at Gray (Haute-Saône), 29 *vendémiaire* IV.

90. A.N., F^{15}255, letter from commune of Neufbrisack to District of Colmar (Haut-Rhin), s.d.

91. A.N., F^{15}373, letter from *hospice civil* of Morlaix (Finistère) to Minister of Interior, 21 *pluviôse* VIII.

92. A.N., F^{15}2818, letter from the *Commission de la police administrative* of Paris on troubles at the Maison Nationale des Invalides, 15 *ventôse* III.

93. Arch. Mun. Bordeaux, H40, report from the commandant of the 11ième Division, Janaury 1793.

94. A.D. Rhône, 1L903, report of the *Comité militaire* in Lyon, 2 June 1793.

95. Arch. Hôtel-Dieu de Lyon, E.$^{HD.}$ 1613, *mémoire* of 13 August 1791.

96. C. Jones, *op. cit.*, p. 325.

5 *Bienfaisance*
and outdoor relief

Hospitals, of course, could never cope adequately with every category of poverty, even in those times when they were not so desperately starved of finance. Traditionally the *hospice* would provide a sanctuary for those who, through the onset of old age or because of serious infirmities, were no longer able to look after themselves or who did not have families in their village able or willing to look after them at home. As we have seen, the facilities offered by hospitals had never been generous, even at the height of Ancien Regime charity, and in the Revolutionary years their provision for such people became a sad travesty of their founders' intentions. The Revolutionary authorities, aware of the extent of these failings, came increasingly to question the suitability of local hospitals as the major providers of such routine relief. Were hospitals, they asked, either the most beneficial or the most economical way of tackling such problems? What suitable alternative means could be adopted? Did people have to be institutionalized before it became feasible to offer them assistance? To questions such as these the *Comité de Mendicité* and its successors vigorously applied themselves.

Institutional relief did have certain fairly obvious disadvantages. For one thing it was expensive: the fabric of the buildings had to be maintained, the staff paid and fed, and the patients' basic needs attended to. The patient himself and his family would be relieved of virtually all responsibility for his welfare, and the full burden would consequently fall, in most cases, on local poor funds. For another, the numbers of poor were increasing, as reports from all over France continually reminded the government. In the Year VI even the beggars of the Faubourg Saint-Marcel in Paris were moved to petition the Directory, pointing out in plaintive tones that their customary sources of informal charity had all but dried up and that they were being left totally destitute, rebuffed by passers-by who had been hit by inflation and deprived of the aid which had previously been supplied through the local *curé de paroisse* or the monasteries of the Paris basin. Now, they complained, the churches at whose doors they had been in the habit of begging had been unceremoniously closed, and the *nouveaux riches* of the Revolutionary years showed not the slightest concern for their plight.[1] Men who had previously managed to make ends meet by seasonal work and short-term begging were now being forced to seek help from the public authorities, exactly at the time when the hospital services were under the most severe pressure. Besides, hospitals were not intended for the starving able-bodied poor: outside the *dépôts de mendicité* which had been opened during the previous twenty or thirty years, there was very little provision made specifically for them. Nor were hospitals necessarily well positioned geographically to cope with the additional influx of destitute patients. Rural areas were especially disadvantaged, as hospitals had tended to be sited in the principal centres of population: in Year VI the *Conseil des Cinq-cents* itself recognized this unhealthy imbalance and urged that more be done for the country districts where three quarters of the people of France still lived. When the bulk of assistance was organized institutionally, they argued, 'vous ne secourez que les villes, et vous laissez les campagnes . . . sans assistance et sans mode déterminé pour y pourvoir'.[2]

The obvious alternative was that of *assistance à domicile*, the making of cash payments to those families who were unable to keep themselves alive by their own efforts. The advantages were clear: it was relatively cheap to administer, those helped would be allowed to preserve their independence and their dignity, and it was a flexible means of assistance which still allowed relatives and others to offer their help to the needy and which could tie the amounts awarded to the seasonal vagaries in the degree of hardship suffered. Above all, there were not the fixed overheads of the institutional system. Yet it was precisely over this question that the basic dualism inherent in the Revolution's attitude to poor relief became most marked. A certain cynicism persisted in the attitude of authority towards the poor, for it was assumed that any system of assistance given without regular inspection and surveillance would of necessity be abused on a massive scale by *gens sans aveu*, that generous provision of aid would go far to discourage industry and create idleness and mendicity instead of curing them. And so it became accepted that two different sorts of provision were necessary – the payment of sums of money to the genuinely needy, counterbalanced by a more repressive approach to the able-bodied beggar, for whom the only kind of aid available would be that provided by a term in the *dépôt de mendicité*.[3] In the eyes of contemporaries they were dealing with two starkly different social problems, and the remedies, to be effective, must be equally distinct. Only in this way could they hope to fulfil their aim of relieving misery, while at the same time rooting out idleness and *vagabondage* in the French countryside.

As with hospital provision, the Revolution's answer to problems of poor relief lay in thorough investigation and national legislation. But it was understood from the outset that social problems were by their very nature highly localized, and that therefore it was only appropriate that local initiative and, wherever possible, local finance should be encouraged. The law of 25 May 1791 accurately reflected the early devolutionist spirit of the Revolution when it established the principle that municipal councils should take charge of poor relief, and it instructed them to set up local *commissions de bienfaisance* without delay. These commissions were to carry out two essential tasks: that of investigating the extent and distribution of poverty in their regions, and that of allocating the available resources to families in need. It was in many ways a crisis measure, made necessary by the sudden collapse of the parish system: yet it would seem to have worked well, the municipal commission for Paris distributing some 862,150 livres in the two years that followed its inception on 1 October.[4] Again and again it was stressed that only by leaving decisions and diagnoses to local people would the real pockets of misery be identified and the distinctions pinpointed between the deserving poor, who should be helped, and the idle scroungers, who must be deterred. In this way, too, as Lebrun argued in a report to the Directory in

Year V, the waste incurred by over-heavy bureaucracy could be avoided, authorities would be forced to tailor their budgets to the current economic climate, and the whole field of *bienfaisance* would become more rigidly subjected to the dictates of what he chose to term 'the true principles of political economy'.[5] They were brave words, but how well, we must pause to ask, did this local emphasis work in practice?

It certainly resulted, as on the national plane did the *Comité de Mendicité* itself, in the collection and analysis of vast numbers of statistics. The local *bureaux*, whether at municipal or cantonal level in rural areas or run by the sections in the larger towns, spared themselves no trouble in the task of identifying pockets of genuine misery and bringing these to the notice of the elected bodies. *Commissaires* were most diligent in investigating supposed abuses and in following up the petitions of those in need: in many respects they were fulfilling, in the towns as much as in the countryside, the functions which the *curé* had traditionally executed in the rural parishes of the Ancien Regime. It was, indeed, a perfectly logical transference of responsibility following the breakdown of church–state relations that stemmed from the Civil Constitution of the Clergy in 1790, and in cities it was a glaring necessity, given the inadequacy of the old parish system: it is interesting to find that one of the first requests for sectional control of assistance came in a petition from fifty citizens of the Section de la Fontaine de Grenelle in Paris, who protested against the scheme, which the Assembly was then considering, to set up new parish committees to assume this responsibility.[6] And the results achieved by these lay *bureaux* were impressive. They drew up lists of those in their area deemed to be in serious need and submitted their names to the local councils, often accompanied by recommendations and comments on the state of their health: in a sense they could be said to have been carrying out some of the tasks performed by a modern social services department. Thanks to such efforts, the social texture of towns and cities became apparent as never before, with the ghettoes of extreme misery exposed and the reasons that lay behind that misery tentatively suggested. Their labours were both useful for contemporaries and a valuable primary source for historians of the period.

Their most startling conclusion was the proof they offered of the wide catchment area for the indigent: few ordinary working-people were ever exempt from the danger that one day they, too, might be numbered among the *pauvres*. Aurillac, which drew up its lists in conformity with the law in Year II, provides a good case in point, that of a market-town with a fairly precarious hinterland where poverty was endemic.[7] In all the list contained 383 names, those of the sick, the weak and the elderly, the unemployed and those who could no longer hope to find work. The majority of them were women, widowed and without occupation, or simply too old to work: often they were afflicted by blindness, paralysis or chronic bad health, which merely added to their already overwhelming problems. Seamstresses and lacemakers, their eyesight destroyed by long hours of labour in failing light, seem to figure especially prominently among them. Of the men, most had the standard jobs of the labouring classes of their locality: they were unskilled and semi-skilled, manual workers and day-labourers, stonemasons and weavers, shoemakers and tailors from Aurillac and its suburbs. But others, too, were vulnerable, and among the *indigents* were listed such as an organist who had become unemployed through illness, an engraver, and two former policemen, the *archers de ville*. Though vulnerability increased with years – it is no accident that the age-group 60–64 is so heavily represented – some relatively young men were numbered among the indigent, as were others whom hard work or physical frailty had aged before their time. The chart of age distribution, indeed, like that of occupational range, goes far to show how large were the sections of Cantal society that were at risk (table 3):[8]

Table 3

Age	Number of poor
Under 30	7
30–34	21
35–39	13
40–44	33
45–49	28
50–54	46
55–59	38
60–64	80
65–69	47
70–74	34
75–79	24
80 and over	12

In large cities the sections busied themselves enthusiastically with gleaning information of various kinds about the incidence of need and conducting regular censuses to establish how best the limited funds available should be distributed. The value of this work was much appreciated by the Convention, which gave them full support and encouragement: in a report on Paris in the Year IV, for instance, Lecloy, the deputy for the Somme, praised sectional diligence in this field in a city whose very size had created a dreadful social problem and had turned it into 'ce grand hôpital de la République, où se trouve le ramas de tous les vices et de toutes les infirmités humaines'.[9] Their statistics illustrated graphically the extent of the inequalities thrown up by these expanding cities, where the new professional and commercial classes were coming more and more to live apart from the unskilled labourers and the *gagnedeniers* of the *faubourgs*. In Bordeaux, for instance, the poor and the immigrants from the countryside were huddled together in the overcrowded and ill-constructed alleys of the Faubourg Saint-Seurin and the Faubourg Saint-Julien, in dilapidated lodging-houses and dank, miserable *chambres garnies*. There, sections like Dix-août and Liberté drew up lists of their poor – 1,527 and 1,800 respectively – which contrasted bleakly with the wealthy merchant areas of the waterfront, such as Simoneau and Brutus, areas which offered no evidence of such misery and which asked for little aid from the municipal council.[10] Similarly in Lyon, there were revealed pockets of densely-packed squalor in Vaise, Croix-Rousse, and various of the poorer central areas of Lyon itself, a misery that was made more grinding by the very high rates of unemployment in the silk industry. In the Section de la Concorde, the poor quarter around the Port Saint-Paul on the Saône, almost every family was in receipt of the indemnity to the poor in 1792: there were some tenement stairs, indeed, where every single inhabitant was dependent on public relief.[11] The 1793 census gave the population of the section as 3,074, of whom 454 breadwinners were unemployed, bringing misery to their families and affecting in all 1,191 people, well over one third of the total number of inhabitants.[12] The unhealthy dependence of the Lyonnais on a single industry, silk, was reflected in the men and women forced to turn to public assistance. The bread indemnity of the Year II is a case in point, and the house-to-house survey on which it was based provides a useful index of poverty. In the Section de la Rue Juiverie, for example, there were 221 men in receipt of the indemnity, of whom no fewer than 171 were *fabriquants*, the small-scale artisans of the silk industry, and all but twenty were in some way dependent for their livelihood on the failing fortunes of the *Grande Fabrique*.[13] Similarly in the Rue Thomassin, out of nearly three hundred poor in receipt of the indemnity, over two thirds of those who had had some sort of employment were directly linked with the textile trade, either in weaving or in stocking- or hat-making.[14] Thanks to these sectional statistics and the hard work cheerfully undertaken by so many sectional officebearers, the nature of poverty was for the first time diagnosed with some accuracy so that appropriate relief could be prescribed.

Often the *bureaux* would go further and suggest solutions to the larger problems of their localities. These sometimes amounted to little more than local grumbles and complaints of government neglect – it was never hard to persuade people in the Franche-Comté or the foothills of the Pyrenees that Paris was arrogantly rejecting their appeals for help – but they could also be constructive. In 1791 the villages around Lons-le-Saunier were asked to explain just why they were suffering so badly, and their replies were listened to with care and respect. Chaussin, for instance, blamed the poor quality of the soil, the lack of manure, and the excessive levels of taxation; Saint-Aubin listed the high price of land and the recent livestock losses as major contributory factors to its economic embarrassment; and Rochefort pointed to the damage caused in the commune by hailstorms and flooding, while also emphasizing the doleful effects of high taxes.[15] Similarly in the Cantal the analysis offered was richly varied and marked by the local experience that resulted from such consultation. Murat pointed, with some justice, to the impossibility of obtaining a decent living for the entire population from a rocky upland soil where agricultural work was impossible during seven months of every year. Riom placed the level of taxation at the top of its list of grievances; Montsalvy stressed the lack of fodder in the department which effectively prevented farmers from keeping their cattle over the winter months; and Laroquebrou claimed that bad roads, blocked passes, and generally poor communications with the outside world were largely responsible for its economic backwardness and therefore for the exaggerated numbers of *pauvres*. In

many cases the only form of aid they could suggest was the grant of money to compensate impoverished peasants for losses caused by climate or disaster, but not all saw
the problem in such narrow terms. The Canton of Saint-Flour suggested that, as
wood was scarce, the authorities should encourage tree-planting on wasteland and
along roadside verges; it further asked that priority be given to keeping country
roads open and passable throughout the winter months, and – with remarkable
foresight – that a school be established in every parish to educate the local children.[16]
Local understanding combined with local statistics to suggest relevant solutions to
the problems posed by popular misery.

   What the *bureaux* remained desperately short of was the money needed to carry
out these ambitious schemes, a shortfall for which, as in the case of the hospital services, the Revolution itself was in no small measure responsible. The reduction in
charitable giving which was so detrimental to hospital finances similarly attacked the
effectiveness of the *bureaux*. In Rouen it was noted that the product of the Church
quêtes had fallen away quite disastrously and that the charitable work of the Dames de
la Miséricorde in the city had not been assumed by the laity.[17] The sums which the
curés had been able to inveigle out of rich parishioners were no longer being spent on
the relief of poverty, and no appeals to humanitarianism could achieve as much
response as the church had done for generations. Legacies could also present unfore-
seen problems to the Revolutionary authorities, since they were generally assigned to
specific purposes, not all of which conformed to the new mood of equality and
bureaucratic rationalization. The town of Lesparre in the Gironde, for instance,
boasted a *fond de charité* to the value of fifty livres which had been established by the
duke and duchess of Nevers for the most impoverished girl in the *seigneurie*; the
thirty-six parishes that composed the *seigneurie* had to compete for the award, which
was bestowed amidst considerable pomp and ceremony, since the benefaction laid
down that 'la fille la plus pauvre de chaque paroisse concouroit au sort qui se tiroit la
dernière fête de Pâques [*sic*] en présence de la justice du lieu qui en dressoit procès-
verbal'.[18] In every way this sounds like a most humiliating performance for the poor
girls of the area, and it is hardly surprising that the practice was discontinued after
1789. But it did mean that the town was poorer to the tune of fifty livres in its provision for the poor. From all over France came similar reports, all indicating that with
the collapse of the old order new burdens had to be assumed by the public purse and
giving a vivid glimpse of the extent to which eighteenth-century charity had been
random and unpredictable. In the Bouches-du-Rhône, for example, suffering was
caused in Allauch because the local *seigneur* ended a long-established tradition
whereby he distributed bread to the poor workers of the commune during the winter
months when there was no farm-work to be found; at Auriol part of the income from
tithes had been used to provide clothing for destitute farm-workers, another source
of relief that was swept away when tithes were abolished; and in Tarascon, a town
whose importance was derived largely from the salt trade, the abolition of the *gabelle*
caused widespread unemployment and more than doubled the numbers in need of
state aid.[19] Such changes could occasion untold misery, and the Revolution, albeit
not wilfully, was in large measure responsible for causing as well as alleviating

neglect. Small charitable associations were callously suppressed because of their religious parentage; private initiative by independently-funded *bureaux d'aumônes* was stifled; and the closure of the gilds also terminated a useful source of social provision.[20] In extreme cases, like Saint-Etienne, the economic plight of the town, coupled with the suppression of the Dames de la Miséricorde, effectively ended all outdoor relief for the local community.[21]

Their financial straits undoubtedly reduced the freedom of action enjoyed by the *bureaux*, since it made them almost totally dependent for their resources on grants from central government. It is true that there were some local initiatives to raise money in the Revolutionary years, but these played a relatively minor part in the financing of poor relief. Sectional collections could take the place of alms-giving in the Ancien Regime, and in town after town hard-pressed local authorities relied on such appeals if they were to prevent starvation and the spread of criminal activity among the poor. These collections, together with forced loans from the richer members of the community, did prove reasonably fruitful: three subscriptions opened among the *sectionnaires* of Le Havre between Year II and Year IV raised sums of 15,875 livres, 12,860 livres, and 16,220 livres for distribution among the town's poor, a substantial relief in a period of steadily mounting unemployment.[22] Clubs, too, saw it as part of their duty to raise regular sums of money for charitable purposes, though the resources at their disposal never appeared adequate to the huge demands made on them. The *Amis de la Liberté* in Bordeaux, for instance, in common with clubs and societies throughout France, was by 1793 distributing aid on a regular basis to some three hundred destitute women, besides organizing special collections to fit out soldiers for the war effort.[23] The idea of a *taxe* on the wealthier citizenry was always popular, especially in the most deprived areas where funds were lowest and where envy of those still in work and still able to maintain their families was unavoidable. Yet it never seems to have been systematically applied, remaining an occasional device to be resorted to in moments of acute stress. Refusal to contribute was viewed as a highly egotistical and even counter-revolutionary gesture, with the result that even foreign nationals resident in France were induced to pay their share. In Le Havre in *nivôse* III, for instance, we find that American ships' captains contributed a total of 6,325 livres to the town's poor fund, and that even the American consul saw fit to make a sizable donation of four hundred livres.[24] Other sources of local aid were somewhat random, varying widely from town to town and often dependent on nothing more methodical than the whim of local officials. The Section du Mail in Paris, for example, helped finance its own social programme by confiscating the profits of a local gambling den.[25] But, like many such ploys, it was more an indication of the willingness of the section to show initiative than a lucrative source of regular finance.

Most of the money for poor relief came, like that for the hospital service, from the national government in Paris, which made grants totalling many millions of livres for the relief of poverty, to be divided among the departments in accordance with the reports which they sent to the *Comité de Mendicité*. Indeed, for a substantial period of 1793 and the Year II it was into such grants that the government channelled the bulk

of its charitable efforts, showing a clear preference for poor-relief schemes *à domicile*
over the claims of the hospitals. The *Comité* had in its third report to the National
Assembly repeated its conviction that home relief schemes enjoyed distinct benefits
since fixed costs and overheads were saved and all the money disbursed was spent
directly on the relief of suffering; in hospitals, by way of contrast, these overheads
constituted 'la dépense principale'.[26] The Convention now attempted to bring this to
fruition. For the needy, those who were sick or old and hence unable to work, state
grants and pensions were proposed. An ambitious decree of 19 March 1793 set out the
structure of the new policy: assistance payments were to be treated as 'une dette
nationale', money was to be disbursed in accordance with the percentage of the
population too poor to pay tax and at a rate related to the daily wage level in the
department, and cantonal agencies were to be set up to supervise its distribution.[27] A
further decree on 28 June 1793 detailed the pensions to be paid to abandoned
children, the children of the poor, and to *vieillards* and *indigents*, a natural extension of
the previous measure which laid out the basis of the Revolutionary welfare state.[28]
These laws were both evidence of the Convention's sincerity and of the importance
attached to pension schemes, but neither was ever put into effect and they remained
dead letters until their final annulment in *frimaire* of Year V.[29] They can be seen as a
statement of intent, as a manifesto outlining the philosophy of Revolutionary *bienfaisance*, but not as practical measures bringing relief to the poor.

More ambitious still was the decision in Year II to draw up a *Grand Livre de Bienfaisance Nationale* as the ultimate measure to destroy popular misery. It was felt by
many deputies that, with hospitals and *dépôts* heavily concentrated in the cities, it was
in the countryside that hardship and neglect were greatest; some, like Barère, were
prepared to argue that the country regions were in any case more worthy, more
patriotic than the cities, producing food for others to eat and providing their sons to
fight in the armies. Speaking on behalf of the Committee of Public Safety in Year II,
Barère urged that countrymen should therefore be given preferential treatment, and
in a lyrical passage a little reminiscent of William Jennings Bryan a century later in
the United States, he thundered out his reasons:

> Dans l'ordre de la nature, la culture et la fertilité des campagnes doivent obtenir la priorité
> des regards du législateur. C'est à la racine qu'il faut arroser l'arbre; les villes ne font que
> consommer les fruits que le commerce accapare, manipule, et agiote au gré de son avarice.
> Dans l'ordre de la bienfaisance nationale, les campagnes doivent passer avant les villes.[30]

From this premise was evolved the proposal to establish a *Livre de Bienfaisance
Nationale*, as a means of ending mendicity in the countryside and sharing out more
equitably the funds available for assistance. The towns were deliberately excluded
from his scheme on the grounds that there relief was already available and could be
channelled through the agency of hospitals and *hôtels-dieu*. What Barère proposed
was that in each department a book be opened containing the names of those who fell
into certain categories of *pauvres* and who were adjudged to be in urgent need of
help: the number of inscriptions was to be proportionate to the population of the

department to ensure that every part of the country was given its fair share of the resources. Those to be assisted were *cultivateurs vieillards*, the most important category, men who had toiled hard in all weathers for over thirty years and who, in Barère's eyes, deserved better than near-starvation or a few miserable years withering away in the poorhouse; *artisans vieillards*, rural tradesmen who had lived in villages or hamlets all their lives, who were to be awarded slightly less (130 livres per year as against 160 livres for agricultural workers) on the grounds that 'les métiers sédentaires occupent des vieillards quoiqu'estropiés' and that they could therefore continue to supplement their pension by working; the widows of farm-workers; and widows and mothers bringing up two or more children unaided. Barère's scheme was adopted by the Convention and became law on 22 *floréal* II.[31] It is important not only as the first major step taken to favour rural workers in a country where much of the worst poverty was to be found on the land, but also as a symptom of the new energy shown by the Convention in removing the causes of indigence in France.

The scheme for the *Livre de Bienfaisance* was the most ambitious and comprehensive to be dreamed up by the Revolution, but the huge scale of the project did not in itself guarantee its success. It was, indeed, typical of the most grandiose phase of Jacobin welfare legislation, soon – like the schemes for hospital finances – to be overtaken by the financial implications of inflation, the military build-up, and the anti-interventionist preferences of the Thermidorian period. But in the short run it certainly captured the imagination more effectively than any other welfare scheme, offering a safety-net to the most needy groups throughout rural France in those very parts of the country where relief had been minimal in the past. Departments and districts set about the task of sifting applications and drawing up their definitive lists: for the category of 'cultivateurs vieillards ou infirmes', for instance, the regulation quota was four hundred names for each department, to be increased by four for every thousand inhabitants in those departments where the rural population exceeded 100,000 souls. The rules were strict and somewhat arbitrary: towns and villages of under three thousand people could be classed as rural for the purposes of this measure. And where the number of claimants exceeded the number of pensions available, it was laid down that the dispute be settled by age, the oldest paupers being given an absolute priority.[32] Not surprisingly, the most lively response to this measure came from those parts of the country which benefited the most, the rural departments of the interior. Large towns were excluded by the terms of the law, and in districts like Bordeaux there is no evidence that the claims of the rural population of the city's hinterland were ever much heeded. But in a department dominated by pastoral or agricultural work, the drawing-up of the *Livre de Bienfaisance* was the most important single act of revolutionary *bienfaisance*. In the Hérault, for instance, we learn that over four fifths of the agricultural communes participated in the scheme and that the department's book contained in all one thousand names. As required by the law, the authorities celebrated this dramatic advance in social provision by holding that most typical of Revolutionary festivals, the *Fête du Malheur*, in the streets of Montpellier on 27 *pluviôse* III.[33]

It was, perhaps, an over-optimistic celebration, for the scheme was never able to live up to the huge expectations it encouraged. Inflation quickly eroded the benefits conferred: widows and mothers of large families were especially unfortunate, trying to struggle to survive on a miserable sixty livres per year. Those without the documentary proof of a birth certificate or marriage certificate could find themselves refused, and now they could no longer hope for aid from other sources such as the Ancien Regime *miséricorde* or the *curé*'s parish charity. The aged and infirm soon discovered that they, too, had been deceived by the rhetoric of the Year II, once the Thermidorians lost their predecessors' passion for universal welfare schemes paid for out of the public purse. The *Grand Livre de Bienfaisance Nationale* became increasingly desultory during Year III and Year IV, till finally the whole scheme was abandoned in Year V, summarily terminated by the same law which reversed the decree of 19 March 1793.[34] From that moment the economics of *bienfaisance* was to be extremely hazardous, with pensions even more vulnerable than were the hospitals to the whim of central government. It is true that from Year V other sources of income were mobilized to help, but the revenue received could never play more than a marginal role. The bulk of the product of the new tax on ticket sales to theatres and *spectacles*, for instance, was assigned to relief projects, but this was never sufficient to guarantee a stable income.[35] It was especially derisory when viewed against the backcloth of the late 1790s, of increasing popular misery and near-starvation in all corners of France, or when compared with the steady rollcall of small charitable *fonds* which had been destroyed since 1789, usually through the attack on the clergy or the abolition of tithes. By the middle of the decade the habit of charity had been so far undermined that virtually all poor relief outside the formalized environment of institutions had disappeared.

The extent of human need and misery during the Revolutionary years is graphically illustrated by the plaintive pleas of those seeking assistance and the large piles of semi-literate petitions which accumulated on the desks of officials in *mairies* and local *bureaux*. These were frequently the most heartrending of documents, simple statements of utter helplessness from people reduced to desperation and indigence. Guillaume Laurent, a peasant from l'Arbresle in the Lyonnais, had inherited his small patch of land from his forefathers, but in 1793 he was forced by dire poverty to write to the district for help: his two cows had died, and he and his nine children were on the verge of starvation, the brittle family economy shattered by the loss of two animals worth some 240 livres.[36] In towns, loss of employment could have a similar impact. Louis Perray, who had earned his living as a bookkeeper to the *brocanteurs* at the market on the banks of the Seine in Paris, found himself redundant in 1791 when the market was closed down, and within two months he was obliged to sell all his possessions in a desperate attempt to retain his dignity and his independence.[37] Or again, the onset of old age could force people to apply, reluctantly and often shamefacedly, for assistance. Men like Santoux, an *officier de santé* in Bordeaux who at the age of eighty was forced to write a begging letter to the local Jacobin club, the *Club national*, mingled a certain shame with a fierce and deeply-engrained pride. He began, in the shaky handwriting of a very old man:

Pardonnez à un homme de 80 ans s'il vous importune par ses lettres; à mon age, les facultés s'affaiblissent, la mémoire n'est pas toujours présente; et je n'ai que mes réflexions pour me rappeler les objets que je peux obmetrer [sic].[38]

After Year II the chances that such pleas would be sympathetically answered were very much reduced as local authorities found themselves unable to honour even the most pressing of their financial obligations.

In such a self-consciously politicized society as that of Revolutionary France, moreover, it was only to be expected that some degree of politicization would creep into the allocation of assistance. Sectional officeholders and the men serving on local *bureaux* were, after all, interested in civic affairs precisely because of their political awareness, and by Year II public life was thoroughly impregnated with a Jacobin conception of morality which could not but affect their approach to applicants for aid. Given that the sums available for distribution were limited, it was only natural that preference might sometimes be given to those whose record of Revolutionary commitment remained untarnished and whose patriotism was proven. Though few towns openly admitted to being influenced by political considerations, it is perhaps symptomatic of the new mood that urgent appeals for assistance during the Jacobin period were almost always couched in terms deeply deferential to the Revolution and accompanied by certificates testifying to the applicant's unassailable *sans-culotte* virtue. When Charles Bertonnet, a seventy-four-year-old Paris demolition worker who was deaf and partly paralysed as a result of a fall, sought aid from public funds in 1791, he enclosed proof of his patriotism and a certificate to show that his poor health had been incurred as a result of injuries received while he was helping to demolish the Bastille, an excellent Revolutionary task at which 'il a travaillé avec plus d'ardeur et de zèle qu'un jeune homme'.[39] One Rupallay, from Rouen, claimed in Year II that it was his patriotism, his ardent love of liberty, which had roused the wrath of local counter-revolutionaries and *aristocrates*, evil men who had treated him so badly that he was unable to resume his normal work.[40] This appeal was answered most generously – Rupallay was given an annual pension of six hundred livres – though it is impossible to state with absolute certainty that the award was made solely for political reasons. More explicitly political was the *bureau* in Le Havre, which openly rejected applications for aid on political grounds. Applicants were asked specifically political questions, such as what they thought of the king's execution, the assassination of Marat, the closure of the churches, and the deportation of priests; whether they knew of any *émigrés* or refractories who had surreptitiously returned to France; whether they would reveal the names of those who were harbouring them. In Le Havre the *bureau* was almost an extension of the political police. Marc-Antoine Chenel had his claim rejected because 'il n'est ni bon père, ni bon mari, ni bon patriote', an interesting mixture of social and political moralizing. Guillaume Gausse, a man of fifty-one with five children, three of them in the armies, was nevertheless refused aid on the grounds that he had failed to perform his *garde* service and had given no proof of his patriotism. And Pierre Bonimare, indigent and a father of three, was equally dismissed without any help by the *bureau* on account of alleged political shortcomings, since he had lamented the death of Louis XVI and had not accepted the Republican constitution.[41] For simple men who had seldom given serious thought to political questions, a political catechism of this sort could form an insuperable obstacle and effectively condemn a whole family to destitution.

The lot of the civilian poor was not eased by the increasingly importunate demands of the military and their dependants for the limited sums which the government did make available for assistance. For just as hospitals came under pressure to treat sick and wounded soldiers as their very highest priority, so the promises of pensions and *primes* made to recruits and their families seemed the most sacred of the social debts which Revolutionary governments incurred. As more and more troops were thrown into the various campaigns of 1793, Year II and Year III, so the toll of wounded and bereaved mounted inexorably, and funds were insatiably gobbled up in furnishing the pensions and the medical care which this demanded.[42] The government's record in honouring these obligations was much better than its performance in caring for the *invalides* and *vieillards* back in civilian life. Similarly it made an honest effort to tackle the problems of devastation and destruction occasioned by war and civil conflict during 1793 and Year II, when constant troop movements over French territory damaged crops and when cottages and holdings in the war zones were liable to be razed completely. A decree of July 1792 clarified the areas in which government would accept some measure of responsibility. Those who had suffered should apply for compensation to their local councils, providing evidence of their loss either in the form of entries from their account-books or (in the case of the poorer peasants, who kept none) of testimonies from neighbours. The only people excluded from the benefits of the decree were declared enemies of the public weal – those who could supply no evidence that they were resident in the area, those who had opposed requisitions imposed by law, and those who had done nothing to retard the advance of the enemy.[43] In principle, the Convention agreed that compensation should cover three major areas of loss: the destruction of crops; houses and farms burned down or wrecked in the course of the fighting; and all property, including furniture, personal effects, cattle, woods and vineyards, destroyed as a result of enemy action.[44] It is interesting to note that, in spite of shortages of funds, the government did try its utmost to make fair assessments and settlements in the majority of cases. In ventôse II, for instance, the Convention put twenty million *livres* at the disposal of the Minister of the Interior to be shared out among those citizens who had suffered losses resulting from both civil war and the ravages of foreign armies.[45]

Some of the largest claims for compensation came, significantly, not from the frontier areas but from the departments affected by counter-revolutionary outbreaks. Zangiacomi's report in Year V on the scale of devastation and of government aid noted that of the six departments where losses were heaviest only two were in the east (the Meuse and the Bas-Rhin), against four in the west (Loire-Inférieure, Vendée, Deux-Sèvres, and Maine-et-Loire).[46] It is an eloquent testimony to the ferocity of the civil war in those departments, and one that is further underlined by the government decision to reduce their tax liability for Year VI by nearly nine million francs, a measure deemed necessary because of the sheer scale of the devastation. It was estimated, indeed, that about two thirds of the surface area of the Vendée had been seriously damaged, one half in the case of the Loire-Inférieure and the Maine-et-Loire, and one third for the Deux-Sèvres.[47] The city of Lyon also suffered considerably from the siege by Republican forces during the federalist interlude in the summer and autumn of 1793; here again, it was the poor who suffered most, the ordinary workers and artisans of Vaise and the Croix-Rousse, whose humble silkworkers' homes were blasted by the siege-guns in the last weeks of the revolt. In the months that followed, some two million livres were earmarked for compensation. But the *cahiers* of claims leave us in no doubt about the reality of the suffering that had been caused. A large number of people had lost all their property in the bombing of the suburbs: the dossier of claims for Vaise, for instance, lists forty-six families, many of them poor, who were reduced to total misery and helplessness. Jean Guinard, an illiterate Lyon stonemason, appealed for aid as he had lost everything he owned, 'laquelle consiste en lit, meubles, outils, marchandise, linge d'homme et de femme'; others submitted rather pathetic claims for the few shattered sticks of furniture that they had once possessed.[48] Some, of course, had lost more than property in the siege. A gauzemaker's widow, Jeanne Giraud, wrote to the municipal authorities explaining that because her husband was paralysed and bedridden she had had to stay with him in the city during the siege, with the result that she was now both widowed and penniless, her husband having been killed and her home shattered by the Republicans' siege-guns.[49] A wool-carder who himself had volunteered for army service found on his return to Lyon that his house had been destroyed and his wife killed: he rather poignantly assessed the total extent of his loss at a mere 586 livres.[50] And another Lyon woman could write in despair that she was reduced to utter destitution, as her husband had been killed and she was left with three children to support, one of them a boy of ten who was blind; with the public workshops closing, she told the city authorities in Year III, she saw no possible way in which she could continue to look after them.[51] Such cases, a mere sample of the human misery concealed behind the Lyon siege of 1793, illustrate the degree of suffering inflicted by war on the civilian population, suffering which revolutionary governments had little choice but to assuage. But by adding to the demand for scarce resources, the casualities of war were unconsciously diverting money from civilian pensions and from the everyday social problems which the Revolution had ambitiously set out to solve.

The new emphasis placed on *assistance à domicile* for the old and infirm was a humane and progressive extension of changes already taking place during the Ancien Regime, however much it may have been vitiated by financial frustrations and by rival government priorities. It was not, of course, intended to be available for all; nor was it seen as a replacement for those forms of closed, institutional care in which supervision played as important a part as relief. The treatment reserved for the seasoned *vagabond* in Revolutionary France was, quite deliberately, very different: it was never a part of the Revolutionary creed that a man had the right to choose a life of idleness, and it was generally accepted that those who refused to conform must be severely punished.[52] One of the very first steps taken by the Revolutionary authorities was to order the repatriation to their canton of origin of jobless workers arrested for begging in the streets of Paris. By the terms of the law of 30 May 1790, all 'mendiants et gens sans aveu' in Paris who had not had a fixed address for at least six months (a year in the case of foreigners) were compelled to ask for passports indicating the route they would follow to return home.[53] This policy was a more drastic version of previous legislation to encourage voluntary repatriation, and it was viewed in the towns and villages of the provinces with a certain despair. For, though it was undeniable that it reduced the depths of misery in the capital itself, in many of the surrounding regions it merely exacerbated existing tensions and increased the latent animosity that had always marred relationships between Paris and its provinces. The law placed the onus for paying beggars their allowance of '3 sous par lieue' on the local officials in the towns along their route, and for departments like the Loiret, criss-crossed with highways and lying strategically between Paris and some of the poorer agricultural areas of the country, it implied considerable extra expenditure. There was not even any guarantee that the government would reimburse them; yet the misery of the expelled beggars would brook no denial.[54] For the *indigent*, returning to his native parish and to the certainty of unemployment, it was a recipe for misery and malnutrition of the sort which he had already known and which had driven him to beg in the first place. Nor could he expect much sympathy from the authorities once he resumed his life of *vagabondage*, since for persistent offenders Revolutionary governments continued to prescribe the same kind of cures as had been favoured by their predecessors – including transportation for those who refused to respond to milder treatment. A decree passed at the height of the Jacobin period ordered that such *vagabonds* be transported to Fort-de-la-Loi in the southeastern corner of Madagascar, where new buildings were to be erected to house them and an armed force stationed to enforce law and order.[55] At its most extreme, the Revolution's attitude to beggars was utterly penal.

Transportation remained an extreme solution, resorted to only rarely. The normal reaction of the authorities throughout the Revolutionary years was to send able-bodied beggars to the local *dépôt de mendicité*, an institution which always fell rather uneasily between its charitable and its punitive functions. Even the *Comité de Mendicité* in Paris seems to have found the purpose of the *dépôts* a little ambivalent, occasionally revealing their penal aspect by referring to them as 'maisons de correction'. Its decree of 1790 made provision for thirty-four *dépôts* throughout France, the smaller and less economic of them having been closed down, which were to house 6,650 inmates at an annual cost of some 1,350,000 livres.[56] It was stressed that these houses were not to be thought of as prisons, but admitted that their main purpose was to reform the beggar and rehabilitate him, 'rendre le coupable meilleur et d'en faire un homme utile à la société'. At local level, the *dépôt* soon came to be seen in less humanitarian terms, and the puritanical approach of many Revolutionaries ensured that a spell in the *dépôt* was little different from a mild prison sentence. The attitude of Clochard, a Bordeaux architect who made a formidable reputation for himself in the city as the principal administrator of *bienfaisance* and poor relief, was typically unyielding.[57] Aged and infirm paupers should be made to do light work to help the economy of the *dépôt*, and they should be provided with living conditions that were adequate without ever being comfortable. No one should ever be put in the position of being attracted into the *enclos*. As for the able-bodied, they should be made to suffer a much harsher regime. They should be put to work, in cleaning up the harbour or sweeping the streets, or in providing hard manual labour for municipal public works schemes. Only when they obtained a job would they be allowed to leave the institution, and should they subsequently be caught begging yet again, Clochard demanded that they be punished by being confined to the *dépôt* 'for all time'. It was a regime in which discipline was severe, mealtimes strictly observed, and leisure very closely limited and supervised. In most *dépôts*, like the Grand Bureau des Pauvres at the Hôtel-Dieu in Paris, religious observance was insisted upon, and priests were in regular attendance, at least till dechristianization was unleashed on the *dépôts* in 1793. The overall impression is one of constant regulation and inspection, of a regime which alleviated the purely physical aspects of poverty but which did so by increasing the psychological cruelty involved.[58] In this respect the Revolutionary authorities were merely building on the achievement of their predecessors, since in the twenty years before 1789 the *dépôts* had become increasingly punitive in both function and aspect.

That is not to suggest that the authorities were unconcerned about the welfare of the *pauvres*, or that care was not taken to ensure that decent basic standards were maintained. The *Comité de Mendicité* was always open to new ideas, from whatever source they came, and many of the administrators in the *dépôts* showed themselves to be kindly, humanitarian men who were deeply and properly concerned that suffering should be alleviated. Clochard himself in Year X was still suggesting improvements to the existing regime, and he quoted the progress made elsewhere in Europe, in Holland, England, and even Sardinia, in support of his case.[59] More immediately, the day-to-day management of the *dépôts* showed that considerable thought was being given to the problems involved, while at the same time they were struggling to balance a very precarious budget. The staffs were sometimes surprisingly large: at the *dépôt* in Lyon, for instance, they numbered forty-one in Year V and were paid a total of 8,050 livres per year in wages; besides medical staff, some of them had special training to allow them to tend particular groups of patients, like the insane, the incurable, and those suffering from venereal diseases.[60] Food was rather unvaried, but was always adequate and compared not unfavourably with the often pitiful diet of the poor in the French countryside. Bread was everywhere the staple food of the poor, and it is striking that in the *dépôt* in Bordeaux five or six times as much was spent each year on bread supplies as on the rest of its provisions, which consisted mainly of beans, potatoes, milk, and a little meat.[61] Again, the government laid down firm standards which *dépôts* were forced to follow, and regular inspections took place, reporting on food, cleanliness, and general standards of maintenance. In Lyon in 1791, for instance, the inspectors' report, though generally favourable, did recommend improvements, notably in the quality of the meat and the wine served to the inmates.[62] Occasionally, even the rather sombre routine might be broken if the political situation demanded it. When the federalist revolt in Toulon was finally crushed and the rebel port fell into Republican hands, even the poor at the *dépôt* in Grenoble were allowed their moment of celebration: the Department of the Isère, overjoyed by the news, thoughtfully voted that wine should be sent to the *dépôt* to allow them to join in the public revelry, 'pour les faire participer à l'allégresse publique sur la conquête de Toulon par les Français'.[63]

The general picture of life in the *dépôts* does, however, remain a sombre one, and the moments of light relief for the inmates were few. In part this was because, as in so many aspects of Revolutionary *bienfaisance*, the actual level of assistance attained fell increasingly short of the high goals set by the *Comité de Mendicité*. The financial problems besetting civil hospitals, which cut back assistance payments and aborted valuable pension schemes, continually affected the management and efficacy of the *dépôts*. The one at Lyon had run up an annual deficit of 800,000 livres by Year IV,[64] and within two years it had become totally dependent on government funds. There were, as we have seen in other connections, very considerable dangers inherent in such a dependence, and the *dépôt* was predictably languishing in great distress. Patients' rations were cut back, suppliers were refusing necessary provisions, and in *ventôse* VI the administrators were being compelled to close down parts of their service and to turn away indigent men and women from outside the Department of the Rhône when they presented themselves, desperate and diseased, in search of help. Venereal patients, in particular, who had traditionally travelled to Lyon from a wide area of central and southeastern France to be cured, were now being sent back to their native communes where no medical treatment was available.[65] And with reduced resources the *dépôt* was forced to cope with more beggars, more *vagabonds*, more inmates, not only because of the increase in the level of misery in the community at large but also because all the alternative sources of assistance were drying up.[66] By Year VI the treasurer was demanding that a grant be made available to them to cover the funeral expenses of those of the inmates who had died over the previous four years. Otherwise, he made it clear, the *dépôt* could no longer afford to provide even a simple burial in the cemetery at La Guillotière.[67] Such instances illustrate graphically the yawning gulf between the standards set by the legislators in Paris and those attained in the individual *dépôts* of provincial France. Again, it was the inmates, the poor and helpless, who inevitably suffered.

Who were these inmates, the able-bodied poor so abused by contemporary commentators and reviled by pamphleteers? In Bordeaux in the first frenzied months of 1790, when the local police and *garde nationale* devoted themselves unstintingly to the task of rounding up *mendiants*, the police files are unusually rich. The majority of those arrested were male, mostly young men aged between seventeen and twenty-five, with trades or unskilled work when they could find it – as *vignerons*, *portefaix*, *charpentiers*, *menuisiers*, and *tisserands*. Very few worked on the land, which is rather surprising in view of the large contingent of agricultural workers who migrated to Bordeaux every year to seek their fortunes, and one can only assume that by the time of their arrest they had already been sucked into the pool of unskilled labour in the city. Interesting, too, is the inclusion among them of a large number of sailors, accounting for one third of the total arrested, who claimed to have been with the navy at Blaye or Libourne and to have resorted to begging every time the fleet was in port.[68] Clearly the trades represented among beggars varied somewhat with the locality, but always they mirrored very faithfully the standard employment pattern of the local population. In La Rochelle, as in Bordeaux, the call of the sea was strong, and again we find sizeable numbers of sailors, ships' carpenters, cooks and others who had been paid off at the end of a voyage and had turned to mendicity in the lean weeks that followed.[69] At Rouen those arrested included a high proportion of deserters from the armies;[70] in Lyon the *mendiants* were predominantly unemployed textile workers.[71] The women generally gave their profession as *couturières, ouvrières en soie, blanchisseuses, cuisinières, journalières, domestiques* – in short, the everyday occupations in the eighteenth century of the working classes. Domestic servants found life especially difficult as they grew older and faced the prospect of solitary poverty in some ill-heated garret, without the security of a pension, once their working life was over.[72] It was a bleak outlook. For all of them, men and women alike, the *dépôt* represented the ultimate indignity, the lowest level to which they could sink; and yet it offered food and shelter and a certain measure of companionship. Denis Mauguin, a thirty-three-year-old bachelor from the Section de la Fraternité in Paris, had been crippled since childhood, and the only way in which he could stay alive was by hobbling around the streets begging from passers-by.[73] Nicholas d'Huiq, an octogenarian from the same section, had been a tailor until poverty and old age had forced him to give up what little tailoring he was still able to do; latterly he had earned a few sous by dispensing holy water at the door of the church of Saint-Louis, until the church was closed down by the Revolution and his last hope of maintaining himself was brusquely withdrawn.[74] Such men, having forgotten the dignity that independence alone could bestow, were glad to seek a refuge in the Paris *dépôt*.

From this it becomes clear that the poor confined to the *dépôts* may have been rather more desperate and marginally more deeply sunk in misery than the people in receipt of *assistance à domicile*; they were likely to be more unsettled individuals, more willing to uproot themselves when famine threatened and take to the city streets or to the highways; they were certainly more unlucky. But they were not a race apart. Like the *bons pauvres*, they were ordinary people overwhelmed by the odds they faced in everyday life, men and women with no special skills to offer who had taken to begging as their last remaining hope of maintaining themselves. Often they had come to the cities in the first place as migrant workers in search of employment and had ended their stay there exactly as they had begun it, alone, friendless, and unable to cope. In the Section du Bonnet Rouge in Paris, of forty-four beggars whose commune of origin is known to us in Year IV, only seven were Parisians, while six came from the Creuse, and others from as far as Lorraine, the Franche-Comté, and Marseille.[75] Very few of those arrested in Bordeaux for mendicity belonged to the city itself: a large number had come from the rural areas of the southwest in search of work, and others claimed to have travelled from much farther afield, from Poitou and the Limousin, from Brittany and Lorraine, from Provence and especially from the Auvergne.[76] The pattern was very similar in La Rochelle, where few local people were confined to the *dépôt*, which was used instead for incomers caught begging in the town's streets, incomers from much of western France, from the Massif Central, and, in the case of seamen, from foreign ports like London and Trieste.[77] This bias need not surprise us. Local people, after all, generally had someone to vouch for their good character; their poverty could be explained away to the authorities, who would not necessarily be unsympathetic; and they would possibly have the broken vestiges of family life to fall back on when disaster struck. Not so the immigrant worker, driven to the towns by poverty, unable to return to the miserable farmstead he had left behind, and now forced to be self-sufficient in an alien and often highly suspicious society to which he could never fully belong. Repatriation as a solution to the problem of poverty could seduce only urban administrators, since to the poor themselves it was totally unrealistic. Of thirty-six men and women arrested in the Section des Quinze-vingts in the Faubourg Saint-Antoine in Year II, all declared that it was their wish to remain in Paris and resisted any pressure to return to their home village.[78] They knew that they had no choice but to stay and continue their life-long struggle to make ends meet. And if they failed in that struggle, as often they were bound to fail, it was they who were most likely to be accused of *vagabondage* and con-demned to the harsh, restrictive regime of the local *dépôt*.

Their lot would have been less pitiable if the *dépôts* had, as the *Comité de Mendicité* intended, been reserved for those caught begging. But the very fact that the regime in the *dépôts* was harsh and punitive encouraged the authorities to use them for a rather wider clientele, with the result that, as in the last years of the Ancien Regime, they were often allowed to become virtually indistinguishable from prisons. *Vagabonds* were, after all, referred to them by the courts, which tended to see a spell in the *dépôt* as a fitting punishment for minor criminals and a deterrent to those who might be tempted to devote themselves to a life of crime. In Lyon the District administration recommended in 1791 that the increasing problems of lawlessness in the country areas around the city could be tackled only by rounding up all the 'filoux, escrocs, et vagabonds' and locking them up in the *dépôt*.[79] In Year IV, a woman who was per-sistently causing trouble in another of Bordeaux's hospitals, the Incurables, was ordered to be moved to the *dépôt de mendicité* in order to cure her of her disruptive ways by making her conform to the strict discipline of the house.[80] In Bourges the deputy on mission to the Cher in Year III even saw fit to transfer two men who were serving ten-year prison sentences, on the grounds that the regime in the poorhouse was more suited to their requirements.[81] The inmates, indeed, were often a somewhat shady cross-section of men and women on the verges of criminality, whom the communal life of the *dépôt* could easily turn into hardened criminals. Those sent to the *dépôt* in Rouen illustrate this fairly graphically. In 1790 the inmates included not only a rich assortment of *vagabonds* but others of a more clearly criminal persuasion: men convicted of complicity in thefts, of stealing silver, of horse-stealing, of arson, of armed robbery and highway robbery were numbered among them.[82] One man had been arrested for the theft of silver from a castle where he had been given alms; another, a young man of thirty, was serving a life sentence in the *dépôt* after the death sentence passed on him in 1787 had been commuted.[83] It is hardly sur-prising in these circumstances that the poorhouse administrators were moved to write to the municipal council to complain about the uses to which they were being put and to point out that they were not a house of correction.[84]

Those convicted of moral offences were also frequently incarcerated in their local *dépôt*, despite the protests of the houses themselves. It had long been established practice to accept prostitutes for purposes both of detention and of cure, since the majority of them were suffering from some form of venereal disease and they posed a considerable threat to public health, especially to the health of the army and navy. In most poorhouses a very high proportion of the women admitted were venereal patients: of one hundred women occupying beds in the *dépôt* in Bordeaux in *pluviôse* III, no fewer than ninety-two were noted as suffering from venereal disease, a figure that elicited neither surprise nor dismay.[85] Indeed, it was confidently expected that prostitutes who found themselves attacked by syphilis and other venereal complaints would sooner or later present themselves for treatment. In Toulouse girls seeking a cure would frequently make a declaration that they were *mendiantes* precisely because they knew that this would get them admitted to the *dépôt*, where they would be treated free of charge: it was a popular and much-practised ruse among the *filles de joie* of the area.[86] As a result, the *dépôts* came to be used for all sorts of moral offenders for whom no more appropriate provision was made by the eighteenth-century authorities. In Rouen the inmates included girls arrested for 'libertinage public', for 'concubinage' with members of robber bands operating in the hinterland of the town, and for incestuous marriages.[87] Many of these girls were pitiable creatures, deserving compassion rather than retribution, born into depths of misery from which they had never succeeded in making their escape. At Auch a woman of twenty-six, mentally retarded and aged before her time, had worked as a prostitute since early childhood until she had been confined to the *dépôt* in 1788.[88] Another twenty-six-year-old prostitute, in Rouen, had taken to the streets after her mother was burned at the stake for infanticide.[89] Men, too, might be sent to the *dépôts* for sexual offences or because they were suffering from venereal disease. One such was François Pavie, who was reported to the guard on the Porte Saint-Hillaire in Rouen by a girl whom he had tried to seduce: after various attempted cures, such as hot baths and bleeding, he was finally sent to the *dépôt* on the grounds that he suffered from a form of sexual deviance and would, without provocation, accost and caress complete strangers of both sexes. As the surgeon knew of no cure, there was apparently no alternative to a spell in the poorhouse.[90]

To make matters worse for the *pauvres valides*, there was no attempt to segregate the old from the debauched and the criminally minded. In many provincial towns the *dépôts* were also made to double as asylums. Rouen's poorhouse was a mecca for the insane from several departments in Normandy, which made no alternative provision, and from February 1793 this indiscriminate mixing of widely differing categories of patients was still further complicated by the use of the *dépôt* for the treatment of epileptics.[91] In short, the poorhouses were fast becoming dumping-grounds for social misfits and those callously ignored by a medical profession as yet unable to offer any effective treatment. As might be expected, internal discipline suffered badly and the morale of the poor and the staff alike plummeted. The old especially, those whose only crime was that they were no longer able to lead independent lives, found the surroundings and the regime most humiliating. Violence was an everyday occurrence, with inmates attacking their fellows as well as the staff of the institutions; it is symptomatic of the widespread fear and of the danger to life and property that in Year V the administrators at Le Havre should have asked the municipal council to supply them with a gun so that the *gardien* could be armed in emergencies.[92] At the Bicêtre in Paris the problem was exacerbated still further by the decision to house convicted criminals there, including men under sentence of death: as the *économe* rightly pointed out, it was most disspiriting for the indigent who were forced to mingle with them, and the lack of security also meant that it was almost impossible to prevent such prisoners from committing suicide.[93] Furthermore, the herding together of beggars and prostitutes in the poorhouses could only encourage the spread of venereal disease, which reached epidemic proportions in some *dépôts*. Vice was rampant, and many of these institutions basked in a well-merited reputation as schools for immorality, where the young and innocent were taught by hardened criminals and seasoned whores. Paganel, reporting to the Convention in Year III on the condition of the women in the Salpêtrière, phrased it neatly when he wrote that 'à l'époque de leur sortie, elles ont presque toutes mérité une perpétuelle réclusion'.[94]

Between the ambitious designs of the *Comité de Mendicité* in its early years, when Frenchmen could still persuade themselves that poverty could be conquered, and the more confused and punitive aspects of many of the *dépôts de mendicité*, there is a stark and cruel contrast. Of course apologists could point out that those who were put into the *dépôts* were not a cross-section of the poor but rather the most hardened of *vagabonds*, and that the expansion of home-relief schemes was intended to reduce the degree of reliance placed on institutional care for beggars. But the reality by the mid-1790s was very different, for if the Revolution had seen the *dépôts* in a constructive light as merely one prong of a multi-pronged approach to social provision, the other prongs were by then largely eaten away by inflation and decay. The progressive collapse of pension schemes and home relief spelled disaster, too, for the *dépôts*, obliged to serve as an underfinanced catch-all for the failures of Revolutionary society and quite unable to cope with the multiplicity of demands placed upon them. A decree of the Consulate in Year IX intimated the full extent of the misery incurred: from the following year, whereas men in prison would receive a daily ration of bread and soup, those in the *dépôts de mendicité* would be forced to survive on bread alone unless they agreed to undertake hard manual labour which would be rewarded by a richer, less monotonous diet.[95] The state now saw its obligations to the beggar and the *vagabond* as being quite minimal, and the work ethic triumphed over any humanitarian considerations. In some respects this was the logical extension of much of the thinking and the legislation of the previous decade, but when combined with the collapse of the ambitious pension schemes announced in the early years of the Revolution, it hardly constituted the 'destruction of mendicity' which had been so confidently proclaimed in those wildly optimistic reports to the National Assembly back in 1789 and 1790.

Notes to chapter 5

1. A.N., AD.XIV.[11], 'Pétition des pauvres de Paris' (from the Faubourg Saint-Antoine), *prairial* VI.
2. A.N., AD.XIV.[7], *Conseil des Cinq-cents*, letter of 26 *nivôse* VI.
3. A.N., AD.XIV.[9], reports of Dutramblay de Rubelle (n.d.) and of Bô (Aveyron) in Year II.
4. A.N., AD.XIV.[6], Law of 25 May 1791 and report on the working of *commissions de bienfaisance*.
5. A.N., AD.XIV.[7], report entitled 'Opinion de Lebrun', 15 *vendémiaire* V.
6. A.N., AD.XIV.[10], petition from the Section de la Fontaine de Grenelle, 30 December 1791.
7. Arch. Mun. Aurillac, *sans côte*, document entitled 'Tableau des patriotes indigens, dressé conformément à la loi du 13 ventôse II'.
8. Arch. Mun. Aurillac, *ibid.*, statistics drawn from the lists drawn up by the *Municipalité* in Year II.
9. Report of Lecloy (Somme), dated 12 *vendémiaire* IV, quoted in A. Tuetey, *L'assistance publique à Paris pendant la Révolution*, III, p. 127.
10. Arch. Mun. Bordeaux, L66, 67, 68, statistics on *Secours aux indigents*, 1793–an II.
11. A.D. Rhône, 31L23, *Section de la Concorde*, lists of those in receipt of the indemnity of 1792.
12. A.D. Rhône, 31L23, *Section de la Concorde*, census return of 1793.
13. A.D. Rhône, 31L96, *Section de la Rue Juiverie*, register of those in receipt of the bread indemnity of Year II.
14. A.D. Rhône, 31L160, *Section de la Rue Thomassin*, register of those in receipt of the bread indemnity of Year II.
15. A.D. Jura, L861, communal returns on poor relief to the District of Lons-le-Saunier, 1791.
16. A.D. Cantal, L161, 'Population: états de population des districts par cantons et communes', return of 1790 to the *Comité de Mendicité* in Paris.
17. A.D. Seine-Inférieure, L2622, 'Mémoire concernant les pauvres des paroisses de la ville de Rouen', 1790.
18. A.D. Gironde, 9L64, District de Lesparre, *mémoire* on *fonds de charité*, 1790.
19. A.D. Bouches-du-Rhône, L494, reports on poor relief from the communes of Allauch (1790), Auriol (1790), and Tarascon (1792).
20. Arch. Mun. Marseille, Q^{3}1, revenue supplied by Marseille gilds for the *Incurables*.
21. Arch. Mun. Saint-Etienne, 3Q249, 'Etat des revenus des établissemens de secours à domicile dans l'arrondissement de Saint-Etienne', 9 *brumaire* IX.
22. Arch. Mun. Le Havre, Q1, account of income of *Bureau de Bienfaisance*, 25 *ventôse* II–30 *frimaire* IV.

23. A.D. Gironde, 12L18, *Amis de la Liberté*, letter of 1 June 1793.

24. Arch. Mun. Le Havre, Q1, gifts recorded in *nivôse* III.

25. A.D. Seine, VD*948, *Section du Mail*, letter to the *maire* of Paris, 13 August 1793.

26. C. Bloch and A. Tuetey (editors), *Procès-verbaux et rapports du Comité de Mendicité de la Constituante, Troisième rapport*, p. 395.

27. A. de Watteville, *Législation charitable*, I, pp. 17–18.

28. *ibid.*, pp. 20–4.

29. *ibid.*, p. 20n.

30. A.N., AD.XIV.⁹, Barère, *Premier rapport fait au nom de Comité de Salut Public sur les moyens d'extirper la mendicité dans les campagnes et sur les secours que doit accorder la République aux citoyens indigens*, 22 *floréal* II.

31. A.N., AD.XIV.⁹, *Décret sur l'extinction de la mendicité des campagnes*, 22 *floréal* II. Mothers with two children under ten who agreed to wean a third child were eligible for assistance, as were widows who had one child under ten and similarly agreed to wean another. The payment for these women was fixed at forty livres, supplemented by an extra twenty livres if their children were still alive at the end of the year. (Details of the legislation are contained in a MS. document in A.N., F¹⁵1862).

32. A. de Watteville, *op. cit.*, pp. 29–31.

33. C. Jones, *Poverty, vagrancy and society*, p. 303.

34. A. de Watteville, *op. cit.*, p. 42.

35. *ibid.*, p. 42.

36. A.D. Rhône, 3L179, petition from Guillaume Laurent, of Bully (Canton de l'Arbresle) to the District of Lyon-campagnes, 13 January 1793.

37. A.N., F¹⁵247, petition from Louis Perray to the *maire* of Paris, 16 August 1791.

38. A.D. Gironde, 12L28, petition from Santoux to the *Club National* in Bordeaux, Year II.

39. A.N., F¹⁵247, petition from Charles Bertonnet to the *maire* of Paris, 29 July 1791.

40. A.D. Seine-Inférieure, L2620, petition from Rupallay, 24 *fructidor* II.

41. Arch. Mun. Le Havre, Q10, *Secours aux indigents*, 'Liste des malheureux et patriotes de la Section de la République', 29 *ventôse* II.

42. For further discussion of military pensions, see chapter 8.

43. A.N., AD.XIV¹¹, report and decree of compensation to be paid to those who had lost property in the war, drawn up by Tardiveau (Ille-et-Vilaine), 31 July 1792.

44. A.N., AD.XIV¹¹, report by Maignet (Puy-de-Dôme) on the evaluation of war losses in frontier departments, n.d.

45. A.D. Rhône, 1L988, letter from Minister of Interior to the Department of Rhône-et-Loire allocating a grant of two million *livres* to the department, 14 *ventôse* II.

46. A.N., AD.XIV¹¹, report by Zangiacomi on compensation to the victims of war damage, 3 *germinal* V.

47. A.N., AD.XIV¹¹, report by Dubois (Vosges) on tax reductions for departments ravaged by the Vendean war, 26 *germinal* VI.

48. A.D. Rhône, 1L989, declaration of loss by Jean Guinard.

49. A.D. Rhône, 1L991, letter from Jeanne Giraud, 26 *frimaire* II.

50. A.D. Rhône, 1L989, declaration of loss by Charles Beluze.

51. A.D. Rhône, 1L989, declaration of loss by *veuve* Lanoy.

52. See above, chapter 2.

53. A.D. Seine-Inférieure, L321, decree of 30 May 1790.

54. A.N., F¹⁵101, letter from Department of Loiret to the *Comité des secours publics*, 23 March 1792.

55. A.N., AD.XIV.⁹, decree of 11 *brumaire* on the transportation of beggars.

56. Sixth report of the *Comité de mendicité*, 'Sur la répression de la mendicité', June 1790, in C. Bloch and A. Tuetey, *op. cit.*, p. 523.

57. A.D. Gironde, 4L134, Clochard, *Observations utiles au sujet des secours que la mendicité rend nécessaires* (printed brochure, 18 January 1793).

58. A.N., F¹⁵1861, report on poor relief in Paris, May 1790.

59. A.N., F¹⁶937, Clochard, *Projet pour détruire l'indigence* (Bordeaux, 30 *messidor* X).

60. A.D. Rhône, 1L1226, *Dépôt de Mendicité de Lyon*, payroll on 16 *floréal* V.

61. A.N., F¹⁵2790, *Dépôt de Mendicité de Bordeaux*, balance sheets, 1786–94.

62. A.D. Rhône, 1L1229, *Gestion du Dépôt de Lyon*, report to the Department of the Rhône, 28 September 1791.

63. A.D. Isère, L61, minute of the Department of the Isère, 3 *nivôse* II.

64. A.D. Rhône, 1L1229, *Gestion du Dépôt de Lyon*, minute of 20 *germinal* IV.

65. A.D. Rhône, 1L1229, letters to the Minister of the Interior, 17 *nivôse* VI and 3 *ventôse* VI.

66. A.N., F¹⁵435, letter from the administration of the *dépôt* at Lyon, 11 *fructidor* V.

67. A.N., F¹⁵435, claim to the Ministry of the Interior from the *dépôt* at Lyon, 8 *nivôse* VI.

68. A.D. Gironde, 4L134, dossier on those imprisoned for mendicity in February, March and April 1790.

69. A.D. Charente-Inférieure, C219, files of the *dépôt de mendicité* at La Rochelle for 1789.

70. A.D. Seine-Inférieure, L321, *Dépôt de Mendicité de Rouen*, minute of 1791.

71. A.D. Rhône, 1L1229, list of inmates at the *Dépôt de Mendicité de Lyon*, *germinal* IV.

72. A.N., F¹⁵1861, Plan for alleviating the lot of retired domestic servants, 24 December 1790.

73. A.N., F¹⁶968, *Section de la Fraternité, tableau de mendicité*, *dossier* Denis Mauguin.

74. A.N., F¹⁶968, *Section de la Fraternité, tableau de mendicité*, *dossier* Nicholas d'Huiq.

75. A.N., F¹⁶968, *Section du Bonnet Rouge, tableau de mendicité*. The statistics are taken from a list of fifty-three beggars of both sexes.

76. A.D. Gironde, 4L134, list of those imprisoned for mendicity, *op. cit.*

77. A.D. Charente-Inférieure, C219, files of the *dépôt de mendicité* at La Rochelle for 1789.

78. A.N., F¹⁶968, *Section des Quinze-vingts*, declaration of 3 *germinal* II.

79. A.D. Rhône, 2L96, *District de Lyon-ville, Police générale*, letter from the District dated 23 February 1791.

80. Arch. Mun. Bordeaux, Q4, letter from Clochard to the *Municipalité du Sud*, 12 *messidor* IV.

81. A.D. Cher, L565, letter from the *représentants-en-mission* in the Department of the Cher, 5 *floréal* III.

82. A.D. Seine-Inférieure, L1369, register of beggars in the *dépôt* at Rouen, November 1791.

83. A.D. Seine-Inférieure, L1376, *Dépôt de Mendicité de Rouen*, fourth register of admissions.

84. A.D. Seine-Inférieure, L1365, letter from the *dépôt de mendicité* in Rouen to the Municipal Council, 5 October 1790.

85. A.D. Gironde, 4L134, *Dépôt de Mendicité de Bordeaux*, list of inmates for *pluviôse* III.

86. Arch. Mun. Toulouse, 3Q1, 'Mémoire abrégé, et situation annuelle, de l'Hôtel-Dieu de Toulouse', 1790, p. 4.

87. A.D. Seine-Inférieure, L1369, register of *mendiantes* in the *dépôt* at Rouen, November 1791.

88. A.N., F¹⁵2811, register of the *dépôt* at Auch (Gers) for 1791.

89. A.D. Seine-Inférieure, L1369, *op. cit.*

90. A.D. Seine-Inférieure, L1365, report by the *chirurgien* at the *dépôt* at Rouen, 27 October 1790.

91. A.D. Seine-Inférieure, L1366, report on the state of the *dépôt* in February 1793.
92. Arch. Mun. Le Havre, Q15, letter to the Municipal Council of Le Havre, 27 *nivôse* V.
93. Letter from Julien Leroy, *économe* at the Bicêtre, on 11 *nivôse* III, quoted in A. Tuetey, *op. cit.*, III, p. 393.
94. Report of Paganel and Merlino to the Convention on prisons and *maisons de santé*, 28 *vendémiaire* III, quoted *ibid.*, III, p. 89.
95. A.N., F¹⁵104, decree on the *dépôts de mendicité*, 23 *nivôse* IX.

6 Job-creation schemes and public workshops

If, as was suggested earlier, the real distinction in eighteenth-century France between those who could and those who could not maintain themselves and their families was between people in work and those reduced to begging and other temporary expedients, then it becomes obvious that none of the solutions already examined could ever aspire to solve the problem of destitution. Hospitals could care for the sick and the injured, look after the aged, and nurse abandoned babies. Cash grants and institutional provision could serve to assuage the most glaring evils of misery and malnutrition. But neither solution could ever get to the root of the problem of poverty: they were no more than palliatives applied after the event, well-intentioned gestures to cure the worst symptoms of the disease without being able to tackle its fundamental causes. The only radical solution, in the eyes of many contemporaries, lay in schemes to create employment for the able-bodied poor, whereby the state would assume a major role in providing jobs for those willing and able to work but condemned to idleness and penury by economic forces beyond their understanding or their control. This point is made again and again in the minutes and reports of the *Comité de Mendicité* in 1790 and 1791, which saw the increase in the country's population over the previous half-century as constituting a quite insupportable burden unless a commensurate number of new jobs could be created. This, said the Committee, had not been achieved by the governments of the Ancien Regime, a failing which it ascribed less to the political outlook of those governments than to the backward state of French agriculture, and it went on to suggest that it was the duty of the Revolutionary administration to ensure that the expansion of job opportunity kept pace with population growth:

> Pour que l'augmentation de population assure le bonheur d'un Etat, il faut qu'elle marche avec l'accroissement de travail, et la France ne se trouve pas aujourd'hui dans cette proportion.[1]

Work, the Committee rightly recognized, was the key to any successful scheme for effective *assistance* in the context of French society at the end of the eighteenth century.[2]

Again, as in so much Revolutionary activity in the social field, there was little that was truly original in this realization: it was far from being a staggering innovation on the part of the legislators. What was new was the extent of government commitment, rather than the concept of job-creation itself. For that concept had been stressed in many of the papers produced in the later eighteenth century under the intellectual influence of the humanitarian movement, and these had often achieved a wide circulation among the more liberal politicians of the day. In the 1780s, for in-

stance, Rouen alone produced a flurry of memoranda advocating a more constructive form of poor relief than the simple repression of prison or the *dépôt de mendicité*. A
mémoire of 1787, typical of many, emphasized the sterility of pouring funds into establishments where overheads were high and where the impetus to reform was non-
existent, and argued that a more efficient solution would be, quite simply, to create
the jobs which could restore to the poor that valuable will to work which was so
integral to their morale and which had been destroyed by their experience of mendicity. Lamenting the harm which existing social policies had done to French
agriculture, the author went on to suggest that the provision of employment would
not only reverse this trend but would also create wealth and happiness far in excess of
the limited resources consigned to the scheme. For, he argued, the creation of
employment meant more than simply jobs; it was a recipe for the achievement of that
ideal of all eighteenth-century reformers, the banishing of poverty itself. He goes on
to explain:

> Ce n'est pas le défaut de biens qui constitue la pauvreté. C'est le défaut de travail. Un
> artisan qui exerce un métier est aussi riche que celui qui cultive six acres de terre dont il est
> propriétaire. Les enfans du premier, qui sont formés au travail du père, ont plus de
> ressources que les enfans du second qui ont divisé entre eux les six acres de terre.[3]

In a faltering, pre-Keynesian manner the point was effectively made: that in a rural
area in particular the economic and social well-being of the entire community
depended on everyone being gainfully employed.

The Ancien Regime reformers did not confine themselves to the expression of
general principles or the enunciation of benevolent platitudes. If Rouen is taken as a
model, then many of their suggestions for the provision of jobs were both sensible
and well tailored to the needs of the locality. The *Assemblée Provinciale* for the
Généralité of Rouen took it for granted in 1787 that the case for establishing some
form of workshops for the unemployed was so obvious that it scarcely required to
be stated, and proceeded instead to suggest some of the general rules that should be
applied when such an establishment was under consideration.[4] In the first place, they
believed, it was in the rural areas that the need was most glaring, especially in those
rural parishes which lay in the immediate environs of towns, where misery had been
observed to be particularly harrowing. Too often, maintained the *Assemblée*, such
foundations had in the past been made dependent on the availability of local charity,
with the result that local *ateliers* had been established in villages where voluntary provision was high but where the incidence of poverty was not necessarily most
widespread. In future, they argued, more use must be made of state money, and
pressure be put on the royal government to increase its contribution, since, in the last
analysis, 'la bienfaisance de Sa Majesté n'attend point sur cet objet le concours de ses
sujets'. And in the second place they urged that, since it was the public purse which
would be paying the greater part of the cost of this scheme, the public should equally
derive palpable benefits from it. Schemes of public works, therefore, must be seen to
be useful to the community: for this reason, they advocated that much of the effort be

concentrated on road-building schemes, on the construction of the local tracks and *chemins vicinaux* which it was the responsibility of the villages themselves to maintain. Other suggestions were equally utilitarian. Ludel, the commissioner with responsibility for supervising the supply of gunpowder to the armies, noted how difficult it was to obtain labour to sift the soil and extract saltpetre, the most basic ingredient of gunpowder in the eighteenth century; and he went on to suggest that this problem could be admirably solved if the *ateliers* were opened and the destitute set to work on this mechanical, back-breaking task.[5] There seems to have been a general acceptance that such workshops would do much to overcome the economic problems experienced by seasonal agricultural workers, problems that were particularly acute in Normandy.

The example of Normandy is by no means unique, although it is true that the region was suffering very acute economic problems in the decade before the Revolution because of the serious recession in the textile industry, in which many of the poorer people, especially around Elbeuf, were employed; in that area alone, Kaplow estimates that some 15,300 people had jobs in the various textile trades in 1788.[6] Anxiety was widespread, especially following the 1786 trade treaty with England; this exposed local industry to direct competition with the more modern and mechanized factories of Manchester and their products, which local merchants openly admitted to be of a substantially higher quality than those they wove themselves. Their protests were vociferous.[7] The Manchester manufacturers had succeeded in obtaining access to their secrets in those sectors, like dyestuffs, where the French believed that they had been in a distinct lead; they had the advantage of cheap coal from the pits of Lancashire, whereas coal in Normandy cost four times as much; and they had installed costly machinery on a scale beyond the wildest dreams of most firms in Elbeuf. The report of 1787 on the state of commerce in Normandy, indeed, sounded an intensely gloomy note. For it was not only cotton textiles that were losing out to English competition; the woollen trades, too, worth twenty million livres a year to Elbeuf and Louviers, were facing fierce competition from the products of Leeds and Bradford, Halifax and Norwich. And linen manufacture was also being threatened by cheap imports, from Ireland and especially from Scotland, where, the Rouen merchants believed, wages were at the very lowest levels since the people lived in perpetual poverty, surviving on a very limited diet of quite shattering monotony: in Dunfermline, they complained, the working population in the linen industry 'ne se nourrit que de pommes de terre ou d'avoine délayée dans l'eau'.[8] This dismal economic climate may explain the exceptional level of interest shown in *ateliers de charité* in pre-Revolutionary Rouen, especially as the majority of reformers seem to have seen it as their main function to prevent the onset of short-term economic disaster. But interest in such schemes was general throughout many parts of the country. Already various provincial academies – most notably the *Académie* of Châlons-sur-Marne in 1780 – had explored the benefits to be derived from a programme of public workshops,[9] and Turgot had attracted a great deal of interest by putting such a policy into practice during his term as *intendant* at Limoges.[10] As in so many other fields of charitable activity, the Revolutionary authorities were building on ideas and projects already discussed in considerable detail by their predecessors in the 1770s and 1780s.

They were also to draw on the underlying attitudes of the eighteenth-century reformers, attitudes which had not only led to a rather moralistic categorizing of the poor themselves but which also attempted to pass judgement on the various methods of poor relief. By the 1780s there would seem to have been a general acceptance in towns like Rouen that the provision of *ateliers* was both inexpensive and fruitful, since it encouraged diligence in the community and also produced an end-product, whether in the form of a new road surface or of some rough-woven hemp, which was of value to society. Moreover, it saved the money which would otherwise have been used for what many saw as the more profligate aspects of poor relief – the distribution of *bienfaisance* or the expense of keeping paupers in an *enclos* – from which the community derived no tangible return. As with many other aspects of public expenditure, charity was already coming to be viewed in terms of the strictest husbandry. A complaint to the *Commission Intermédiaire* in Rouen in 1788, for instance, was brutally critical of the decision to make economies totalling two hundred thousand livres in the region's roadbuilding programmes; these economies were seen as totally false in view of the extra alms that would have to be distributed as a result and the additional fifty thousand livres that would be required for the upkeep of poorhouses.[11] It seems to have been generally recognized that a co-ordinated overall policy for the region was desperately needed, the sort of policy which could only be rationally envisaged once the Constituent Assembly had ordered the collection and processing of the relevant statistics in 1790. Efficiency and economy remained the keynotes of this policy throughout. Humanitarian considerations were taken into account, of course, but always within the confines of the strictest budgeting. And any discussion of the provision of workshops seldom went unaccompanied by more menacing prescriptions for those who were unwilling to work, or by thinly-veiled fears that, were conditions in the *ateliers* made too attractive, then roving bands of vagabonds would immediately descend upon the locality.[12] Repression was never far from the mind of the eighteenth-century administrator.

These same anxieties can be detected in the legislation that set up the Revolution's own scheme for *ateliers de charité* in 1790. It was stressed – both in the letters-patent of the king ordering the establishment of these workshops and in the decree of 19 December 1790 which allocated fifteen million livres to the workshop programme in Paris and the departments – that the scheme was envisaged not as a regular part of France's charitable provision but rather as an emergency measure taken to stem the bitter hardship which many workers were temporarily suffering. The circumstances of that winter were such as, in the rather optimistic wording of the decree, 'ne peuvent se reproduire'.[13] Even such emergency legislation, however, had to be carefully circumscribed to avoid abuse. It was made abundantly clear that the *ateliers* were intended only for those men and women who, through no fault of their own, were genuinely made redundant and were, as a consequence, reduced to misery and helplessness. They were not to provide a new form of shelter for vagabonds and men hardened to a life of begging and idleness: that, more than anything else, appears to have been the deepseated fear haunting the proponents of the scheme. It was of the foremost importance that no reform should in any way harm the prosperity of agriculture or industry by attracting labour away from them. And yet the scheme must provide succour to the greatest possible number of those in genuine need.[14] In an attempt to satisfy all these at times conflicting aspirations, the legislators decreed that the existing workshops already in use in Paris and other cities, and widely believed to have been abused by tramps and other petty criminals, should be immediately closed down. Wage levels were avidly discussed, the aim being that of finding a nice balance between the minimum needed to support a family and the maximum that could be paid without making the *ateliers* seem too attractive to those employed in the private sector. Finally, it was deemed advisable to pay the sick and the able-bodied on a totally different basis, the sick receiving a fixed sum for each day's attendance at the workshop, but the *valides* being dragooned into working really hard by a system of piece-rate payment.[15] In such ways the Revolutionary authorities believed that they had created a system of public workshops whereby poverty could be alleviated in accordance with the best humanitarian principles, but without encouraging idleness amongst the poor or involving the state in massive additional expenditure. It was a scheme that was wholly compatible both with their concern for economy and with their rather patronizing attitudes towards the less fortunate members of their society.

Priorities, clearly, had to be established in the spending of the fifteen million livres allocated, since no sum of money, however generous, could hope to solve the social problems of France at a stroke. Given that the very nature of the project was one of emergency aid, some areas could submit claims for especially urgent consideration – areas like Lyon, where the silk industry had been devastated by the economic recession and by the emigration of many of its richest customers,[16] or like Le Havre where the abolition of the slave trade was to add to the already high unemployment figures in those industries connected with the Atlantic trade.[17] But, following the disastrous harvests of 1789 and 1790, there were few areas of the country that could not impress on the Assembly the extent of their losses or submit heartrending accounts of localized misery. Again, from many regions came the not unreasonable request that, since much of their unemployment was seasonal in incidence – almost a basic truism in a society that was still predominantly rural – there could be no adequate antidote that did not channel at least part of its resources into some form of winter employment for farmworkers. As Bosc, the deputy from the Aube, was to point out in the Year VIII, in a farming economy like that of France prosperity and confidence in the currency were alike dependent on the steady maintenance of the workforce throughout the year: that confidence was lost and foreign trade suffered disastrously during those months when penury engulfed a substantial proportion of the people and when, as a direct consequence, 'la majorité des transactions sociales sont suspendues'.[18] It was a point that was well taken. Throughout the Revolutionary years the various committees and commissions concerned with employment and poverty looked with favour on plans for short-term schemes of useful works that would help boost the economy. More generally, they also seem to have recognized that, since unemployment, like misery itself, was a highly localized problem, only local solutions could have any chance of being effective. As a result, as with the *Comité de Mendicité*'s other concerns like poor funds and *dépôts*, research on unemployment was conducted in very considerable detail, with statistics being collected by the departments and forwarded to Paris. Money tended to be voted in the form of departmental allocations, leaving the local administrations with the final responsibility for deciding upon the ways in which it should be spent.

In keeping with the highly devolutionist spirit of the administrative reforms of 1790, the early schemes for public workshops seem to have been most flexible. Claims were submitted by departments on the basis of local circumstance and grants made accordingly: in 1792, for instance, the Vendée asked for 60,000 livres for *chemins vicinaux*, and the Pyrénées-Orientales, which had suffered badly from the effects of earlier neglect, specified necessary schemes of roadbuilding, river-dredging, and bridge works across the Agly.[19] In turn, departments distributed the money they received among their districts and cantons so that they could make the best possible use of it to relieve local pockets of poverty. The District of Bourges, for instance, was allocated thirty thousand livres of the departmental grant to the Cher in 1791, a sum which they spent almost entirely in organizing road-maintenance schemes in the more remote parts of their area.[20] In this operation the role of central government and of the *Comité de Mendicité* in Paris is rather akin to that of a referee, examining submissions from various parts of the country, commenting on their apparent worth, and attempting to maintain a degree of equity in the apportionment of resources in accordance with the size of the local population and with the level of suffering and degradation. Legislation in this sphere aided rather than imposed the implementation of *ateliers de charité*, although most authorities were naturally eager to take advantage of the benefits offered.

Once again, it is impossible to ignore the effects of other Revolutionary policies in this area of charitable provision, and here – in contrast to the plight of so many hospitals – we may conclude that these effects were generally beneficial to the community. Sizeable sums of money, on top of the initial block grant of fifteen million livres, were enthusiastically allocated to what the authorities almost unanimously saw as one of the most constructive means of ending the problem and the national shame of popular misery. And the happy coincidence that this was being advocated at the same time as various religious orders were being suppressed meant that monasteries, convents, and other religious buildings were falling vacant, which the Revolutionary leaders regarded as being eminently suitable for conversion into workshops. The opportunity was not missed. In June 1790, for instance, two Parisian religious houses, those occupied by the Récollets in the Faubourg Saint-Laurent and by the Dominicans in the rue Saint-Jacques, were cleared of their confessional trappings and unceremoniously converted into *ateliers*.[21] Similarly, in the Year II, three churches in Saint-Etienne were designated for conversion: the Eglise Sainte-Ursule became an arms store, the Eglise des Pénitents a *magasin des fers* for the powerful *Manufacture* in the city where so many of France's firearms were made, and the Eglise

Saint-Etienne a workshop to provide jobs for some of the many men and boys who faced starvation as a result of lengthy unemployment.[22] In these circumstances it is hardly to be wondered at that the poor of Saint-Etienne, in common with their counterparts in many other French towns and cities, should have greeted the dechristianization campaign with such overt enthusiasm, or that local government in departments like the Loire should have become such convinced and dogged dechristianizers. At times, indeed, their enthusiasm was carried to excess, and in the Year III one indignant local merchant was to complain that in the process of converting one of the churches into an *atelier* for ironworkers, the municipal council had trespassed on to his property, demolished one of his walls, sequestrated part of his garden, and dismantled a bridge linking his house to an adjoining meadow.[23] The opportunities presented by the dechristianizers seemed endless, and not only local sections and clubs, but also town councils, deputies on mission, and *armées révolutionnaires* throughout wide areas of provincial France were eager to maximize the benefits which they could derive from the church's discomfiture.

Once the idea of setting up a network of *ateliers* had come to be accepted, attention naturally focused on the kind of work that ought to be provided. Should priority be given to the towns or to the countryside? Was need greater among men or among women? Should some attempt be made to provide jobs for the sick and handicapped as well as for those who were simply out of work? Such questions were posed and re-posed in the pamphlet literature of the day, and they were mulled over endlessly by the members of the *Comité de Mendicité* in Paris. Quite clearly, the workshops were never seen as an independent project in their own right, but rather as one of a number of ancillary social innovations which might help to alleviate misery. For this reason discussion was often somewhat confused, and schemes for *ateliers* vied for scarce funds with other favoured ideas, including the provision of poorhouses and outdoor relief which we have already examined.[24] Benefit societies and insurance schemes for working people also commanded widespread support among the politicians of the 1790s, and plans abounded in the early years of the decade for various forms of *caisses d'épargne, de prévoyance, d'économie et de secours*, savings schemes which were deemed to encourage a sense of thrift and responsibility among the poorer, more vulnerable groups in society. The project of Lafarge, presented to the Assembly in 1790, was particularly popular, since it excised the profit motive and proposed what was virtually a basic form of state social security which would guarantee a pension to a poor man if he made economies throughout his working life.[25] This plan, known universally in Revolutionary Paris as the 'tontine Lafarge', was put into effect with the opening of the first insurance society in April 1791.[26] It was not alone of its kind. The need to stimulate small savings was one of the dominant themes among the philanthropists of the day, and the Revolution's official encouragement of such projects gave them an added impetus. There were, in particular, several proposals to improve the lot of that most vulnerable of all social groupings, domestic servants, by providing them with some form of insurance against sickness, accident, or pregnancy – the sort of eventualities which had reduced so many servants to indigence or to prostitution during the Ancien Regime. In Paris, just such a scheme was implemented as early as January 1790, offering substantial benefits to those women able and prepared to contribute six livres per year to the benefit fund: they were to receive payment for medicines and for days lost through illness, to receive an additional subsistence payment for two months in case of indigence, to be compensated in the event of broken limbs, and to receive twelve livres towards the costs of childbirth should they become pregnant.[27] The aim of all these ideas, and of the many reformers who urged the adoption in France of benefit societies on the English model,[28] was the same: to improve the condition of the poor and to avoid the desperate pitfalls of sudden, pauperizing unemployment. The *ateliers* must necessarily be seen as an integral part of this same general strategy.

One implication of this ideal was that the sorts of work which the *ateliers* would cater for must be those most representative of local employment patterns. It is true that there were occasional demands that workshops be set up to provide jobs for particular sections of the deprived population, like the plan by Merlino, the deputy for the Ain, in Year III for a shop to be opened in Paris to serve the needs of blind workers, a group who were, he said, particularly adversely affected by the vast rise in the cost of food and other essentials.[29] But such requests, worthy as they were, were also highly untypical. More customary were insistent demands, from spokesmen and councillors all over France, that the *ateliers* must be geared to the needs of the majority in the community and not to the specialist skills of the few. Labouring and basic manual jobs had to be given priority if sizeable numbers of destitute families were to be given even a modicum of assistance. In particular, as the commune of Mamers was quick to maintain, there was little purpose in opening *ateliers* in any of the luxury trades which had been so important during the Ancien Regime. In part, no doubt, this point was made to underline the needs of small towns like Mamers, a textile town which had shared in the general slump that had ravaged employment prospects in the upland areas of Normandy at the beginning of the Revolutionary period, whose staple product lay firmly at the cheaper end of the textile market. But the argument was expressed in moral as well as purely utilitarian terms. Luxury goods, it was suggested, were an unstable base for future economic development, since they were subject to very great trade fluctuations and could be totally wiped out by international war or competition. Furthermore, wage levels in the luxury trades were intolerably low: it would be far better for the economy and for the social well-being of the population if money were invested in more basic trades, employers of large workforces that would fit easily into local traditions of manufacturing. Only in this way, urged Francis Nibelle, speaking on behalf of his district in 1791, could an *atelier* be grafted on to the existing industrial structure and fashioned into a socially valuable institution, into 'un établissement dans lequel un honnête citoyen puisse trouver, sans rougir, une ressource dont il seroit privé si elle n'étoit le fruit de son travail'.[30] His contention, supported by many of the same general tenor, evoked a ready response.

A glance at the numerous lists of public works schemes that were given the official stamp of approval during the Revolutionary years would suggest that Nibelle got his way and that the bulk of government aid went to precisely the kind of basic, unskilled or semi-skilled occupations which he recommended. It is true that the *Comité de Mendicité*, as early as 17 March 1790, had asked whether there were not more interesting forms of employment than roadbuilding which could be offered to the unemployed and had called upon public authorities to display some imagination in formulating suitable alternatives.[31] It is also the case that in some areas ingenious methods were devised to bring the general public into the debate on the provision of workshops – a splendid if somewhat rare instance of participatory politics at local level. In the Jura, for instance, where the Department found itself in January 1791 with some eighty thousand livres to spend on public works schemes (its share of the fifteen millions from the national treasury), the councillors at first discussed proposals which seemed to them to be useful and worthy, such as the draining of marshes, the digging of canals, and the restocking of forests. But in the end, searching quite genuinely for inspiration, they invited the citizens to come forward and suggest their own ideas, 'en conciliant à la fois les secours qu'en doit tirer la classe indigente et laborieuse avec l'avantage général qui doit en résulter', and a competition was launched for the best ideas, with a gold medallion promised to the winner.[32] It was a bold initiative, calling on the people to analyse the economic problems of their locality and to suggest viable solutions. And yet the final outcome was little different from that espoused in other parts of the country: overwhelmingly, the jobs provided were of a hard, manual variety for men and those dependent on monotonous repetition for women.

It was in the rural areas that the majority of the schemes were approved, and it was there, too, that the range of opportunity was most limited. For unemployed farmworkers were not the most flexible kind of labour, and *ateliers de charité* were never permitted to undertake agricultural work on their own account. It was therefore predictable that most rural *ateliers* took the form of heavy outdoor work, of digging ditches and mending roads: the *Comité de Mendicité* was being no more than realistic when it expressed the fear that all public works risked being reduced to roadmaking and general labouring. The works, of course, had to answer a manifest public need, and the Revolutionary authorities were well aware of the soul-destroying sense of waste that would ensue if men were merely being employed to fill in potholes or squander their time and energy on minor works undertaken only in order to provide them with jobs. But, whatever the rationale and however ingenious the presentation, most of these schemes amounted to little more than labouring and rough *terrassements*. In the Ardennes, for instance, the District of Sédan proposed to repair local roads 'pour faciliter le transport des bois nationaux et communaux', to continue the military road from Remilly to Mouzon, and – more originally perhaps – to develop tobacco-planting in the vicinity.[33] Lons-le-Saunier, besides much-needed road repairs, proposed drainage schemes, the digging of wells and ditches, and earthworks to prevent flooding when the local rivers burst their banks.[34] Many of the largest grants made by the *Comité de Mendicité* to local authorities were allocated to exactly such drainage and transportation schemes, like the 50,000 livres awarded to the Isère in 1791 to build dykes to protect good farming land against flooding. Canal works and river works were especially favoured, for the digging and repairing of

canals and navigation channels would increase ease of transport between key areas of
the country. Six hundred thousand livres, the largest single sum granted to any
department outside Paris in 1791, was awarded to the Yonne to finance work on the
Canal de Bourgogne, for instance, while sums of 150,000 livres were set aside for
such major schemes as the digging of the Canal de Beaucaire at Aigues-Mortes in the
Gard, clearance work on the Rhine in Alsace, and excavations to deepen the harbour
at La Rochelle.[35] Such work may, indeed, have been physically hard and intellec-
tually undemanding. But, as the village of Lambesc in the Bouches-du-Rhône
tellingly intimated in 1790, rough physical work like roadmending was in many
ways the most suited to the needs of their population, especially during the winter
months when agricultural work had ceased to be available. More sophisticated
ateliers might be well tailored to the needs of towns, but in rural areas there were
often no suitable buildings for conversion into workshops; besides, such workshops
could do positive harm to the local community:

> Tout y est presque cultivateur; les bras sans cesse tournés vers la terre ne seroient guère
> propres à un autre genre de travail; il seroit même dangereux pour les communautés de
> campagne d'accoutumer le peuple à des ouvrages qui pourraient dans la suite le dégoûter
> du travail précieux de l'agriculture.[36]

Yet the public works schemes for men devised in urban areas were often
remarkably similar to those opened in the countryside, with the emphasis solidly on
outdoor projects demanding hard physical labour. It is true that there was rather
greater variety than in rural departments, with quarrying around Paris, ironfound-
ing in Saint-Etienne, and some mine-working at Tarascon providing welcome relief
among the rather monotonous lists of road-repairs proposed by every department in
the country.[37] But these were exceptions to the norm. Even in Paris, relief soon came
to take the form of standardized schemes of labouring on public utilities and demolition work, employing large gangs of navvies at the least expense to the public purse.
Among the projects proposed by the *Comité de Mendicité* in November 1790, for instance, were construction work on the Quai d'Orsay, digging out the Canal de
Saint-Maur, and demolishing the Porte Saint-Bernard and the Tour de Vincennes.
Such tasks were chosen specifically because they were labour-intensive and would
mop up many of the beggars and unemployed workmen who were coming to be
regarded as a major nuisance in the streets of the capital.[38] In a celebrated pamphlet
on the *ateliers* to be provided in Paris, J. P. de Smith provided a plausible justification
for such ideas, arguing that the most suitable outlets were roadbuilding and
roadmending, which would help communications within Paris and would in this
way assist industry, and organized street-cleaning, an aspect of policing which, he
believed, was sadly neglected.[39] Above all, these projects had the great advantage in
his eyes of involving menial work which posed no threat to the prosperity of existing
enterprise and would attract none except the most desperate and the most necessitous.

For women there would seem to have been little disagreement about the most appropriate form of work that the state could provide: in all those areas where provision for women workers was made (and they were considerably fewer than for

men), it took the form of an *atelier de filature*. Already in the Ancien Regime such workshops had gained acceptance as an appropriate form of poor relief for destitute women, for those thrown out of work by economic crisis or unable to hold down a position in domestic service. Turgot, for instance, had given active encouragement to such projects in the Limousin, on the grounds that it was a suitable alternative to the hard physical labour of *terrassements* for those without the necessary physical strength. In Paris, too, there were precedents for this form of charity: earlier in the century the *curé* of Saint-Sulpice had been in the habit of distributing yarn to the poor of his parish on which they could work at home, and in 1779 Lenoir, the lieutenant of police, had established an office at the Porte-Saint-Denis, subsidized to the tune of around twelve thousand livres per year, for the distribution of yarn.[40] Once again, therefore, the Revolutionary authorities were doing little that was truly novel in extending the scheme of *ateliers* for women after 1790, but they did bring a new urgency and a much greater financial commitment to what they saw as one of the most worthwhile ideas to have emanated from the Enlightenment. A decree of May 1790 ordered the establishment of a new network of workshops in the spinning trades, where women and children might find suitable employment. In Paris alone, workshops at Chaillot and Picpus kept one hundred and twenty spinning-workers in employment until 1791, and thereafter much bigger ventures, such as the converted monasteries of the Jacobins and the Récollets, were opened to replace them.[41] Against the backcloth of steadily rising female unemployment in the city, their supporters could present these *ateliers* as a considerable achievement and as a victory for common sense and humanity. At the peak of the movement, in 1791, the various Parisian workshops were providing 4,800 jobs for women and children in the spinning trades.[42] Even in the Year II, indeed, the Récollets were still providing much-needed jobs in a socially-deprived area of the Faubourg Saint-Laurent, though the scale of the operation had been greatly reduced and much of the initial euphoria had worn off. In all, in Year II, eighty-six boys were employed in the carding process, with as many again performing the more menial task of the *éplucheur*, plucking and cleaning the raw wool. In the workshop itself, 163 women operatives were spinning yarn, helped by a further 330 outworkers spinning for them in their own homes; and a subsidiary workshop gave employment to over a hundred more.[43] Nor were the economic benefits confined to the workers themselves, for the conversion work needed to open these workshops was often long and expensive, providing invaluable jobs for tradesmen and building labourers.[44]

Although in terms of employment the benefits derived from the workshops may seem to have been incontrovertible, the scheme was not greeted with universal acclaim by contemporaries. In part, no doubt, this was due to the fact that popular misery in 1790–3 remained visibly obvious, with perhaps nine thousand Parisian women reduced to indigence in 1791, a figure far beyond the limited resources of the *ateliers* provided.[45] But there were other criticisms, too, which suggest strongly that the notion of artificially injecting state-inspired and state-financed employment into the existing market economy was still too novel, too revolutionary, to command a general acceptance. The cost of the scheme gave rise to much adverse comment, and critics were quick to ask whether interference in the workings of the economy was a fitting or a wise way to spend public money. It is true that job creation was not cheap. The sums spent on building work alone at three Paris *ateliers* between their foundation in 1790 and January 1793 – the Jacobins, Récollets, and the rue de Bourbon – totalled nearly 87,000 livres.[46] And wage bills soon piled up to provide the critics with further ammunition: in the single financial year of 1790–1, for instance, the Jacobins paid out 15,380 livres to its employees, and the Récollets a further 10,500 livres.[47] Yet, unlike other forms of *bienfaisance*, the provision of jobs did produce a return in the form of the yarn spun by the workers, even if in some areas this return seemed somewhat derisory. The Atelier de Charité de Saint-Michel in Aix-en-Provence is a good instance of this, an *atelier* which in its first year of operation was so expensive in terms of the construction work required that it was forced to survive almost entirely on gifts and loans. The expenses for the year totalled over 64,000 livres; the total income from the cotton spun by the workers was only 567 livres and sixteen sous. Indeed, in the case of Saint-Michel income from the tax on tickets to the local theatre and from the alms given for the *soupe des pauvres* both exceeded the money raised by selling the finished yarn.[48] There could be no more conclusive evidence that the workshops must be viewed solely in the context of social provision, of poor relief, and not as an early example of public enterprise.

Cost was not the only basis for the doubts which increasingly came to be expressed about the desirability of these workshops. There was also the wider question of internal discipline for people who were, in the eyes of respectable society, hardly to be distinguished from beggars and vagabonds. For the atmosphere in the *ateliers* frequently appears to have been immensely easy-going, with a laxness of work discipline that contrasted strikingly with that in the *dépôts de mendicité*. Only in the rooms reserved for children was some attempt made to control the workers and subject them to firm rules and regulations: but there the *atelier* had an educative function as well as a purely social one, with schoolmasters not only teaching the rudiments of the trade, generally the spinning of cotton thread, but also instructing the children in religion and the catechism.[49] The general picture was quite different, and indiscipline among the workforce, male and female alike, came to be seen as a major abuse which risked undermining the entire enterprise. In Paris the police were alert to the dangers of riot and disorder heralded by the opening of any new *atelier*, and in January 1791 the *commissaire de police* responsible for the area around the Temple complained bitterly about the unruliness of the workers, advocated setting them on the task of cleaning up the local streets – a task for which his department had at least nominal responsibility – and concluded by demanding vigilance and the strictest surveillance from the city authorities.[50] Since the opening of a new workshop was commonly believed to attract beggars from neighbouring areas, this alarm is easy to understand. Women workers were no more amenable than their male colleagues, and the *ateliers de filature* soon developed a most unsavoury reputation for insubordination and rowdy behaviour. Complaints in 1791 focused on the total lack of authority within the institutions and described in graphic terms the extent to which supervisors were mocked and subjected to strings of oaths and obscenities by the women and were pursued by cat-calls in the streets around the workshops. Women from the Récollets, it was alleged, were allowed to roam the streets in the middle of the morning, spreading the spirit of rebellion to their fellow-workers at the Jacobins. And there were descriptions of an 'orgie' in the same workshop, when the women defiantly downed tools, ran shouting and screaming round the cloister, and finally left to enjoy the soothing atmosphere of the neighbourhood bars, 'y raffraîchir leur gozier échauffé par les cris'.[51] The supervisor of the workshop, not unnaturally, wanted some clear definition of his authority, so that he might hope to impose a modicum of discipline on his workforce. But such reports also served to arouse the worst fears of many Frenchmen about the whole role and future of the *ateliers*.

They had certainly good reason to believe that abuse was rife in the public workshops of Paris and other large cities. In 1791 the scale of the operation burgeoned, apparently uncontrollably, until by June of that year Liancourt was compelled to inform a shocked Assembly that the Paris system had virtually broken down, with unemployed workers from all over France presenting themselves in the capital and demanding that they be given jobs. The degree of abuse and the level of expense alike, he claimed, were vast: Paris at that moment had thirty-one thousand men employed on public works schemes at a cost of 900,000 livres per month, a sum swollen still further by the 50,000 livres paid in wages to the fourteen hundred men working on the Canal de Bourgogne.[52] Supervision was scanty, as in the women's *ateliers*, and work was simply skimped or neglected. And he went on to suggest that men without any real need of public subsidy were succeeding in obtaining employment after the very minimum of inquiry by the authorities. These were not the sour reflections of a jaundiced member of the Assembly, horrified by the scale of the public works programme to which his government had committed itself. Allegations of abuse came from all sides, not least from among the poor themselves, from those of the workers who were angered by what was happening around them and were fearful lest the workshops gain a reputation for rioting and indiscipline. Some ninety of the workers employed by the *atelier* in the Section du Roule in Paris went so far as to petition their section in Year II to complain that honest men were working on the project side by side with miscreants, patriots with the enemies of the Revolution, and that as a result order had frequently broken down. They were afraid, they added, that the workshop would be closed and that the genuinely indigent citizens would, like the troublemakers, find themselves condemned to unemployment and penury once more.[53] Where huge sums of public money were being distributed with only the most minimal auditing, allegations of fraud and pecculation were always credible. In Aurillac, for instance, where the Department had followed the normal practice of paying the money directly to the local councillors, rumour of scandal was rife, and in 1792 commissioners were appointed to report on the work executed during the previous two years. They found that very little had in fact been done and very few men and women employed. Much of the money paid to the *officiers municipaux* was still in their possession; in other cases the work done had cost over four times what it was worth, besides which the quality of the workmanship was scandalously bad; and there was evidence that, whereas the *officiers* had been paid in specie by the Department, they had paid all their own bills in fast-depreciating *assignats* and had coolly pocketed the difference.[54] In too many cases, neither those employed nor those in charge of the schemes inspired any degree of public confidence.

Concern was also expressed about the wider economic implications of public works projects on such a grandiose scale. Besides the effects on the public purse, legislators and others were concerned that they should not in any way harm existing firms or damage the livelihood of artisans and master-craftsmen. Given the nature of the work prescribed, there was little danger that the state would put private interests out of business as a result of direct competition: that most obvious of pitfalls had been avoided. But was there not a real danger that the provision of alternative employment in the workshops would have a distorting effect on the labour market? Would not the lax discipline of the *ateliers* attract workers away from more demanding employers whose regime was stricter and where the work expected was of a higher quality? It was a very real danger, for the workers in the public sector soon began to obtain greater rights and privileges than their counterparts with independent masters. When, for instance, the women at the Jacobins petitioned the municipal council for a pay rise in June 1793, the council listened to their plea with obvious sympathy and understanding. Furthermore, on those occasions when women were dismissed by the direction of the *ateliers* for some offence, they could and frequently did appeal against the decision over the heads of the administrators to the Department of the Seine, which would look into their complaints, almost assuming the functions of a court of appeal.[55] Again, this was a privilege unheard of in the works and shops of industrial Paris, a privilege that appealed to many men and women already in employment elsewhere in the city. Employers not unnaturally began to complain that they were losing skilled workers, who were betraying their skills by transferring to an easier life in the public workshops. Even the sections, which had championed the setting-up of the *ateliers* and had in many cases opened subscriptions to finance public works projects for their own districts of the city,[56] baulked at this very serious development. The Section du Temple, for instance, alerted by a petition from the *maîtres charpentiers*, who were worried by the losses of craftsmen they had sustained since the opening of the workshops, went so far as to ask the administrators of all the Paris *ateliers* to check the credentials of men who sought work, to refuse to hire anyone who was already a skilled building-worker, and to send any skilled men whom they already employed back to their former masters.[57] In agreeing, the Section de la Grange-Batelière noted the serious and deleterious effects which such losses were having on the standing of various trades in the city.[58]

None of these fears and grievances can, of course, detract from the valuable social work that was provided by the *ateliers* during the early years of the Revolution. For if there were abuses, there were also success-stories, the many thousands of men and women for whom the workshop meant the difference between being able to cope and being thrown back into helplessness and destitution. Many of those who were helped were worthy people, reduced to poverty by bad luck or by economic recession, or by the effects of the war or the Revolution itself: people like *citoyenne* Leclerc of the Section du Panthéon, who sought employment in a public workshop, the Jacobins, because she had four children to support, her husband was fighting for France on the frontiers, and, as she said with just a tinge of bitterness, her section was failing to carry out the promises of maintenance which it had made to her husband when he enlisted.[59] Sadly, such cases tended to be lost amidst the more strident howls of abuse increasingly directed against the workshops, and, as government cash became even scarcer, the *ateliers* were subjected to rigorous review. Already in 1792 the number of new schemes opened was severely cut back, and no longer were public works seen as the obvious answer to the problems of unemployment. From 1791 no new schemes were started in Paris, and those people already employed on public projects who had come to Paris from the provinces were to be assisted to return to their area of origin.[60] As for the *ateliers de filature*, they survived until Year III, when a government report accused them of wasting valuable resources and of harbouring 'l'improbité, la paresse, la débauche, protégées par l'esprit d'insurrection'. Thereafter it was only a matter of time until they were closed down altogether, by a decree of 29 *prairial* III which roundly condemned the poor quality of their output and the 'charge onéreuse' which they imposed on the state.[61] The same pattern was followed in the provinces, with the brave new world of job-creation schemes which had been launched in 1790 petering out rather miserably within two or three years. In 1792, for instance, the Department of the Puy-de-Dôme, disenchanted by the abuses which were alleged to be sweeping its *ateliers*, peremptorily ordered their closure.[62] By Year III the experiment was largely over, leaving thousands of workers destitute and bewildered, like the shoemakers who had found employment in an *atelier* in Aix-en-Provence, having left their homes to come to do work which they saw as useful for the welfare of the Republican armies, and who now, without explanation, were faced with even greater hardship than before by being released on to the labour market at the same moment as so many others. Their perplexed outrage is easy to understand.[63] For yet again the Revolution had failed to live up to its initial promise: indeed, in this instance its practical achievement was even more faltering and shortlived than in other fields of *bienfaisance*. Yet again the appeal of humanity had seemed for a brief moment to be heard and answered, only to be forgotten once the dictates of finance demanded it.

Notes to chapter 6

1. 'Plan de travail du Comité pour l'extinction de la mendicité', decreed by the National Assembly on 21 January 1790, in C. Bloch and A. Tuetey (editors), *Procès-verbaux et rapports du Comité de Mendicité de la Constituante, 1790–1791*, part 2, p. 312.
2. See, for instance, the *Premier Rapport du Comité de Mendicité*, 12 June 1790, *ibid.*, p. 330.
3. A.D. Seine-Inférieure, C2121, *Mémoire sur la mendicité* (MS. 1787).

4. A.D. Seine-Inférieure, C2111, *Registre: procès-verbal des séances de l'Assemblée Provinciale de la Généralité de Rouen*, minute of 19 November 1787.

5. A.D. Seine-Inférieure, C2121, Ludel, *commissaire des poudres, Projet sur la mendicité*, 1787.

6. J. Kaplow, *Elbeuf during the Revolutionary period: history and social structure*, esp. pp. 24–9.

7. A.D. Seine-Inférieure, C2111, *Rapport sur l'état du commerce* (1787).

8. *ibid.*, folio 8.

9. M. Bouchet, *L'assistance publique en France pendant la Révolution*, p. 72.

10. F. Dreyfus, *Note sur les ateliers charitables de filature de 1789 à 1795*, p. 125.

11. A.D. Seine-Inférieure, C2121, letter to the *Commission Intermédiaire* of Rouen, 18 June 1788.

12. A.D. Seine-Inférieure, C2173, reply from the *Assemblée Municipale* of Rouen to the minute of the *Assemblée Provinciale* of 19 November 1787, *op. cit.*, n.d.

13. A.D. Rhône, 1L1170, law of 19 December 1790 on the construction of *ateliers de charité*.

14. A.D. Rhône, 1L1170, *Lettres-patentes du Roi sur l'Assemblée Nationale*, 31 August 1790.

15. A.N., F^{16}936, decree of the National Assembly of 31 August 1790.

16. A.D. Rhône, 1L520, 522, documents on the fortunes of the silk industry during the Revolution.

17. Arch. Mun. Le Havre, F^{2}7, statistics on Le Havre trade during the Revolutionary years. Already in 1790, ships' carpenters were being laid off because of the recession in the Atlantic trade, and in March they staged a rising in protest (Arch. Mun. Le Havre, F^{2}8, letter from the *Direction Générale des Ports* to the *Conseil Municipal* du Havre, 13 March 1790).

18. A.N., AD.XIV^6, Bosc (de l'Aube), *Rapport sur les moyens d'assurer du travail aux ouvriers pendant cet hiver, et de raviver l'industrie* (16 *brumaire* VIII).

19. A.N., AD.XIV^{10}, *Secours publics*, distribution of funds for relief work, 22 January 1792.

20. A.D. Cher, L497, *Ateliers de charité*, account of expenditure for 1791.

21. A.N., AD.XIV^6, *Ateliers de charité*, letters-patent of Louis XVI dated 18 June 1790.

22. A.D. Loire, 842L, bills submitted in Year II by workmen employed in the conversion of these three churches into *ateliers*.

23. A.D. Loire, 842L, letter from a Saint-Etienne merchant, Testenoire, to the Municipal Council, 7 *floréal* III.

24. See above, chapter 4.

25. A.N., AD.XIV^6, plan of Lafarge, presented to the National Assembly in October 1790.

26. A.N., AD.XIV^6, *Observations sur la Tontine Lafarge*, 1807.

27. A.N., AD.XIV^6, Plan for a *caisse de secours* for domestic servants working in Paris, guaranteed by the Municipal Council, January 1790.

28. A.N., AD.XIV^6, Project of J. Marsillac, a hospital doctor, in 1792 is a good instance of this.

29. A.N., AD.XIV^6, Plan for an *atelier* for the blind, presented by Merlino (Ain), 25 *prairial* III.

30. A.N., F^{16}937, F. Nibelle, *Mémoire sur les moyens de bannir la mendicité à Mamers et dans les autres villes où il y a fabrique de toiles* (1791).

31. C. Bloch and A. Tuetey, *op. cit.*, p. 8.

32. A.D. Jura, L861, *Département du Jura*, minute of 10 January 1791.

33. A.N., F^{16}966, suggested *ateliers de charité* in the District of Sédan (Ardennes), 1791.

34. A.D. Jura, L861, suggested *ateliers de charité* in the District of Lons-le-Saunier (Jura), contained in reports to the District in 1791.

35. A.N., AD.XIV⁶, Liancourt (Oise), *Rapport fait au nom des Comités des Finances, d'Agriculture et Commerce, des Domaines, et de Mendicité*, 16 June 1791, p. 7.

36. A.D. Bouches-du-Rhône, L863, letter from the commune of Lambesc, 8 September 1790.

37. A.D. Loire, 842L, report of Year II; A.N., F¹⁶966, report on *ateliers de charité* from the District of Tarascon (Ariège).

38. C. Bloch and A. Tuetey, *op. cit.*, p. 178.

39. J. P. de Smith, *Des ateliers de secours établis à Paris et aux environs* (1791).

40. F. Dreyfus, *Note sur les ateliers charitables de filature de 1789 à 1795*, p. 126.

41. *ibid.*, p. 127.

42. *ibid.*, p. 128.

43. A.N., F¹⁵3567, *Filature des Recollets*, report for Year II.

44. A.N., F¹⁵3578, report to the Municipal Council of Paris on the *ateliers de filature*, 23 October 1792.

45. F. Dreyfus, *op. cit.*, p. 128.

46. A.N., F¹⁵3578, *bordereau* of bills presented since 1790, dated 14 January 1793.

47. F. Dreyfus, *op. cit.*, p. 127.

48. A.D. Bouches-du-Rhône, L863, *Atelier de Charité de Saint-Michel* (Aix-en-Provence), documents on *gestion*, 20 October 1790–23 August 1793.

49. A.D. Rhône, 1L1170, *Atelier de la paroisse Saint-Irénée* in Lyon, report for 1790.

50. A.D. Seine, VD*1662, *Section du Temple*, letter from Department of Police, 4 January 1791.

51. A.N., F¹⁵3567, report of the *chef d'atelier* at the Recollets, 1791.

52. A.N., AD.XIV⁶, Liancourt (Oise), *Rapport fait au nom des Comités des Finances, d'Agriculture et Commerce, des Domaines, et de Mendicité*, 16 June 1791, p. 6.

53. A.D. Seine, 4AZ.269ᵗᵉʳ, *Pétition des travailleurs des travaux publics de la Section du Roule*, Year II.

54. A.D. Cantal, L322, District of Aurillac, report on works concerned with the establishment of *ateliers*, 1792.

55. A.N., F¹⁵3575, *Filature des Jacobins, Rapport au Bureau Municipal*, 18 June 1793.

56. B.N., N.A.F.2654, *Section du Mont-Blanc*, register of *travaux publics*, f. 93.

57. A.D. Seine, VD*1661, *Section du Temple*, extract from the deliberations of 4 May 1791.

58. B.N., N.A.F.2654, *Section du Temple*, register of discussions, f. 142.

59. A.N., F¹⁵3575, *Section du Panthéon*, petition from *citoyenne* Leclerc.

60. A.N., AD.XIV⁶, Liancourt (Oise), *op. cit.*, p. 7.

61. F. Dreyfus, *op. cit.*, p. 129.

62. L. Accarias, *L'assistance publique sous la Révolution dans le Département du Puy-de-Dôme*, p. 71.

63. A.D. Bouches-du-Rhône, L863, District of Aix, letter from workers at the *atelier de cordonnerie* in Aix-en-Provence, 18 *floréal* III.

7 The *Enfants Trouvés*, 'une dette nationale'

In a society like Revolutionary France it was predictable that the attention of the legislators should focus sharply on the lot of children and on the particular problems of caring for them. In part this was a reflection of the intense family-consciousness of the French themselves, the widespread belief at all levels of society that it was one's duty to have children to perpetuate the spirit of liberty which the present generation had won for themselves and their descendants. This was a moral as much as a political judgement, and it was held as tenaciously by the *sans-culottes* of the Paris sections as it was by the politicians in the Convention and on the floor of the Jacobin Club. The good *sans-culotte*, in Vingternier's famous definition, was a family man who lived simply with his wife and children on the fourth or fifth storey;[1] homeliness and the simple pleasures of family life were not so much respected as turned into moral imperatives by the social canons of the age.[2] In the same vein, family men were offered some degree of protection from military requisition, while bachelorhood was denounced and equated with egotism. But it was not entirely a question of morality, even once allowance has been made for the new puritanism engendered by the Revolution. Especially after the declaration of war in 1792 there were far more practical reasons of state which could be cited in defence of family life. Population was seen by many as a source of future strength, both on the battlefield and in the economic sphere, as a weapon that could be used in the Republican cause to drive back the forces of darkness and further the spread of liberty across Europe. Sons, in particular, were welcomed as future soldiers, and motherhood came to be honoured by the state: by the Year II it was relatively common for parents to justify their own patriotism by pointing to the sons they had raised for the armies, a favoured first line of defence in the event of interrogation by the local *comité de surveillance*. It was during the Jacobin months, too, that mothers were wont to be portrayed as Republican heroines, marching solemnly in the endless processions of the *fêtes nationales*, draped in *tricolor* sashes and proudly bearing banners proclaiming to the world that they had given four, five, or six children to a grateful Republic.[3] For France in the 1790s was a country kept buoyant by a fundamental and unquenchable optimism, looking to future generations to build on present achievements and to ensure the permanent gains of the Revolution. In such a society, despite the grinding poverty and the terrible deprivations of the present, children were the source of future hope, the guarantee that all the sacrifices had not been in vain. They soon became idealized, like the youthful faces smiling dreamily into a red dawn, which in the twentieth century have symbolized the *Jeunesses Communistes* on innumerable French walls and billboards. And that very idealization ensured that children would receive high priority in matters of social policy.

Once again, the Revolution was building on the work of its predecessors, and especially on the research and reform plans produced by the humanitarian movement of the 1770s and 1780s. Awareness of the social and intellectual deprivation of large sections of the children of France was not new; indeed, the tragic loss of human potential had given rise to much consternation in the previous half-century, when concepts of equal opportunity and such educational theories as those propounded by Jean-Jacques Rousseau had gained a wide readership and appeared glaringly at odds with the reality of French society. In the Revolutionary years the contrast was even more apparent, and intellectual outrage was caused by what was seen as a horrific betrayal of the basic principles of liberty and equality. In particular, the Revolution emphasized two spheres of activity where it was felt that previous efforts at reform had been inadequate – the intensely practical issue of the level of care available to poor and abandoned children (an area in which the state had accepted only the most perfunctory responsibility during the Ancien Regime), and the more intellectual question of the best type of elementary education that should be offered to the children of France. The second of these lies outside the scope of this study, though, like *bienfaisance*, it was an area where the basic egalitarian and anticlerical instincts of the Revolution played a major part in defining policy.[4] But the question of the *enfants trouvés*, of young children orphaned or abandoned for others to raise, was one that alerted the social conscience of the French Enlightenment and was to be a major element in the social policy of the Revolution. Already in the last years of the Ancien Regime public concern had been sufficiently awakened to their plight to provoke a degree of state intervention, notably in the wake of the harsh recession of 1779, and a number of provinces and *pays d'états* had even begun imposing taxes specifically for this purpose.[5] But these were no more than the piecemeal beginnings of a policy towards *enfants trouvés*: the reality of large numbers of innocent, abandoned foundlings in the hospitals of France presented to the men of 1789 an unanswerable case for the kind of blanket welfarism in which some at least among them so passionately believed.

These children generally fell into one of two distinguishable categories of neglect – those who had been abandoned because their parents were too poor to raise them themselves, and those who were illegitimate and genuinely unwanted, abandoned in many cases by the mother in desperation lest she lose her job in service and be reduced to begging.[6] Sometimes the parentage of the child was well known in the community. Priests would recommend that babies of indigent parents be taken into care in cases where the additional child would destroy the nicely-balanced domestic economy of a very poor household. On other occasions, pathetic tear-stained letters would be found attached to babies, pleading with the authorities to care for them since the mother or the parents were simply unable to do so. Or else the mayor or municipal council might themselves intervene, as happened at Cussac in the Canton of Oradour-sur-Vaize (Haute-Vienne) in Year II, where the mayor interceded on behalf of a servant-girl who was too poor to care for her newly-born son, 'car elle est obligée de servir en qualité de domestique pour se procurer sa nourriture et entretien'.[7] But such cases were in the minority. More often, the baby would be anonymous, abandoned by society to be cared for by the local *seigneur*, or the *curé*, or the hospital. Eighteenth-century France was a society where such abandonment was taken for granted as a normal event in the lives of the poor, one that was made necessary by grinding poverty and by years of bad harvests. It was tacitly assumed that thousands of illegitimate babies would have to be abandoned each year, and, unless the child died as a result of its exposure, it was unlikely that any serious criminal charge would be brought against the mother. As Olwen Hufton makes clear, until about twenty years before the Revolution little distinction was drawn by hospitals between legitimate and illegitimate children: it was simply assumed that all *enfants trouvés* were the unfortunate victims of their parents' loose living, so that, when legitimate babies were admitted, they were nevertheless *réputés bâtards*.[8] All were received with an equally fatalistic acceptance and all subjected to the same stereotyped regime.

Illegitimacy posed particularly serious problems for the authorities in cities and large towns. Recent research on the *déclarations de grossesse* that were kept in all French towns in the eighteenth century suggests that the contrast between town and country was astonishingly high, ranging from one or two per cent of births in rural areas to figures as high as 17 or even 20 per cent in Paris and certain of the larger cities. More significantly, the illegitimacy rate in these cities was rising steadily throughout the century.[9] In industrial towns like Lyon, pre-marital conception was becoming very much more common among the operatives in the *Fabrique*, and marriage itself was seen almost exclusively in terms of procreation. This is clearly demonstrated in one of the poorer weaving areas of Lyon, the Paroisse Saint-Georges, in the second half of the century, where Maurice Garden has found that between 10 and 20 per cent of first babies were born within three months of marriage.[10] Not all promises of marriage, of course, were kept; they were often hastily made by young men on the Sunday *promenade* to girls who, anxious for security in the lonely city, were willing to agree. Many of the *ouvrières* in the silk industry were country girls, strangers in Lyon, and only too happy to dream of marriage and be reassured by the tantalizing prospect of some modest improvement in their economic status. Richard Cobb's splendidly impressionistic essay on Revolutionary Lyon shows just how vulnerable were the young immigrant workers of the city to social pressures, to the quest for economic security and, not least, to the prospect of companionship.[11]

The Revolution served to increase these pressures and temptations in a number of ways, and especially through the mobilization of the young men in the population as regular soldiers or as National Guardsmen. Even more than previously, the French population became mobile and peripatetic, forced to take to the roads to join their battalions, to return on leave or to hospital, to find alternative employment in a period of economic recession. In a garrison town like Strasbourg, with troops passing through to fight in Germany, with artisans crossing freely from the Rhineland or the Black Forest, and with a large transient population of carters and bargees servicing the armies, illegitimate births were predictably high. The fathers listed in the city's *déclarations de grossesse* reflect the social texture of Strasbourg: a *sergent des grenadiers*, a captain in the Douzième Régiment des Chasseurs, a corporal from Brittany, a servant who had crossed the Rhine with his master, a *compagnon ceinturier* from the Limousin, a *garçon maçon* from Holland 'qui a quitté la ville pour retourner dans son pays'.[12] The picture is a consistent one, of servant-girls from Strasbourg being deceived by *gens de passage*, whether soldiers on their way to the front or tradesmen who, like Agricol Perdiguier in the following century, were passing through on their *Tour de France*, without either ties or responsibilities in the region and eager for what casual sexual relations they could find. The babies born of such affairs almost always ended up in public care, adding to the large numbers with which towns like Strasbourg already had to cope. For cities not only recorded higher illegitimacy rates within their own boundaries: they also attracted from the hinterland many of the village girls who had got themselves pregnant. They were known to be better supplied with charitable institutions, and, above all, they were anonymous, hidden from the censorious eyes of the family and from the shame of the village. So single girls, frightened and destitute, would move to the cities, girls like Barbe Hardi in Strasbourg, 'ouvrière brodeuse, native de Lunéville, qui, n'ayant jamais habité cette ville, est venue se réfugier ici pour faire ses couches et reclamer la charité de la Nation pour son malheureux enfant'.[13] In many instances de Montlinot was right to lay the blame for the pregnancy not on the artisans of the cities in question but on farm labourers back in their native villages – 'des valets de ferme ivrognes et grossiers', as he rather colourfully phrases it – and on the rich and pleasure-seeking bourgeois who had few qualms about the misery they caused or about the girls they made use of.[14]

Of course this problem was not new, but the increased numbers of children being taken into care in the Revolutionary years caused alarm and despondency among the authorities. It was partly a reflection of increased poverty, an index of the worsening lot of a large section of the population, and it is perhaps instructive that this increase had been a source of complaint for some years before 1789. The exact numbers of babies abandoned in this way cannot be known, although contemporaries were seldom reluctant to propose plausible statistics. In a letter to the *Comité de Mendicité* in May 1790, La Millière went so far as to claim that the number currently in care in France was 22,410, adding for good measure an estimate of their cost which, with endearing confidence, was exact to the nearest denier.[15] Such figures were undoubtedly exaggerated to impress the Committee, but it is true that the number of abandonments in the last thirty years of the Ancien Régime was rising steeply. Tenon, citing the statistics for Paris in the eighteenth century, shows that the numbers of *enfants trouvés* taken into care had risen from 1,738 in 1700 to 2,401 in 1730 and 3,785 in 1750; between 1770 and the outbreak of the Revolution the numbers exposed each year ranged between around 5,500 and 7,500, with a peak in the famine years after 1770.[16] Rising costs alarmed hospital administrators, as did the feeling among many commentators that family life itself was decaying and that moral standards were becoming much too lax. The hospitals for *enfants trouvés*, in the words of a member of the Académie at Châlons in 1777, constituted 'le tombeau de l'amour maternel'.[17] By legalizing divorce, the Revolution was, in the eyes of many more Catholic and more conservative Frenchmen, giving fresh encouragement to a highly regrettable trend.

Even if the Revolution had not facilitated divorce, there were many other reasons that could be adduced for the increase in the numbers of children in care – the harvest failures, the loss of production in pre-Revolutionary industries, the large number of widows and orphans created by the Revolutionary wars, the rapid rises in food prices and the grinding slowness of the government in paying out desperately-needed pension instalments. All played a significant part in disrupting the delicate balance of the family economy in the years after 1792, and the admission figures to hospitals and *dépôts* reflect the worsening economic outlook for ordinary people. In particular, military service greatly swelled the ranks of young widows and of *filles-mères*, left to look after babies and young children long after their fathers had been killed in Italy or on the Rhine. Young children were among the most pitiful victims of the war, and almost always they ended up being cared for by the state. At Thionville, for instance, the local hospital in Year III was caring for two abandoned orphans, of German parentage, whose father had been killed in battle and whose mother had met her death at the hands of the Revolutionary Tribunal in Metz. The same hospital accepted responsibility for Louis Plessis, an orphan boy from Fougères in Normandy, who at the age of twelve had already had his fill of adventure:

> Cet enfant, aussi orphelin et abandonné, a perdu ses parents à la guerre de la Vendée, a suivi un bataillon de volontaires, qui l'a laissé très malade sur le pavé de cette ville.[18]

It was the vast increase in the numbers of young children in care which persuaded the Revolutionary authorities by Year IV that a strict, legalistic definition of *enfants trouvés* must be enforced if the state were not to be burdened with charges for which it had no responsibility. Too often, as the Minister of the Interior explained in year V, departments were including in their quotas of children babies whose fathers and mothers were known, where the father had been killed on the frontiers and where the unmarried mother, left alone to raise the child, was unable to cope. This, he stressed, was quite inadmissable, since the hospitals were intended only for children who had been exposed and abandoned by their parents, whereas the *fille-mère* had a right to a state pension to help her raise her offspring.[19] The fact that the pension was risibly small – the maximum payable was a mere eighty livres per year – and that the law which established it was never put into effect helped ensure that the children of unmarried mothers continued to figure on the lists of *enfants trouvés* in every department of France.[20] The Minister might object that this led to widespread administrative confusion, or that it entailed a serious decline in standards of morality and discipline among children in care.[21] Hospitals might, in similar vein, complain about the extra burdens imposed on them, and some local authorities even tried to enforce *déclarations de grossesse* and the immediate registration of births specifically in order to make such abandonment more difficult.[22] But bureaucratic ordering of this kind did nothing to disperse the problem, and the hospital service in the Revolutionary years continued to be hard pressed by the rapid increase in the numbers of abandonments.

The concern shown by the authorities was the greater in that the institutions set aside to receive and care for abandoned children were patently incapable of raising them adequately. Babies exposed in the hours after birth were in any case weak and sickly; facilities in the hospitals and *dépôts* for *enfants trouvés* were cramped and disease-ridden; and eighteenth-century ideas of sanitation and medication were likely to kill as many as they could save. In keeping with current fashion and the orthodox ideas of the day, babies would be taken at a very early age from the city hospitals to wet-nurses in the countryside, often having to survive long journeys in open carts and carriages on cold winter days in their quest for what the authorities optimistically hoped would be a more healthy environment.[23] Many of the children suffered at birth from diseases inherited from mothers who were riddled with syphilis or emaciated by the effects of chronic malnutrition. Nor was childbirth made any easier or any safer by the lack of expertise by so many French midwives, women of the village or the *quartier* who had received no training in midwifery and had little notion of basic hygiene; this problem, claimed a pamphleteer in Marseille in the 1780s, was especially serious in seaports, where a woman in labour would have little choice but to call on the services of a neighbour, of 'une femme confidente de son in-conduite, n'ayant aucune connaissance de l'art d'accoucher et très peu soigneuse de procurer à l'enfant qui va naître les secours dont il peut avoir besoin'.[24] Midwifery, indeed, had never come to be regarded as a subject worthy of special training or study. These dreadful conditions go far to explain the quite terrifyingly high death rates that were recorded in eighteenth-century hospitals among the children in their care. At a country hospital like the one at Issoire in the Auvergne, for instance, the statistics for the twenty years before the Revolution show the extreme precariousness of the existence of such children. In 1785 twenty-five babies were entered in the hospital register; but in the same year there were sixteen deaths, three among babies under one month, six among those in their first year, and the remaining seven of children aged between one and six. Furthermore, as the *intendant* wrote in 1777 that some forty-five babies were abandoned in Issoire every year, it must be assumed that those who were still-born or who died during their first day of life were not entered in the hospital records.[25] Other statistics merely add to the impression that the *Enfants Trouvés* in many towns were little more than *mouroirs* where weak, undernourished and underprivileged children were neglected and allowed to die. Of the two thousand or so babies taken each year to Paris from the provinces, some nine tenths regularly died before they were three months old.[26] And local returns at the end of the Ancien Regime from various parts of the country confirm the same grisly impression. In the Midi, for example, Léon Lallemand has shown that in the ten years from 1763, 56 per cent of *enfants trouvés* in Toulon died in their first year of life, 48 per cent in Tarascon, 38 per cent in Sisteron, and 41 per cent in Apt.[27] When account is taken of the numbers dying in early childhood, these figures become even grimmer.[28]

In large measure the awakening of public interest in the lot of these children in the years after 1770 is yet another instance of the greater humanity and public conscience that resulted from the Enlightenment. To Montlinot and men like him it was an outrage that so many young children should be allowed to die for want of proper treatment, an outrage that owed as much to public indifference as to the lack of skills in the hospitals. The sense of human waste appalled him, the lack of training provided, the dismal air of fatalistic wretchedness that hung over the children themselves. In Paris, he pointed out, some 105,500 children were cared for in the fifteen years from 1772, yet only 14,430 were still alive, and of these no more than five or six hundred had been taught a trade. The cost was vast – nearly fourteen million livres – and the end product risible: even in terms of cost-effectiveness no one could justify the exercise, which had become an 'effrayante consommation d'hommes et d'argent'.[29] In Bourges, reformers were struck not only by such bleak statistics as these but also by the dreadful sense of gloom and futility, the sheer joylessness of the children's lives in institutions where 'ils ne vivent que pour sentir le poids affreux de leur triste existence' after being rejected by their elders and treated more cruelly than animals.[30] But not all the impetus to reform was so clearly humanitarian in tone. The waste of public money was widely resented, compounded by the strong suspicion that all the children in care were not bona fide orphans or illegitimate children from the immediate area. In the Revolutionary years, as during the previous decade, there was considerable outcry against 'outsiders' who, it was believed, were causing the crisis to the existing facilities by seeking aid in towns to which they did not belong. The poor, it was widely accepted, deliberately travelled to cities where provision was rumoured to be good so that they could then abandon their babies with a clearer conscience – hence the vast rate of exposure in the capital and in the Auvergne, where the king was until 1790 *haut justicier* of Riom, Clermont and Issoire and where hospital provision was, as a consequence, unusually good.[31] Characteristically, Montlinot's report on Soissons in 1790 insisted that in that area children were frequently abandoned by tinkers and other *marchands ambulants* who were little more than 'des espèces de vagabonds', with dire results for the local hospitals. Even more serious was the effect of foreign foundlings, abandoned in French towns where provision would be made for them: in Soissons, he points out, 586 children out of a sample of 3,240 were foreign, mostly from across the frontier in Belgium, where few social amenities existed and where the poor were utterly indigent.[32] His Enlightened, humanitarian outlook did not extend to those who, he felt, were seeking to abuse French charity and generosity.

Both these attitudes survived into the Revolutionary period, when, as in so many other areas of social provision, they tended to become highly charged with idealism and political principle. Especially in the *Comité de Mendicité*, the humanitarians received respectful attention, and the rhetoric of the period was undoubtedly theirs. More important, perhaps, is the fact that much of that rhetoric was turned into legislation, that the Revolutionary state did in several ways assume responsibility for the welfare of the poor and the illegitimate alike. The ending of seigneurial jurisdiction in 1790 did much to force their hand, since one of the duties of the *seigneur* in the Ancien Regime had been to care of all local children found abandoned on his land. In most cases this had meant that the nobles had shouldered part of the cost of the *dépôts* to which these children had been sent, but with the abolition of their privileges in 1790 their obligations were also removed and responsibility for foundlings reverted to the state.[33] Henceforth they were to be cared for by the local authorities, who accepted the principle of public intervention and agreed to treat them not as a despised burden but as *les enfants naturels de la patrie*, children who would grow up to be valuable citizens and who by 1793 were usually destined for service on the frontiers or in ancillary trades servicing the armies of the Republic. Such citizens, whatever their origins, could not but share the full benefits of citizenship and equality before the law, and both national legislators like La Rochefoucauld-Liancourt and local administrators like Clochard in Bordeaux worked hard to achieve this goal.[34] In legal terms they undoubtedly succeeded, their success crowned in Year II by a decree which guaranteed that in future illegitimate children were to enjoy the same rights of succession as those born in wedlock.[35] With the rights of the church cut back and and divorce officially instituted, the moral as well as the economic stigma on bastardy was effectively reduced. It could never, however, be totally erased, and the increased cost of maintaining the *enfants trouvés* had the unfortunate side-effect of encouraging further grumbling and carping at a service which some continued to see as a costly subsidy to licentiousness and irresponsibility. Throughout the Revolution there were those who urged that the expense be pruned and that the fathers of illegitimate babies be registered and compelled to pay the cost of their basic foodstuffs.[36]

Finance, of course, was one of the principal obstacles which the legislators encountered in their attempt to guarantee the rights of illegitimate children and to treat their care as *une dette nationale*. As we have seen, every other aspect of social provision was blighted by inflation and by the shortage of government funds as the Revolution progressed, and the *enfants trouvés* shared fully in that deprivation. Admittedly, there is some evidence that where private charity did still remain significant after 1790 it was to these unfortunate children that people felt moved to make donations: in the Puy-de-Dôme Accarias notes that even the clergy still made occasional gifts, like the sum of 40,000 livres donated by Dom Gerle, superior of the Chartreuse at Port-Sainte-Marie, in March 1790 to be invested for the benefit of the new *Enfants Trouvés* in Clermont.[37] But these private acts of charity were insignificant when compared with the sums donated in the Ancien Régime, as even sympathy for innocent abandoned children could never hope to equal the religious motivation of the *fidèles*. The result, once again, was an almost total dependence on government grants, which became more and more inadequate as the years passed: in this respect the *Enfants Trouvés* were treated in exactly the same way as all other hospitals and *ateliers* and suffered the same serious shortages. In 1790, before the abolition of feudal dues, the *Manufacture* in Bordeaux could depend on an independent income of over 142,000 livres, largely from rents, country estates, interest charges and feudal exactions: but by Year V its revenues had been cut to just over 43,000 livres as a result of Revolutionary legislation, a sum lower than what it had received from rents on houses and warehouses in 1790.[38] What made this reduction more difficult to bear was the concomitant increase in the numbers of babies taken into care and the uncontrollable rise in the rate of inflation that followed the lifting of the General Maximum. This double pressure on the hospital authorities meant that the standards of care which they could offer were very uneven, and that in many areas the children themselves were made to suffer.

The regime inside the various hospitals for foundlings changed little, despite the consultation of medical opinion by the *Comité de Mendicité* in Paris. Generally it was very strict, with little clear distinction made by officials between an *asile* for abandoned children and a detention centre for young offenders. The president of the Hôpital Saint-Jacques in Aix-en-Provence phrased the ambiguity succinctly in 1790 when he wrote that 'l'oeuvre des enfants abandonnés est une maison de correction pour les enfants au-dessous de dix-huit ans.'[39] This made some sense, inasmuch as there were no alternative institutions available for children who were arrested for minor crimes and offences; but it does underline the curiously ambivalent role which the *Enfants Trouvés* had to fulfil. In many towns parents would request that sons and daughters whom they were unable to control be admitted to the institution for a period of correction. Thus Honoré Heiries, a fourteen-year-old carter's son from Aix, was admitted to the Hôpital Saint-Jacques at his father's request on condition that his father paid for the costs of his board and lodging.[40] Similarly, there were cases of known troublemakers being transferred to the *Enfants Trouvés* by harassed local authorities, like the twelve teenage boys moved in 1793 to Strasbourg, boys 'déjà parvenus à l'age d'adolescens, dont les moeurs et la conduite sont de nature par le mauvais exemple qu'ils ont donné et donnent journellement dans leur hospice actuel'.[41] In such cases there were understandable fears for good order in the institution to which they were transferred, especially as cases of vandalism and rowdiness were not uncommon. Discipline could be harsh, particularly for offences that prejudiced the smooth running of the establishment. In Year III, for instance, in Marseille, we find the authorities facing a group of boys who claimed the benefits of the Declaration of the Rights of Man and refused to accept the discipline imposed by the institution; the administrators, angered by 'ces enfants rebelles', demanded additional powers, including the right to resort to extreme punishments like expulsion, solitary confinement, a bread-and-water diet, and even imprisonment.[42] But there is little evidence that such measures were ever invoked.

The philosophy underlying the care reserved for the children also remained largely unchanged. It was still assumed that they should, in the interests of their health, spend much of their early childhood in the countryside with a wet-nurse, before returning to the institution for training in a trade or, alternatively, undertaking farm work in their village of adoption. This was the traditional way of caring for abandoned children, and though it had come under mounting criticism during the eighteenth century, little had been done to improve it or to investigate its deficiencies. But in the twenty or thirty years before the Revolution, Enlightened opinion was coming to question its efficacy and to ask whether the shockingly high death rate among such children was not directly related to the methods of care employed.[43] The number of children consigned to *nourrices* had risen dramatically in the course of the century, and with that increase had gone a correspondingly huge rise in the number of child deaths. Tenon, a noted surgeon and campaigner on medical matters in the 1770s and 1780s, was one who was in no doubt that there was a direct causal link between these deaths and the system of wet-nursing. Even in Paris, where there was a *Bureau des nourrices* to supervise the allocation of babies and where control was much tighter than in most provincial centres, he noted a death rate of 31–32 per cent in the 1770s; and in Lyon, where the allocation was left unsupervised, it was estimated that as many as two out of every three babies died while *en nourrice*.[44] The death rate caused widespread anxiety, to reformers and the police alike, and further alarm was occasioned by the numerous cases of fraud and abuse which came to the notice of the authorities. Disease spread easily where one *nourrice* suckled several sickly infants; babies were so tightly swaddled that they died; others were left on their own for long periods by mothers who were at work in the fields; there were reports of infants burned in untended fires, scalded in vats of water, even attacked and eaten by pigs.[45] Often the wet-nurses themselves were unable to come to the hospital in the neighbouring city to take charge of their babies, and in such cases transportation was left to the callous, commercial hands of a carter or *meneur*.[46] Above all, the problem was one of numbers: the number of infants in need of suckling far outstripped the number of women who made themselves available for this work, even after the inducement of a wage increase in 1773, and many of the poorer children, those abandoned at birth by their parents, were having to travel long distances from the cities into rural parishes where poverty was rife and ignorance widespread. From Paris, for instance, babies were being taken when only a few days old to wet-nurses in Normandy, Picardy, and the Beauvaisis. Yet the practice continued unchecked, despite the warnings of medical experts and the grimly regular toll of young lives: indeed, so ingrained was the practice that it was not only the poor and those in care who were sent *en nourrice*, but a large proportion of the children of bourgeois and artisans as well. But Tenon's report makes it clear that the most unhygienic conditions, the longest journeys, the poorest and most emaciated wet-nurses and the most alarming death rates were reserved for the poor and the vulnerable, the children designated by the local hospital for *Enfants Trouvés*.[47]

Not surprisingly, the horrendously high mortality figures which characterized the later eighteenth century showed little sign of abatement after 1789, despite the undoubted energy and the paternalistic concern of the *Comité de Mendicité* in Paris. In Limoges, for instance, they were still reporting in 1792 that one fifth of babies were dying in their first year of life and three fifths by the time they were three years old.[48] The reasons are not hard to seek. With the increases in the numbers of children admitted, the segregation of those who were diseased was no longer possible. At hospitals like the Pitié in Paris, where there were 1,600 boys in care, outbreaks of fever were very common and the danger of epidemics was of frightening proportions. It is true that children who caught smallpox and other contagious diseases were removed to the *hôtel-dieu* for treatment and that there were separate wards for patients with skin diseases like the *galle*. But outbreaks of catarrh and inflammation, biliousness and chest infection, diarrhoea and even dysentery were uncommon occurences in the open dormitories of the *Enfants Trouvés*, and many malignant fevers would so weaken children that they died.[49] Since many of the babies admitted were already suffering from serious venereal and respiratory diseases, their chances of life were sadly diminished, and many others risked infection in the fetid, unhealthy atmosphere of the hospital wards. Such limited precautions as were taken to safeguard their lives do not exactly inspire confidence. At Toulouse, for instance, a hospital which took more care than most, the normal procedure was to take babies to the *salle des épreuves* for two weeks on admission, where they were fed on cow's milk 'un peu rechauffé au bain-marie' and given lukewarm baths twice a day until the authorities were satisfied that they showed no symptoms of venereal complaints. Then they were passed to the *nourrices* in the accustomed manner.[50]

This mixture of economic recession and overcrowding, combined with rather primitive medical knowledge, guaranteed that the lot of these children got no better in the Revolutionary years, and most contemporaries were agreed that it actually deteriorated sharply in spite of the more liberal attitudes encapsulated in national legislation. Theory and practice, as in so many aspects of revolutionary social policy, remained wildly at variance. In theory everyone was agreed about the importance of education in preparing these disadvantaged youngsters for adult life and, indeed, some laudable steps were taken by enthusiastic local administrators. At hospitals like the Trinité in Paris, a foundation going back to the thirteenth century, a vigorous apprenticeship scheme was maintained, whereby orphan boys could be instructed in skilled artisanal trades.[51] Most towns did make some effort to find apprenticeships for the boys in their care when they reached their teens, though the very limited sums of money devoted to these schemes – in the financial year 1789–90 Strasbourg spent no more than 733 livres in all – would suggest that they never became a top priority.[52] Even in 1793, when the scheme was more solidly established and links had been forged with local employers, only twenty-five boys from the city's *Enfants Trouvés* were apprenticed in this way, the remaining children being kept in the hospital buildings or sent out *en pension* to private homes in the community.[53] It was not any lack of awareness of the importance of such educational measures that was responsible for this apparent dilatoriness, for there is overwhelming evidence that the Revolutionaries were constantly reminded of the benefits they could confer. In 1790, in a report to the *Comité de Mendicité*, La Rochfoucauld-Liancourt had himself lamented the lack of technical training and indicated that this could only have the unhappy effect of preparing a new generation of *vagabonds*, unable to hold down a job or contribute adequately to modern society. At the Pitié in Paris he noted that the only classes given were in reading, writing, and religion, subjects in which the standard of attainment was lamentably poor. Apart from these lessons,

> Il n'est aucun travail dans cette maison; ces malheureux enfants, destinés à être pauvres toute leur vie, sont façonnés par la charité à l'oisiveté, à l'inertie, et préparés par conséquent à devenir des sujets nuisibles à la société.[54]

Surprisingly, perhaps, in view of the influence of Enlightened opinion with its insistence on the value of education, the Revolutionary period saw no expansion of educational provision for these children. Financial stringency ensured that the level of instruction offered remained very basic, and in some hospitals, like the Hôpital des Enfants in Epinal, it was the first thing to be cut back when funds ran seriously short in Year III.[55] Inevitably in times of acute shortage, administrators looked to answer the children's most immediate needs, and these had to be the provision of food, clothing and heating. Even the most rudimentary education had come to be seen as something of a luxury.

The wards for *enfants trouvés*, whether in separate hospital buildings or as part of more diffuse general hospitals in the local community, were subject to the same financial constraints as the rest of the hospital service, and they suffered from similar degradation and neglect. Rotting, damp buildings could not fail to undermine the health of babies and young children whose resistance level had never had a chance to develop, and the lack of basic maintenance contributed to the poor level of health among the inmates. And, as elsewhere in the service, as Year II gave way to the new spirit of the Thermidorian regime and France saw a return to a free-enterprise economy, so the full failings of the Revolutionary welfare state became obvious to all. By Year III and Year IV it was not only luxuries, however broadly that word is interpreted, which were being desperately discarded. Adequate funds were no longer coming through from the Commission in Paris, and the *Enfants Trouvés*, as one of the most expensive sectors in eighteenth-century hospital provision, suffered badly. Growing numbers of abandoned infants had to be looked after somehow, whatever the state of the hospitals' finances: unlike some of the other hospital services, there was no way in which they could simply be sent home and forgotten. Indeed, however miserly the sums paid throughout the period of the Directory, and however late the depreciated moneys which eventually reached the hospitals, some contribution continued to be made for what everyone recognized as necessary expenditure. The prefect of the Gironde was right in Year IX when he claimed that

> La pénurie où se trouve la Commission des Hospices est principalement occasionnée par les avances qu'elle a fait [*sic*] jusqu'à ce jour pour les Enfants de la Patrie.[56]

But this did not prevent babies from dying in childbirth, because midwives could not be found at the miserable rate of wages that was offered to them.[57] Nor did it prevent young children from lying stark naked in open wards in the many hospitals which had no money to buy clothing for them.[58] In the cash-starved years of the Directory the level of needless suffering among these foundlings rose steeply, and with the private resources of the hospitals already sold off or otherwise alienated, the local administrators could only repeat their increasingly harrowing tales to the authorities in Paris.

With the increased numbers of abandonments and a steady rise in the numbers of war orphans to be catered for, the pressure on space and – more damagingly from the point of view of health – on the severely limited amounts of fresh air in the hospitals became more acute. Overcrowding became a major problem, especially since some of the buildings which had previously been reserved for children were now required for other, more urgent purposes, and the children were sometimes moved into ordinary wards along with the old, the chronically sick, and the dying. In Strasbourg, for instance, the buildings at Stephansfeld were converted into a military hospital in Year IV, and the *enfants naturels de la patrie* who lived there were unceremoniously transferred into the already overcrowded *Enfants Trouvés* in the city.[59] At Gray in the

Haute-Saône the separate provision for children had been terminated and the entire function of the hospital distorted by the conversion of two of its three rooms into a reception hospital for soldiers from the front; and the diversion of scarce funds to help treat those troops was largely held responsible for the state of almost total deprivation that reigned among the children.[60] The needs of wounded soldiers were often most urgent and were allowed to take precedence over those of other patients. Still nearer the front, at Castellane, it was noted that soldiers billeted there required immediate stocks of bandages and dressings, and that the mattresses and linen commandeered for their use would normally have served the needs of the fifty children with whom they shared the building.[61] The fact that the men were frequently in hospital for several weeks or months as they were nursed back to health only emphasized their call upon the limited supplies available. The children, already accustomed to a life of austerity, were condemned to still further suffering.

It was in the years of the Directory – the years of highest inflation and also of the most consistent commitment to foreign war – that the care provided for *enfants trouvés* sank to its nadir. If bedlinen and nightclothes were in desperately short supply, some children were also forced to stay indoors at all times because shirts and articles of outdoor clothing could not be obtained. Especially in the war zones many tailors had been requisitioned for the supply of the army and were not available to work for the account of bad debtors like the local hospital: in Strasbourg, for instance, almost any form of skilled labour was unobtainable except for military purposes, with the result that the gardens were untilled and the fabric of the buildings allowed to fall into serious disrepair.[62] Severe shortages of coal and firewood added to the general discomfort of the winter months. And for much of the period even the most basic foodstuffs were impossible to come by, with the result that many of the children were seriously undernourished. In Marseille in Year IV the treasurer noted bleakly that vegetables were the only form of food consumed in the hospital, since they had no money to buy anything else.[63] Two years later the hospital at Valenciennes gave a detailed account of the food rations it was able to allow the children in its care, rations measured out with the utmost economy to prevent the hospital from sinking to starvation-point: each child was given four ounces of meat once every ten days, plus a daily ration of 'cinq quarterons' of bread. There was no drink provided other than water.[64] The hospital administrators were openly ashamed of the standard of nutrition and the general quality of life they were affording the children, who in many cases were themselves innocent victims of war. But there was little that they could do, except plead with essential suppliers to extend their credit for a few weeks more. It is this desperation on the part of local administrators and registrars, faced by the reality of dwindling resources and soaring indebtedness, which explains their apparent pettiness in attempting to turn away any additional charges. In Marseille, for instance, defensive treasurers became adept at refusing admission to all legitimate children on the grounds that they were properly the responsibility of their parents, and, as in Paris, they became much more severe in turning away any child from a parish outside the boundaries of the city.[65]

Internal rigours and spartan diets were common to all spheres of the hospital service after 1794, and the *Enfants Trouvés* found themselves in exactly the same plight in regard to government funding as other charitable institutions. The children suffered from the resulting shortages and discomforts, but there is no reason to believe that many deaths stemmed from these cutbacks: the service survived this period more or less intact. What did bring its operation to the brink of collapse under the Directory was another, more crucial shortage of money – the increasing inability of the government to pay the wet-nurses for their services. The *nourrices* were, as has been indicated, a fundamental part of the system of child-care, for without them the hospital buildings would have become utterly unequal to their task, overrun by swarming children and susceptible to every form of contagion and pestilence. Yet in most areas the cost of the *nourrices* was the largest single item of expense for the hospital management, and when moneys failed to come through from the national treasury for three or six months it was the most obvious and most immediate form of economy.[66] With the increase in the number of foundlings, moreover, there was by Year II a patent need to attract even more of these women to offer their maternal services, at exactly the moment when the shortage of funds for the purpose began to be most critical. Ironically, it was the government's failure to maintain social welfare payments of another kind – the sums promised to the widows and dependants of men on active service – that was helping to create the crisis by adding significantly to the number of abandonments.[67] As for the nurses, they were for the most part ordinary working women, the wives of farmworkers and rural tradesmen in country villages near towns where hospitals were sited, mothers themselves in the majority of cases, who were willing to share their milk with orphan children. Most of them did it not from any charitable impulse but simply because they needed the money, and there are frequent cases where one woman, tired and drained, was attempting to suckle several babies at once for the local hospital. Indeed, there can have been few incentives other than money, since the job was often unpleasant and even dangerous, with the ever-present chance of catching venereal disease from the discarded babies of prostitutes. It was the kind of job that would be undertaken only by the poor, for whom the modest income could be a means of saving their own families from destitution. That income was modest indeed: in 1790, for instance, the Hospice de la Grave in Toulouse paid them three livres per month in coin and gave them a complete set of clothes for each child once a year. With inflation and successive government cash crises, the real value of such payments was to be steadily eroded in the years that followed. Indeed, under the Directory that same hospital was obliged to pay a monthly wage of 750 livres, and it was admitted that the nurses were still substantially worse off than they had been in 1790. But the nominal cost to the hospital was huge – an astronomical 1,800,000 livres each month.[68]

The greatest fear of all hospital adminsitrators was that large numbers of *nourrices* would suddenly stop caring for their charges at a time when they were so desperately needed, and such was the rate of inflation by the Thermidorian period that that fear was very real indeed. Women could not be expected to continue to wet-nurse infants if they were not paid for their trouble or if the remuneration was so long delayed as to be worthless when it finally arrived: the child in such circumstances would only become a burden on the limited family resources of the nurses themselves, the kind of burden that could easily reduce them in turn to begging or destitution. Yet arrears of pay mounted steadily: at Angoulême, for instance, in Year VII they had still not received any payment for the fourth quarter of Year V.[69] By the following year local arrears could be even longer: at Reims *nourrices* had not been paid for twenty-eight months[70], at Maurs in the Cantal for forty-one months.[71] The steady increase in the price of bread further jeopardized the position of nurses, and many villages, like La Fère in the Aisne, reported bleakly that they were living 'dans la misère la plus affreuse', while the children in their care were dying of cold and hunger.[72] Their plight in the face of inflation is graphically illustrated by a petition from the District of Brioude in the Haute-Loire, which compared the nurses' income level with basic grain prices in the area during 1791 and the Year III. In 1791, they explained, they earned eight livres per month, but grain prices had never risen above four livres: hence 'leur mois suffisait pour leurs nourritures et peut-être au-delà.' Now, in Year III, when their earnings were thirty livres, the price of rye exceeded one hundred livres, with the result that they could no longer afford more than five ounces of bread per day, a totally insufficient diet.[73] It is hardly surprising that a number of *nourrices* were beginning to grumble that they ought to be paid in grain and not in cash, since only grain could guarantee their continued survival.[74] In particular, they blamed the huge rate of inflation on the *assignats*, frequently demanding that the hospitals pay them in coin and not in paper, especially in the case of arrears whose value in *assignats* had already considerably depreciated.[75] Some local authorities tried to resist their demands by finding other means of nourishing their foundlings. Douai in the Nord was one of a number of towns which experimented with animal milk and other forms of artificial feeding, but they met with little success and caused the deaths of almost all the children involved, despite the devoted attention of their staff.[76] Even more desperately, the hospital in Mont-de-Marsan, embarrassed by debts of over 100,000 livres to its *nourrices*, was reduced to using goats as a substitute for wet-nurses, a device which, it freely admitted, 'expose à mort certaine les orphelins qu'on est obligé en quelques lieux d'élever avec les chèvres'.[77]

These solutions were, of course, extreme, but they do illustrate the depths which the service was forced to plumb in the Revolutionary years. For what the Revolution had achieved – and it is a considerable achievement, given the generally docile mentality of the nurses, their lack of organization, and the scattered villages and farmsteads where they lived – was to create a new militancy among the *nourrices*, the sort of mood that would lead them not only to ask for a decent reward for their services but also to back that demand with the threat of industrial action. From all over France reports were being filed in Year III and Year IV that the Convention must raise the grants made for wet-nurses without delay if huge numbers of babies were not to be returned to the hospitals and defiantly dumped on their doorsteps. In the Haute-Marne the *nourrices* were sufficiently organized by Year IV to demonstrate in the streets for more pay, insisting that they would act in unison and keep the children for no more than one further month unless their terms were met.[78] The women understood very clearly that they had entered into a contract with their local hospital to suckle and care for the children, and it was the hospital and the hospital administrators that they rounded on when their pay was blocked. At Sédan, in the Ardennes, the director was not lacking in sympathy for them, since the injustice of what was being done was patent to everyone. But he noted wryly that the *nourrices* did not seem to believe that it was the government in Paris that was holding up payment; instead they angrily attacked and denounced the hospital staff, alleging that they had diverted the funds for their own use.[79] Elsewhere, there were accusations that some infants were being starved and physically ill-treated by nurses determined to be rid of their unprofitable responsibilities.[80] After 1795 rumour and counter-rumour circulated wildly. Continually the nurses were on the point of returning the babies they were suckling; continually the hospital authorities tried to buy them off with promises that the payment would be made in a matter of days; and continually they smarted at the deceit and the bureaucratic inefficiency which had occasioned these smouldering periodic crises to break yet again.

Throughout the years from 1795 to 1800 the whole structure of charitable provision for *enfants trouvés* seemed on the verge of total collapse. Occasionally belated money grants from Paris were received, and a threatening crisis passed once more. Or local short-term expedients might be tried, like the decision of the authorities in Metz in Year VI to pay their *nourrices* by selling off *émigré* lands[81], or the quite arbitrary distinction made at Bagnères whereby only those nurses caring for children under the age of seven would be paid, on the somewhat unscrupulous grounds that the hospital would lack the skills and resources to look after very young children if they were handed back.[82] But the service was constantly tottering on the brink of disaster. For the *nourrices* were being treated very shabbily, their relative ignorance and isolation being played upon mercilessly by a government which could afford to regard them as a lower priority for scarce funds than the war effort or the requisitioning of food for Paris. It was sadly mistaken, however, if it took the threats of the *nourrices* too lightly, for by Year IV and Year V commune after commune reported that babies were already being returned to them, often half-starved and in poor health, to the utter despair of the hospital authorities. 'Ces enfants', lamented one town in the Eure, 'sont absolument tout nuds [*sic*]', and the local *Enfants Trouvés* was so seriously underfinanced that it could not even clothe them[83] At Metz in Year VII a steady flow of young children and babies was being reluctantly received back into the hospital, sometimes as many as half a dozen in a single day, and the director made it clear that some of these foundlings had died in the hospital as a direct result of the government's failure to pay the *nourrices*.[84] There was little that the authorities could do. *Nourrices* would creep up to the hospital gates under cover of darkness, leave their baby, naked or scantily clad, where they were sure that it would be quickly found, and vanish into the night. In short, the worst fears of departments like the Dordogne were being fulfilled, without the departments having any idea what they should do to avert a stream of potential tragedies. Should they, they asked the Minister, seek out these unfortunate women, arrest them and punish them in order to discourage others?[85] The Dordogne, like other departments, knew only too well that the scale of poverty and misery was such that no punishment could hope to have any real deterrent effect, for the wet-nurses, far from being strong and able-bodied, were now on the brink of utter destitution, forced to take to begging to feed themselves and their children. Such was their wretchedness in Year VIII that one canton in the west of France was moved to point out that the real danger to the health and survival of the foundlings came not so much from the threat of abandonment as from the impoverished, run-down state of the women who were asked to suckle them. A *nourrice* drained and withered through the ravages of poverty gave a sickly baby very little hope of survival into adulthood.[86]

Increasingly under the Directory, central government accepted less and less responsibility for even this area of hospital provision, arguing that it no longer endorsed the Jacobin concept of a centralized welfare state and expected the hospitals and *dépôts* to raise at least a sizable part of their own running costs. As with general hospitals, so *enfants trouvés* found their right to manage and lease lands restored in Year V, though without any guarantee that the government would immediately find the properties they required to replace their alienated *biens nationaux*.[87] And by Year VIII the Ministry had another solution which effectively passed responsibility back to the local councils, as new legislation allowed them to raise local taxes, *octrois*, to finance such services. This proved rather too facile an escape-hatch. Writing to the Department of Pas-de-Calais in *ventôse* of that year, in response to a particularly pressing appeal for funds, the Minister of the Interior would accept no responsibility for paying a grant from the national treasury. The *octrois*, he said, had been introduced in order to give back to hospitals some of their independence, and if the current rate was not sufficient to feed and care for the abandoned children in the department, then the tariff could, quite simply, be raised to bring in more revenue.[88] Nothing, it would seem, could be more straightforward. The government also took full credit for several pieces of humanitarian legislation for *enfants trouvés* since Year III, which appeared to raise the quality of their lives, such as the decree of 30 *ventôse* V insisting that children stay with wet-nurses until the age of twelve, when they should be guaranteed some form of industrial or agricultural training by being put to work in a trade or placed with a local farmer.[89] Unhappily, like much of the legislation of the period, this decree read well and suggested a viable, even a compassionate solution, but it was never seriously acted upon, and the conditions of misery and dereliction continued for several years afterwards.

This, indeed, must remain the most damning indictment of the Revolution's social policy in the field of *enfants trouvés*, that so few of its good intentions were carried into effect and that, even by Year VIII or Year X the condition of the children remained deplorable and of the institutions that housed them both shabby and dilapidated. Hopes had been raised and promises made, yet the fears and the insecurity suffered in Year II and Year III were equally prevalent in the first years of the nineteenth century. Nothing had changed, except perhaps that stocks of food and linen had dwindled still further and the directors and *économes* had become accustomed to a new, savagely inadequate norm. At La Fère in the Aisne, the administration reported in Year VIII, almost as a matter of course, that not only had the government failed to pay the grants allocated for the current year, but it was still in arrears for substantial sums due in every year since Year III.[90] Another hospital for abandoned children, at Blangy in the Seine-Inférieure, told a similar story: in this case not a single penny had been paid by the exchequer for four years.[91] Such statistics spelt just as great hardship in Year VIII as at any time in the Revolutionary years: it is significant, indeed, that the bureaucratic turmoil of successive Revolutionary governments should have achieved so little and that it would be several years into the Napoleonic era before the finances of the *dépôts* began to be restored to an acceptable level of stability. Still in Year IX local hospitals faced threats from *nourrices* to return their babies, even though in practice it was recognized that the real danger posed was less to infants already with wet-nurses than to the new generation of foundlings for whom no nurses would be forthcoming. At Soissons the *dépôt* faced the daunting prospect of some 250 to 300 babies being returned to their care[92]; at Auch the authorities desperately appealed to the Minister for emergency aid since they simply could not cope with the numbers of infants being dumped on their doorstep.[93]

For the *Enfants Trouvés* as for other parts of the hospital service, this period around Year IX and Year X was as cripplingly deprived as any in the entire Revolution: it was the period when the government had effectively abdicated all responsibility for direct financing and when local taxes and redeemed hospital property had not yet become sufficiently established to place the institutions' finances on a sound footing. The number of children had greatly increased because of the war, yet the number of women offering their services as *nourrices* had been allowed to fall. The tale of grim suffering had reached its most horrendous point, with young children admitted to the *dépôts* with little or no chance of survival. At Marseille, for example, there was such pressure on the wet-nurses still on the hospital's books that in Year VIII many were being implored to suckle three or even four orphans at a time, while in the *dépôt* itself butchers, winemerchants and other suppliers had become frightened by the sheer scale of the debts owed and for two months the children had had nothing to eat except bread and water. In these straitened circumstances it is hardly surprising that few of the orphans survived: of the 555 admitted in the course of Year VII, only twelve were still alive in *nivôse* VIII.[94] All the worst fears of the hospital managers had come to fruition; and the hopes of the reformers, of the *Comité de Mendicité* and the other social crusaders who faced the new dawn of 1789 with such optimism, had been cruelly dashed. Never, even in the worst period of the *pré-révolution* when hospitals and *enfants trouvés* had been seriously underfinanced, had their failure been on such a monumental scale. Only after Year XII, once the principles of the Jacobin welfare state had been fully expunged, did some vestige of stability begin to be restored.

Notes to chapter 7

1. Vingternier, 'Réponse à l'impertinente question: mais qu'est-ce qu'un sans-culotte?', in W. Markov and A. Soboul (editors), *Die Sansculotten von Paris*, p. 2.

2. R. C. Cobb, 'The Revolutionary mentality in France', in *A second identity*, p. 129.

3. O. Hufton, 'Women in Revolution, 1789–1796', *Past and Present*, pp. 90ff.

4. M. Gontard, *L'enseignement primaire en France de la Révolution à la Loi Guizot*, part 2.

5. A.N., F^{15}101, *mémoire* on *Enfants Trouvés*, dated 1791.

6. A.N., AD.XIV.^{7}, Montlinot, *Observations sur les Enfants-Trouvés de la généralité de Soissons* (Paris, 1790).

7. A.D. Haute-Vienne, L377, letter from the *maire* of Cussac, 5 *floréal* II.

8. O. Hufton, *The poor of eighteenth-century France, 1750–1789*, p. 319.

9. *ibid.*, pp. 320–1.

10. M. Garden, *Lyon et les Lyonnais au dix-huitième siècle*, pp. 102–6.

11. R. C. Cobb, 'A view on the street', in *A sense of place*, pp. 79–135.

12. Arch. Mun. Strasbourg, Div. III, liasse 73, *déclarations de grossesse* and applications for admission to the *Enfants-Trouvés*, 1792–3.

13. Arch. Mun. Strasbourg, Div. III, liasse 73, report on Jean Bastian, *enfant trouvé*, born 12 May 1792.

14. A.N., AD.XIV^7, Montlinot, *op. cit.*, p. 14.

15. C. Bloch and A. Tuetey (editors), *Procès-verbaux et rapports du Comité de Mendicité de la Constituante, 1790–91*, p. 30.

16. J. Tenon, *Mémoires sur les hôpitaux de Paris*, pp. 91–2.

17. C. Bloch, *L'assistance et l'Etat en France à la veille de la Révolution*, p. 119.

18. A.N., F^{15}254, minute of Hôpital Sainte-Elizabeth at Thionville (Marne), *frimaire* III.

19. A.N., F^{15}316, letter from Minister of Interior to Department of Lot-et-Garonne, 12 *ventôse* V. The same view is expressed by a number of other errant departments in Year V.

20. Law of 28 June 1793, repealed in *frimaire* V. The text is in A. de Watteville, *Législation charitable*, 1, p. 20.

21. Arch. Mun. Marseille, Q^{3}17, *Hospice des orphelins de la Patrie*, letter from Minister of Interior, 21 *thermidor* IV.

22. A.N., F^{15}440, edict of *municipalité* of Cambrai, 16 *nivôse* VIII.

23. M. Garden, *op. cit.*, p. 127.

24. A.D. Bouches-du-Rhône, C1733, *Mémoire sur les bâtards*, n.d.

25. B. Bellande, *L'ancien Hôpital Général d'Issoire*, pp. 182–3.

26. S. T. McCloy, *Government assistance in eighteenth-century France*, p. 239.

27. Quoted in B. Bellande, *op. cit.*, p. 186n.

28. This is clearly illustrated by the statistics for child deaths at the hôpital Gras de Sisteron (table 4), which greatly inflate Lallemand's figure for deaths in the first year of life only.

29. A.N., AD.XIV^7, Montlinot, *op. cit.*, p. 12.

30. A.D. Cher, C36, *Discours prononcé en présence des souscripteurs du Bureau de Charité*, 27 July 1787.

31. J. Coiffier, *L'assistance publique dans la généralité de Riom au dix-huitième siècle*, p. 135.

32. A.N., AD.XIV^7, Montlinot, *op. cit.*, pp. 6–10.

33. A.D. Rhône, 1L1139, law of 10 December 1790.

Table 4

Year	Admissions	Number dying under age of six
1767	16	12
1768	16	12
1769	19	13
1770	21	18
1771	14	11
1772	27	21
1773	17	15
1774	21	16
1775	11	10
1776	25	17
Totals	187	145

Percentage dying under the age of six = 77.5 per cent

Source: A.D. Bouches-du-Rhône, C1733, *tableau des bâtards* for Sisteron, 1782.

34. F. Dreyfus, *L'assistance sous la Législative et la Convention*, especially pp. 64–5.
35. A.D. Bas-Rhin, 1L1592, decree of 12 *brumaire* II 'relatif aux droits des enfants nés hors du mariage'.
36. A.N., F¹⁵1862, correspondence with the *Trésorerie Nationale*.
37. L. Accarias, *L'assistance publique sous la Révolution dans le Département du Puy-de-Dôme*, p. 138.
38. A.D. Gironde, 11L27, *Etat général des hospices de Bordeaux, prairial* V.
39. A.D. Bouches-du-Rhône, L858, letter of 14 October 1790.
40. A.D. Bouches-du-Rhône, L858, letter of 28 November 1790.
41. A.D. Bas-Rhin, 1L1593, letter of 11 January 1793 from the *Conseil Municipal* of Strasbourg.
42. Arch. Mun. Marseille, Q³2, letter of 21 *ventôse* III from administrators of the Hospice de la Charité in Marseille.
43. For the information that follows on wet-nursing in the later eighteenth century I am indebted to Dr George D. Sussman of Albany (New York), who has worked extensively on this aspect of Ancien Regime charity. In particular I should like to thank him for lending me two unpublished papers, on 'Wet-nursing in the eighteenth century' and 'Three histories of infant-nursing in eighteenth-century France', in which aspects of the system touched on here are treated at very much greater length.
44. G. D. Sussman, 'Wet-nursing in the eighteenth century', pp. 62–3.
45. *ibid.*, pp. 45–9.
46. *ibid.*, pp. 49–50.
47. *ibid.*, p. 9.
48. A.D. Haute-Vienne, L377, Hôpital de Limoges, minute of 14 April 1792.

49. A.N., F^{15}1861, report on health at the Pitié in Paris, 16 June 1790.

50. Arch. Mun. Toulouse, 3Q1. *Mémoire abrégé et situation actuelle de l'Hôtel-Dieu de Toulouse*, 1790, pp. 6–8.

51. A.N., F^{15}1861, *Comité de Mendicité*, minute on Hôpital de la Trinité, 1790.

52. A.D. Bas-Rhin, 1L1593, Enfants Trouvés de Strasbourg, return for 1789–90.

53. Arch. Mun. Strasbourg, Div. III, liasse 73, 'Etat des enfants pauvres qui le 13 juin 1793 ont été entretenus aux frais de la commune de Strasbourg'.

54. A.N., AD.XIV^8, Rochefoucauld-Liancourt, 'Rapport fait au nom du Comité de mendicité des visites faites dans divers hôpitaux, hospices, et maisons de charité de Paris' (1790), p. 15.

55. A.N., F^{15}276, hôpital des enfants at Epinal (Vosges), 'Plan de comptabilité' for Year III.

56. A.N., F^{15}384, report from Prefect of Gironde on the hospitals of Bordeaux, 25 *vendémiaire* IX.

57. A.N., F^{15}259, Department of Seine-et-Marne to *Commission des secours publics*, 3 *pluviôse* III.

58. The allegation that babies were lying *tous nuds*, that there is no cash for *layettes*, is a common one throughout the Directory in hospital reports on their state of deprivation. Aimed at melting the hearts of government officials, it is a claim that lends itself to exaggeration and poetic licence; yet the dire shortage of such clothing is not in doubt. See, for instance, A.N., F^{15}336, report from the Cantal on 23 *frimaire* VII.

59. A.D. Bas-Rhin, 1L1595, decree of Fricot, *député-en-mission* to the Rhin and Mont-Terrible, 15 *vendémiaire* IV.

60. A.N., F^{15}255, Hospice de Gray (Haute-Saône), report of the *économe* for Year III; A.N., F^{15}268, letter dated 29 *vendémiaire* IV.

61. A.N., F^{15}429, Hôpital Civil de Castellane, letter to Department of Basses-Alpes, 18 *ventôse* V.

62. A.D. Bas-Rhin, 1L1595, Hospice des Enfants Naturels at Stephansfeld, minute of 21 *fructidor* II.

63. Arch. Mun. Marseille, Q^{3}17, Hospice des Orphelins de la Patrie, minute of 4 *ventôse* IV.

64. A.N., F^{15}440, report from hospital at Valenciennes, 15 *prairial* VI.

65. A.D. Bouches-du-Rhône, L858, Hôpital Saint-Jacques, minute of 23 September 1791; Arch. Mun. Marseille, Q^{3}17, minute of 11 *fructidor* III.

66. A.D. Bas-Rhin, 1L1593, Hospice des Enfants Trouvés à Strasbourg, *comptabilité*, 1791–3.

67. A.N., F^{15}1862, petition from commune of Bergerac (Dordogne), 12 *floréal* IV.

68. A.D. Haute-Garonne, L4068, Hospice de la Grave de Toulouse, reports of 22 *messidor* V and *vendémiaire* V.

69. A.N., F^{15}440, petition from Angoulême (Charente), 27 *fructidor* VII.

70. A.N., F^{15}440, *Commission des hospices civils* of Reims, report of 6 *nivôse* VIII.

71. A.N.., F^{15}430, letter from *hospice* at Maurs (Cantal), 21 *pluviôse* VIII.

72. A.N., F^{15}440, petition from La Fère (Aisne), 24 *nivôse* VIII.

73. A.N., F^{15}1862, petition from District of Brioude (Haute-Loire), 12 *messidor* III.

74. A.N., F^{15}1862, petition from Mur de Barrès (Aveyron), 6 *nivôse* IV.

75. A.N., F^{15}440, petition from Langres (Haute-Marne), 6 *pluviôse* IV.

76. L. Lallemand, *La Révolution et les pauvres*, pp. 232–3.

77. *ibid.*, p. 234.

78. A.N., F^{15}440, petition from Langres (Haute-Marne), 6 *pluviôse* IV.

79. A.N., F^{15}430, report on *enfants trouvés* from the *hospice civil* in Sédan, 25 *frimaire* VIII.

80. A.N., F^{15}440, petition from Angoulême (Charente), 27 *fructidor* VII.

81. A.N., F^{15}434, report from Metz on *nourrices*, 2 *thermidor* VII.

82. A.N., F^{15}377, report from Bagnères (Hautes-Pyrénées), 20 *nivôse* VIII.

83. A.N., F^{15}1862, letter from Verneuil (Eure), 6 *floréal* IV.

84. A.N., F^{15}434, report from Metz, *op. cit.*, 2 *thermidor* VII.

85. A.N., F^{15}310, letter from Department of Dordogne to Minister of Interior, 5 *frimaire* VI.

86. A.N., F^{15}440, letter from Canton of Port-la-Vallée (Maine-et-Loire) to Minister of Interior, 12 *nivôse* VIII.

87. Law of 16 *vendémiaire* V, text in A. de Watteville, *op. cit.*, p. 41.

88. A.N., F^{15}377, Minister of Interior to Department of Pas-de-Calais, 9 *ventôse* VIII.

89. A. de Watteville, *op. cit.*, pp. 44–5.

90. A.N., F^{15}429, petition from *Commission des hospices civils* at La Fère (Aisne), 24 *nivôse* VIII.

91. A.N., F^{15}382, letter from *Enfants Trouvés* at Blangy (Seine-Inférieure), 22 *nivôse* VIII.

92. A.N., F^{15}383, letter from Department of Aisne to Minister of Interior, 9 *thermidor* IX.

93. A.N., F^{15}384, letter from *hospice civil* at Auch (Gers) to Minister of Interior, n.d. (reply dated 24 *frimaire* IX).

94. A.N., F^{15}430, report from *Enfants Trouvés* at Marseille, 17 *nivôse* VIII.

8 Military service and the Revolutionary Wars

The social policy of the Revolution has been discussed in the previous five chapters as it affected certain clearly-defined categories of the poor – those who were institutionalized, sick or abandoned, those desperate for a pension or for employment if they were to avoid destitution. Such people came first to the minds of Revolutionary governments precisely because they did form obvious groupings and could be easily categorized by government bureaucracy. Yet, as was made clear at the outset, the poor of eighteenth-century France cannot be adequately defined as the sum total of these bureaucratic classifications: they were a wide, often vague spectrum of the population, people at risk, liable to be plunged by some misfortune into the ranks of the indigent. In a period as interventionist as the Revolution, when ordinary citizens were expected to make sacrifices for the common cause, it is only to be expected that government policy would have a serious effect on the delicate balance of the domestic economy of large sections of the population. And in no sphere was that policy more all-embracing than in that of foreign affairs. For the waging of war against much of the rest of Europe after 1792 so dominated government activity as to have an immediate effect on every other aspect of the French Revolution. As we have seen again and again in reference to particular measures of social policy, the financial appetites of the war were enormous and ate into the budgets put aside for other purposes. The social effectiveness of Jacobin *bienfaisance* in particular was repeatedly undermined by the huge costs of the Revolutionary armies. But of more immediate concern to most Frenchmen, and especially to the young men of the *classes populaires*, was the unpalatable fact that now, to a degree unknown in the Ancien Regime, they were likely to find themselves in uniform, compelled to leave their villages to defend the Republic against its enemies.

The image conjured up by the armies of the Year II is an exhilerating one of dedicated enthusiasm and revolutionary *élan*, with the typical soldier depicted as a young man burning with patriotic fervour and ready to spill his blood selflessly on the battlefield if that sacrifice will help to save his country. The armies themselves are portrayed as a cross-section of the youth of France, as *le peuple armé, la nation en armes*.[1] It is a reassuring picture and one that was to go far to consolidate the patriotic appeal of the revolutionary tradition throughout the nineteenth century, but it takes no account of the doubts and fears that loomed large in the mind of the individual soldier. For the carpenter from Avignon and the farmworker from the Beauce were not shorn at a stroke of their traditions, their prejudices, or their long-established, conservative instincts: they would never come to regard military service with the intense and single-minded passion of a Dubois-Crancé. The quality of next year's harvest, the lot of their wives and children, the ever-present danger of unemployment once they returned from the army, such personal considerations influenced their thinking far more strongly than did the military propaganda of governments in Paris. No doubt the glorious dream of liberating the oppressed races of Europe from the tyranny of kings and princes provided a powerful spur to Revolutionary politicians, but it played little part in motivating the average Frenchman in 1793 or the Year II.

That is not, of course, in any sense to diminish the achievement of the men who devised and organized the revolutionary armies, for their accomplishments were vast. France introduced new methods of recruitment, radical and outwardly democratic, such as the *levée des 300,000* in the spring of 1793 and universal conscription in the Year II. And the victories gained by French arms on the battlefields of Europe in the Revolutionary years bear eloquent witness to the efficacy of these innovations and to the value of the reforms in the conditions of service which the Revolution introduced. These root-and-branch changes included the abolition of corporal punishment for military offences, the introduction of an element of democracy in the election of officers, and the insistence that French soldiers should enjoy all the rights and responsibilities of citizenship, including the right to take an active part in politics and to join political clubs and societies. Collectively, such measures did much to raise the prestige of the army and the social status of the individual soldier.[2] There can be little doubt that their status needed to be raised. The Ancien Regime had nothing but contempt for the art of soldiering, and the king's troops were brutalized by years of bullying and degradation. Those who joined the army were frequently the dregs of eighteenth-century society, who, overcome by misery and hardship, could find no other means of staying alive – the younger son with inadequate land to feed himself and his family, the landless labourer condemned to begging or petty crime, the small peasant whose crops failed, the migrant worker who became disillusioned by the poverty and soul-destroying loneliness of life in a city garret. There was no provision for pensions for soldiers when finally they left the king's service, frequently wounded and broken by years of campaigning, without any family or dependants to whom they could turn. So often ex-servicemen had become pitiable drifters, wandering in solitary helplessness from village to village, flaunting their war-wounds to elicit sympathy and alms. Such was the image of the army that had been familiar to every Frenchman in the years before the Revolution, and it was an image that made the reforms of the Revolutionary years as indispensable to army morale as they were desirable in the cause of common humanity.

Revolutionary historiography has traditionally concentrated on these reforms and has presented the armies of the Republic not only as an effective fighting unit but also as an interesting experiment in democracy in action. They are, of course, right to do so, but I should suggest that that democratic aspect was largely confined to the army structure and institutions, and that one cannot, even in Year II, go so far as to imply that the new *demi-brigades* ever contained a true cross-section of the entire French population. Nor can one seriously maintain that military service, after the first glad morning of the Revolution in 1790 and 1791, was ever in any sense popular. It is true, of course, that the numbers of soldiers were greatly increased and hence that a much wider spectrum of the population had direct experience of army life. But not all sections of society were involved. The aristocrats who had provided the officer class in the Ancien Regime either emigrated – as they did in large numbers – or were stripped of their rank. But what of the bourgeoisie, the very groups in whose interests the Revolution was being carried out and in whose cause the wars were being fought? The sons of the middle classes certainly rushed eagerly to join the National Guard when it was formed in 1790 and took part in the ostentatious public junketings that were the early *fêtes de la Fédération*: it was a patriotic gesture which cost nothing and posed no obvious threat to their wellbeing. Besides, it was fun: they wore the national *cocarde*, often jauntily, in their caps; they handled weapons, albeit not always very skilfully; they strutted around feeling very self-important, stopping innocent passers-by to question them about their movements and their political motivation. It was all a pleasant act of make-believe, a comfortable niche that any provincial *fils de papa* could healthily dream of filling between his adolescent years at the *collège* and his adult life at the *comptoir*. For the bourgeoisie, in the 1790s as during other troubled periods of French history, were adept at recognizing where their true interests lay, and if the *garde* seemed cosily attractive to them, we may be equally sure that the armies on the frontiers most certainly were not. Playing at soldiers was one thing; real soldiering was quite another. And though, as Jean-Paul Bertaud has shown, the middle classes were represented among the officer ranks in the revolutionary armies, their contribution was never commensurate to their numbers or to the benefits which they might hope to derive from the wars.[3]

But it was not only among the middle classes that military service was unpopular during the Revolutionary years. The mass of the population showed less than a compulsive enthusiasm for service. It is true that there were some, among them some of the staunchest Jacobin *cadres*, who were fired with patriotic zeal and won over by the propaganda of the political leadership; such men rushed to volunteer in 1791 and 1792 and formed the vanguard during the first faltering campaigns of the Austrian war. But their enthusiasm did not communicate itself to the majority of the people, and it did not last; even in the spring of 1793 departments were finding it appallingly difficult to fill their quotas for the *levée en masse*. The change in conscription regulations towards increasing compulsion was one that was forced on the Revolutionary authorities by the harsh, undeniable evidence that the voluntary principle simply could not provide the required numbers of recruits. The evidence from the regions was consistent and depressing, that already by 1792 the mood of discouragement had set in, inspired as much by the impersonal national appeal of the new recruitment drive as by the damagingly slow grind of Revolutionary bureaucracy. In the Dordogne, for instance, the response to an appeal for local battalions was far better in 1792 than that to the national recruiting laws, simply because the local requirements seemed relevant and the local officials could command greater trust.[4] And by the *levée des 300,000* of spring 1793 the last vestiges of patriotic enthusiasm were exhausted: those whose sense of patriotism might have been inflamed by a call to arms were already serving on the Italian or the German frontier.

The ones who remained were at best apathetic, at worst openly hostile to service in the armies. It is not hard to understand why, for, despite the legislative reforms and the administrative reorganization of Dubois-Crancé and others, the age-old popular fear of military service and contempt for the job of soldiering remained deeply engrained in many sections of the French population. And after the early campaigns those returning from active service, battered and often demoralized, could not but pass on to the civilian population of their *pays* some concept of the frustrations of army life. The villagers learned with very little prompting to distrust the glossy image of fighting for liberty, of crusading against monarchies and the forces of despotism, that was presented to them by the recruiting-propagandists in Paris. The reality, they knew, was rather different, one dominated by misery and tedium. It was not only the danger, for with that many would have been prepared to cope; it was rather the sheer boredom of army life. They heard from other villagers, from men like Joliclerc, a trooper with the Seventh Battalion of the Var, how he had for several months been sleeping on the same patch of ground waiting for the enemy, wearing the same, often damp, uniform.[5] They listened to Joseph Capellin, a member of the Sixth Battalion of Marseille, who told how, in 1793, supplies had run out and the men had been reduced to eating roots if they were to survive.[6] Or they talked to young soldiers like Louis Deroire, from Amplepuis in the Rhône, who wrote home in Year II from the Pyrenean front to explain how, after four months lying desperately ill in a military hospital in Perpignan, he had found his papers stolen and had been in constant fear of arrest and possible execution.[7] Such stories, often exaggerated as they passed from mouth to mouth in the *cabarets* of French villages, were legion during the war years, and they did nothing to alter the fundamental distrust of the average Frenchman for service in the armies.

It was this widespread reluctance to serve among the generality of the population, and not any deeply-rooted principle, that finally led to the introduction of conscription in Year II. In the early years, with the *levées* of 1791 and 1792, France had been content to rely on volunteers, on those dedicated and patriotic enough to respond to the call of *la patrie en danger*. But the demands of the ever-increasing burden of war proved insatiable and the numbers required escalated sharply. As the American historian, Sam Scott, has demonstrated, the line army was steadily built up, even before the more dramatic expedient of the *amalgame* of February 1793, into a strong fighting force of over three hundred thousand men, many of them the sons of Jacobin militants, the sort of men who were prepared to offer their lives in the Revolutionary cause whether or not conscription was introduced.[8] It was the *levée en masse* of February and March 1793, the call for yet another three hundred thousand troops to bring the total strength of the armies to over half a million men, which finally showed up the inadequacies of voluntarism. Deputies on mission in the provinces, under relentless pressure from Paris to see that their quotas were filled, reported again and again that the required tallies were not being reached, and commune after commune had to admit sheepishly that they were quite unable to find sufficient volunteers. Only the poorest inner-city districts – like the Section de la Rue-Beaubourg in Paris[9] – could with pride proclaim that their quotas were over-subscribed; and only the desperately poor, those without a stake in society, were still coming forward in any numbers, exactly as they had done during the Ancien Regime.

This widespread reluctance to volunteer is faithfully reflected in the broad spectrum of ruses and devices to which communes were compelled to turn if their quotas were ever to be filled. The most common was the adoption of some form of balloting, whereby all the young single men of eligible age would be summoned to the *mairie* or village green, where their fate would be decided by drawing lots. This was, not surprisingly, intensely unpopular among the young, who risked finding themselves arbitrarily separated from their more fortunate friends and despatched to their battalions. Violence and rioting were not uncommon. At Hesdin, in the District of Saint-Pol in the Pas-de-Calais, the military *commissaire*, Darthé, was met by an angry crowd totally opposed to any form of balloting, and the draw had to be abandoned in view of the very real danger of his being lynched.[10] Similarly, at the village of Chasseneuil in the Vienne, where eight names had to be drawn from a possible fifty-three, there were angry murmurings and disturbances which prevented the ballot from being held, though in this case the leaders were noted as being servants of local nobles and were assumed to have counter-revolutionary sympathies.[11] In the Vendée the recruiting laws have long been cited as one of the principal causes of peasant rebellion. And even in relatively loyal areas like the Sarthe, the bland words of reassurance from the deputies on mission cannot conceal the uncomfortable fact that the town of Le Mans came close to open rebellion over recruitment and that much of the surrounding countryside became a prey to collective violence.[12] The law, indeed, was frequently treated with scant respect. At Marcolès in the Cantal, where rioting forced the abandonment of any attempt at recruitment, the local council meekly suggested that those involved in the disturbance should be pardoned, as they were afraid of possible reprisals from the people if they tried to punish any of the offenders.[13] Their attitude was no more than realistic, and there is no evidence to suggest that a single miscreant was ever brought to book.

The other device commonly used by local councils was that of selection *par scrutin*. It was this method that was adopted at Laroquebrou, near Aurillac, and the description we have of the scene outside the village hall is both graphic and instructive.[14] The villagers assembled at a public meeting on an agreed day, and nominations were received for good, patriotic citizens between the age of eighteen and forty, without dependants, who would fill the communal quota in the armies. Each nominee was solemnly subjected to a vote by his peers, the first, a *bouvier* from the countryside beyond the village, being adopted enthusiastically by 77 votes to 14. All the candidates, once nominated, were adopted by an electorate that could be as high as 104 or as low as 66; and almost all those chosen were herdsmen, though they did include a *garcon tailleur* and a *garcon menuisier* among their number. The whole process was conducted against a backcloth of rumbling, threatening noise, which would ebb and flow as the names were shouted out. It was a very random, if superficially democratic, way of raising the necessary levy, an army raised by popular acclaim and approved on the basis of the known patriotism of the nominees. Or so the official documents would give us to believe. In fact such recruitment would seem to have been a thoroughly ill-tempered exercise, conducted in the face of sullen animosity from the mass of the population. Nor is it likely that the people voted on the strength of the candidate's stout Republican qualities; more probably his friends and relatives would rally to his defence, whereas those voting for his inclusion would do so largely from a sense of relief that someone outside their own family and circle of intimates had been selected, thus reducing their own chances of being chosen.

By such expedients and by the liberal use of signing-on bounties[15] the Revolutionary ideal of the nation in arms began to gain substance, an ideal which, it was hoped, would guarantee an equal degree of sacrifice from all the citizens. The law decreed that all were to be liable alike for conscription, without regard for wealth or status. Only certain reserved occupations, necessary for the furtherance of the war effort, were specifically exempted. On 14 March 1793, for instance, the Convention decreed that for the duration of the war those bakers, carters and drivers who could provide evidence that they were engaged in servicing or provisioning the armies should be exempted from serving themselves. On 2 April this privilege was extended to another group of workers whose talents were desperately needed elsewhere – those making guns and powder for the war effort, 'attachés à la fabrication des armes, aux fonderies de canons, aux grandes forges et aux mines de fer'.[16] From rural areas came petitions from *cultivateurs* and *agriculteurs*, peasant farmers complaining that requisition would result in land going out of cultivation and a further diminution of the grain harvest so badly needed for feeding the troops and the munitions-workers. It is very noticeable, indeed, that by the Year II it was countrymen rather than townsmen who were being favoured by requisition panels, such was the fear of famine and crop-failure.[17]

The policy of granting exemptions did, however, have the serious defect that it quickly led to allegations of favouritism and unfairness. Except for a brief period in Year II no serious attempt was made to curb the habit of *remplacement*, and of course the poorer members of the community were rarely able to find the money or influence necessary to gain an exemption or to buy their sons out of the army. As a result, many local Jacobins were resentful when they saw the sons of the upper bourgeoisie regularly and ostentatiously escaping the clutches of the recruiting officer by means of cash payments in lieu of active service; they regarded this, not altogether without justification, as a simple means of favouring those blessed with money.[18] From the Sarthe came the forthright statement that equality was being outraged, since only the poor were being asked to save the Republic: 'Il n'y a que les pauvres à soutenir la République, ceux-là seuls sont contraints de rejoindre les armées, parce qu'ils ne peuvent, faute d'argent, se procurer des exemptions.'[19] Sometimes the allegations were more specific. Giraud de l'Aude, on mission from the Convention, was sufficiently worried by the lack of gunsmiths in Saint-Etienne to issue a decree allowing anyone who would apprentice himself to an *armurier* to leave the ranks forthwith. The result, as the rural commune of Millery angrily protested, was easy to foresee: a number of the sons of the richer citizens of the commune, without any experience of the trade but eager to take advantage of the new dispensation, had immediately withdrawn from the army and retired to the comparative tranquillity of an apprenticeship. Equally predictable was the resentment and the rancour which this occasioned, and the commune was not slow to bring allegations of bribery against parents anxious to buy protection for their children:

> Cela occasionne un grand murmure entre les jeunes gens de notre commune, qui sont partis aux frontières de bonne volonté, disant quel privilège ceux-là peuvent avoir de plus qu'eux parce qu'ils sont riches et que leurs pères égoïstes par le moyen de leur argent ont cherché des protections auprès des maîtres armuriers pour y placer leurs enfants après être enrollés dans le Bataillon.[20]

Even if all the animals were nominally equal, some were clearly believed to be more equal than others.

How much truth is there in such allegations, that it was the poor who were expected to sacrifice themselves in the Revolutionary cause, while the rich and the privileged could remain aloof and secure? There can be little doubt that even in Year II all Frenchmen were not equally liable to find themselves in uniform: the Jacobin Constitution of 24 June might boast that military service was a duty that went hand-in-hand with citizenship, but this was to remain a rather distant, abstract goal.[21] Geography and age both played a part in discriminating against certain groups, since the Republican armies were heavily recruited in frontier areas and regions close to war fronts, and since the average age of the troops was very low: the law permitted the signing-on of adolescents of only sixteen, and in a sample of some eight thousand recruits Jean-Paul Bertaud found as many as 79 per cent aged twenty-five or under.[22] Significant, too, was social class, for though the bourgeoisie did take a fairly prominent role among the officers of the early Revolutionary armies, their ardour had clearly dimmed by 1793 and Year II. The new army, egalitarian and highly politicized, was hardly to their liking, especially as officers could be elected and generals risked being held personally responsible for defeat in battle. Buying oneself out, paying for a substitute to fight in one's place, or making a substantial donation to a patriotic cause often seemed a more attractive alternative to young men of the bourgeoisie safely engaged in civilian occupations. From the lists of conscripts extant in local departmental archives a picture emerges of the kind of men who were drafted into the battalions in these years, and it goes some way to substantiate the charges of social discrimination made by the municipal council at Millery.

In rural areas the men of standing in the local community seldom appear to have served: commune after commune sent in lists of peasants and landless labourers, transport workers and apprentices. In many villages the peasantry, always rather recalcitrant when faced with the threat of conscription, succeeded in avoiding military service themselves, and the local returns were consequently filled with farmworkers, country blacksmiths, and carpenters. The *notable* might supervise recruitment, but he would be unlikely to serve in person; for instance, Pierre Reynier, *officier municipal* of Ceyreste near Marseille, raised nine men for the *levée des 300,000* (five farmworkers, a carter, a shepherd, a servant, and a former seaman) but did not put his own name forward for consideration.[23] More interesting, perhaps, is the very full list of enrolments in 1792 which survives for the District of Lyon-campagnes, the rural communes of the Lyonnais. Here the recruits were bribed with a signing-on bounty of some eighty to 120 livres, and the occupations listed, 243 in all, reflect very faithfully the tasks performed by the *petites gens* of the area. Agricultural work accounts for 127 of them, or 51 per cent of the total, employed, mostly in a lowly capacity as labourers on the soil, and variously described as *vignerons, laboureurs, cultivateurs,* and *jardiniers.* In an area where outworking for the Lyon silk industry was a necessary and welcome source of employment, it is equally unexceptional to find that textile workers are well represented: 41 men from the textile trades, or 17 per cent of the volunteers, were included. Building workers were not especially prominent (15 recruits, or 6 per cent), whereas there were twenty-five *cordonniers,* a group especially noted for their revolutionary commitment. Of the others, few were other than workers or artisans, servants or apprentices, the only possible exceptions being one man who classed himself as a 'bourgeois', a law student, a clerk at the *bureau des postes,* and an actor, a lad of seventeen from Marseille who signed on in a burst of boyish enthusiasm. Almost all the others were local, and almost all were young: sixty-one of them, or 25 per cent, were aged eighteen, and 80 per cent were twenty-five or below. In the Lyonnais at least, it is clear that it was the able-bodied sons of the local farmworkers and artisans who rushed to the defence of the Republic.[24]

In towns the employment patterns were more varied, but the social implications of Revolutionary recruitment were equally apparent. As in the countryside, it is the *menu peuple* of the area, the men performing dull and arduous tasks in manual oc-cupations, who offered themselves for military service. A list of 104 recuits in Marseille during the month from 13 March to 11 April 1793, joining the army in response to the *levée des 300,000* and for service in the Vendée, accurately reflects the industrial pattern of the city.[25] Unlike Lyon, where the silk industry was so very dominant, there was no single trade which totally distorted the Marseille labour market. Of the 104 men, however, it is interesting to note that sixteen were shoemakers and fifteen employed in the tailoring and textile sector. Nine were *savon-niers,* employed in the hot and noxious labour of soap-making, and a further three made candles; ten were stonemasons, employed in the building trades in the city, trades which suffered a serious slump with the onset of Revolution; four were sawyers, *scieurs de long.* The others were mainly journeymen or apprentices in tanning and starchmaking, plastering and cabinetmaking, hatting and glass-blowing. Overall, indeed, Marseille was a working town, a port with a high migrant popula-tion from the rural hinterland, and its recruitment lists reflected these characteristics. Only thirteen of the recruits had been born in the city; the majority had come from the rural southeast, from Provence and the Rhône valley, the Gard and the Ardèche, as well as from the more immediate hinterland of the Bouches-du-Rhône itself.

Such statistics – and they are typical of the pattern in other areas of the country – suggest strongly that Revolutionary recruitment involved a high degree of social in-justice and that the ideal of equality was still far from being reflected in the battalions of 1793. Nowhere was this injustice more glaring than in an area like the Cantal, where rural poverty was intense and where a high percentage of the men and boys were forced to leave their villages every year to do seasonal agricultural work in a less barren area of the country. For when the quotas were drawn up and the *scrutin* was held, many of the young men of these impoverished communes were still harvesting in the Pyrenees or in Spain, or trudging home from their winter labouring jobs in Paris or Lyon. To a District like Murat such seasonal work was an essential element in the battle for economic survival; but it placed the District in an intolerable position when it was ordered to fill a prescribed quota. Many communes were forced to nominate soldiers in their absence, which could lead to bitter acrimony when they returned. Villages short of manpower were also tempted to select recruits from other areas in a bid to conserve what remained of their own population for agricultural work: the commune of Saint-Martin-sous-Vigouroux, for instance, chose only four of its own men out of a quota of eleven, filling it up with outsiders, including a priest from Cézens whom it clearly viewed as a quite admirably suitable candidate.[26] Faced with the same shortage of able-bodied men, the District of Saint-Flour deftly tried to argue that their quota should be cut, on the grounds that, were agriculture starved of labour, famine would endanger the safety of the Republic every bit as much as enemy armies; but this plea was to no avail.[27] More serious for the Cantaliens was the very real danger that their sons, when the draft was ordered, would be seized by the communes in which they were working or through which they were passing at that moment, with the result that they would be included in the battalions of the Rhône, or the Ardèche, or the Puy-de-Dôme. Paris, it was claimed, filled its armies with seasonal workers; and numerous examples of alleged injustice were excitedly discussed by local officials. Saint-Bonnet in the District of Murat was appalled to learn that three men from the village, though carrying certificates allowing them to pursue their trade as *marchands forains* in the Champagne, had been arrested as they were passing through Clermont on their way home and forced to submit to the *scrutin*. The village authorities noted with heavy sarcasm that they were, of course, selected, since Clermont was known to recruit those passing through in order to fill its contingent.[28] And if Saint-Martin-sous-Vigouroux was happy to choose outsiders to fill its own quota, it was less amused when three young men from the village were integrated into the battalions of the Aveyron.[29]

Injustice was only compounded by self-interest and the blatant unfairness of local officials. In their desire to avoid serving themselves and to prevent those dear to them from being called up, local councils and general meetings of villagers were capable of the most unscrupulous distortion of the intentions of the Convention. Two national guardsmen from Arpajon found themselves selected even although they were married with family responsibilities and therefore ineligible in terms of the law.[30] Seasonal workers who succeeded in avoiding conscription elsewhere not infrequently returned to their village to discover that they had been designated for service in their absence. It would seem to have been a general rule of village meetings, indeed, always to select someone who, for whatever reason, was not there to plead his case at the time of the *scrutin*. In Junhac, ten young men from the farthest hamlets in the commune petitioned the administration, claiming that the isolation of their homes had prevented them from attending the recruitment meeting and that for this reason they had, quite unfairly, been picked on.[31] Cowherds living solitary lives high on the mountainside were also much favoured by villagers anxious lest their own families be decimated by recruitment; in March 1793 thirteen *bouviers* from La Besserette complained that the village boys had conspired to send only outsiders like themselves to face the dangers of military service, alleging that 'il s'est formé une coalition entre les garçons natifs de ladite paroisse pour nommer tous les garçons étrangers'. Although their complaint was almost certainly fully justified, it is noticeable that the local council angrily and rather touchily advised that their appeal be rejected out of hand.[32] After all, they had filled the required quota with the minimum of pain or inconvenience to themselves, and that was their principal objective.

Unfairness was further magnified in those villages where the mayor and the local worthies openly altered lists, forged recruitment slips, or otherwise tampered with evidence in order to falsify returns; in one blatant case of malpractice in 1792, when the mayor of Saint-Etienne-de-Maurs forged a list to avoid any possibility of his having to serve in person, the District of Aurillac was sufficiently outraged to suspend him from his duties for a month and ask the *procureur* to consider whether there was any basis for prosecution.[33] Such drastic action was rare; in general mayors could act with complete impunity, basking in the grateful admiration of the local elites. Dissidents could complain and make allegations, like this sweeping condemnation of recruitment practices in Moissac contained in a letter from Saint-Flour in May:

> Le recrutement donna lieu à beaucoup d'injustice dans les paroisses, les municipalités se coalisent avec les riches propriétaires et se concertent pour désigner ou les pauvres ou leurs ennemis personnels, et par ce moyen exemptent leurs enfants, de sorte qu'en général le recrutement ne porte que sur les pauvres. Nous voilà encore, conséquemment, sous l'Ancien Régime.[34]

But such allegations were rarely acted on. Until recruitment legislation was backed by all the rigours of the Terror in 1794, the rich, the influential, the local *notables* who controlled village politics even in the midst of the Revolution, continued to avoid personal service in the armies. The army of the Republic was very largely an army of the poor.

Such blatant injustice was not confined to any single area, and it naturally caused widespread disquiet among the troops, the young who waited anxiously for the next *tirage*, and the families of the labouring classes of society. Obligatory service was something quite novel to Frenchmen, an innovation which seemed to many to constitute an intolerable burden and for which inadequate civic instruction had been carried out by way of preparation. Expectation soon gave way to fear, at least among the 18–25 age-group, for it was they who, overwhelmingly, were to bear the full burden of the war. In particular they were alarmed to find that call-up was open-ended, that there was no *terme* laid down to their period of service, that even on attaining the age of twenty-five they had no chance of being freed from their patriotic obligation. Men whose only crime was to belong to a particular generation, to be under twenty-five on 23 August 1793, were still in uniform in the campaigns of year VII: in Gustave Vallée's chilling phrase, their generation was 'chargée à elle seule d'acquitter intégralement l'impôt du sang'.[35] To that overwhelming injustice were added other, less excusable distortions of an already imperfect system – the part played by local corruption, by jealousies and family feuds and by the naming for service of suspects, political opponents and those least able to create a fuss. Town-country grievances were accentuated, traditional sores reopened: all the hatreds created by militia service seemed to be revived. In one commune in the Dordogne, the *scrutin* lent itself to a novel and highly profitable form of protection racket, with money 'contributions' being openly solicited in return for the promise that the donors would not be nominated for service.[36] At root, the problem was simple:

> Ce qui aggrave les inconvénients de ce système, c'est que les désignations de ceux qui doivent partir sont faites par les collectivités même sur lesquelles pèse l'obligation.[37]

Even the most saintly of local mayors and officials must have realized the extent of the temptation that was suddenly opened up to him.

From the examples cited, it is clear that the revolutionizing of the French army had wide-ranging implications for the mass of the population. The old stigma attached to military service in the Ancien Regime was at least partly rooted out of the popular mentality, and soldiers achieved a status that was previously inconceivable. They were heroes of the Revolution, fighting to save France and her political institutions. They were the nation's first priority in matters of supply and grain requisitioning. They had a privileged position in the affairs of state. But for the ordinary Frenchman what undoubtedly counted most was the fact that he had to do the military service that the government demanded, with all the personal danger, the dislocation of the domestic economy, the neglect of families and relatives which this of necessity entailed. After February 1793 there can have been few families, at least among the *classes populaires*, which did not have a son fighting on the Somme or in the *Armée des Alpes*, or a breadwinner embroiled in the horrors of the Vendée. The army was a force for egalitarianism, as the French Communist Party today is quick to appreciate, precisely because the experience of military service was so very widely shared, if not by the rich and the powerful, then at least by the bulk of the population. But it was also an additional burden which interfered with the already delicate balance of their everyday lives, a burden that weighed especially heavily on the poor and the insecure. To its credit, the government recognized this, and much of the legislation of this period was geared to lessening the soldiers' sufferings and alleviating their more chronic anxieties.

The most nagging of all these anxieties, and one which was widely blamed for the reluctance of many Frenchmen to volunteer for service, was their fear of death or mutilation. As we have seen, in the eighteenth century a family without an able-bodied breadwinner capable of holding down a steady job was almost certain to be condemned to a life of misery and degradation. So it was paramount for any government in the Revolutionary period to take a bold initiative in guaranteeing pensions and other forms of security for the dependants of men serving on the frontiers, a policy that was demanded both by the practical needs of the war effort and by the dictates of humanity. It goes without saying that the government recognized this obligation and quickly urged that the bounties being paid to men on joining the army should be supplemented by an adequate pension scheme for *mutilés de guerre* and for the wives and children of those killed in action. Especially in the early years of the war, between 1792 and the Thermidorian Reaction, there was a strong streak of idealism in the approach adopted to such pensions, as Revolutionary politicians turned their energies to finding a solution that would end the blatant unfairness of existing royal legislation, whereby ordinary soldiers and their dependants had been condemned to near-starvation while inflated gratuities were reserved for the privileged officer class.[38] From 1793 the whole basis on which pensions were calculated was dramatically reformed. The amount paid to a wounded soldier, unable to continue his service and severely incapacitated in civilian life, was now made proportionate to the gravity of his wounds, not to the rank he had held in the army.[39] Widows' pensions, previously calculated as a percentage of their husbands' pay, were also reformed: in *prairial* II Collot d'Herbois introduced a law making all such payments on a flat rate.[40] Even more radical was the thoroughly egalitarian law of 6 June 1793 which stated that, because serious wounds necessarily ended all possibility of a man's promotion in the army, all seriously wounded soldiers, those who had been blinded or had suffered amputations, should automatically be promoted to the rank of *sous-lieutenant honoraire* and rewarded with a lieutenant's pension.[41] It was an ideological solution, one fully in keeping with the mood of France in the Year II and with the needs of a revolutionary army. Certainly no one could allege that the Convention did not care: during the thirteen months of the Jacobin ascendancy, no fewer than twenty-five reports, laws, decrees and addresses were issued on the subject of such aid, many of them insistent that information on the scale of the problem be made available to the Ministry of the Interior, and a special commission was designated to ensure the most equitable distribution of resources in accordance with the law.[42]

Radical reforms were also introduced in the statutes and regime of the Hôtel des Invalides in Paris, the most important and prestigious institution caring for army veterans and *mutilés* during the Ancien Regime. Royal governments had continued to shower favours on the Invalides and had built it into a highly privileged institution, financed entirely by the crown and enjoying in 1788 a budget of 350,000 livres, considerably above the sums allocated to the two great civilian hospitals in the capital, the *hôpital général* and the *hôtel-dieu*. It also enjoyed tax-free status, had sufficient liquid resources to become a substantial investor in *rentes*, and had come to cater for a clientele of officers rather than men to such a degree that the Revolution regarded it with a certain hostility, as a fulcrum of privilege and not as a true source of succour to the needy.[43] Besides, as in the field of civilian assistance, the Revolution retained its distrust of institutional care and encouraged as many veterans as possible to accept pensions in lieu. Dubois-Crancé had even planned to abolish the Invalides entirely, but in 1793 it was finally resolved to sustain a policy of freedom of choice for veterans between a pension *à domicile* and residence in the hospital. What was reformed was the regime and the privileged aura of the Invalides: from 1793 volunteers as well as regular troops were admitted, privileges for officers were abolished, and an attempt was made to democratize the administration of the hospital by having the administrators elected by the *invalides* themselves. It was to be, says Isser Woloch, a model *cité*, caring for four thousand veterans, of whom two thousand would be resident.[44] Under the Jacobins complete equality of food entitlement and living conditions was established, and some basic schooling was introduced to help the *invalides* readjust to the demands of civilian life once they were released on society.[45] It was a bold and imaginative transformation, typical of the very best reformist vision of men like Lacuée, yet destined to be held responsible for the widespread disaffection and spirit of revolt which characterized the hospital under the Directory.

The transformation, indeed, proved sadly short-lived, for neither the idealism shown in the attitude to the Invalides nor the concern that all *mutilés* should receive adequate pensions could survive the ravages of the Thermidorian and Directorial years. In part, as with civilian assistance, this can be ascribed to a change in government priorities and to a loss of will. The Directory might remain committed to the notion that veterans constituted *une dette nationale*, but they had no deep loyalty to Jacobin concepts of equality and quickly restored differentials based on rank and length of service.[46] Turbulence and indiscipline in the Hôtel des Invalides aroused the suspicion in government circles that it had become a dangerous cell of neo-Jacobinism, with the result that stricter surveillance was introduced and detailed medical examinations were imposed to establish the individual soldier's right to remain within its walls. By Year VI, indeed, at the time of the elections, the government openly moved dissidents and Jacobin activists away from the Invalides to alternative quarters at Versailles in an attempt to restore calm to the streets of Paris.[47] But in part, also, the reasons for this change must be sought in the petty practicalities of day-to-day government rather than in political attitudes. The insistence on painstaking documentation before pension grants could be approved meant that the process of awarding pensions became unnecessarily drawn-out and that long waiting lists of applicants became the norm. By *pluviôse* V, for instance, as Woloch shows, whereas pensions had already been granted to 5,150 officers, 5,250 men, and 5,300 war widows, decisions were still pending on a further 4,500 officers, 19,200 soldiers, and 10,700 widows; on the eve of *brumaire* he notes that there was a backlog of over 25,000 troops seeking some form of veterans' benefit.[48] Revolutionary France had no tradition or experience of social administration on this scale; once again the intentions of the legislators risked being swamped in an avalanche of paperwork.

Even more basic was the ever-present problem of finance, as the spread of the war multiplied the demands made on the treasury and as the country faced unprecedented levels of monetary chaos. Even in 1793 and Year II, before the worst inflationary pressures were felt, the implementation of the law was often imperfect and funds were not made available when they were urgently required. Often the actual payments were left to municipal and sectional authorities, and had to be found from the blanket treasury grants which already served such a bewildering multiplicity of disparate purposes. The result was predictable: by 1793 the cash provided was already grossly inadequate, and harassed local authorities found themselves forced to rely on public subscriptions and exceptional levies if they were to meet their obligations to the troops and their families. And amidst all the competing claims made on the public purse, even such a worthy cause as this was bound to lose some of its impetus. Clubs and sections were expected, after all, to find the money to pay bounties to the new recruits and to equip them for battle. Such equipment was far from cheap: in the district of Villefranche-sur-Saône, the costs of fitting out the men raised by the requisition of spring 1793 varied from commune to commune between 240 livres and 320 livres, a very considerable sum that was almost entirely used for purchasing kit and clothing.[49] In Marseille the *Amis de la Constitution* raised over 28,000 livres by public subscription in March 1792 to arm the local battalions, and this was easily consumed in buying 874 rifles and 1100 pikes, a modest enough tally.[50] On such occasions the general public were generous enough in their response, but, especially in times of economic depression like so much of the war years, there were strict limits to the sums that could be gleaned by public appeals. As the months passed and the war claimed more and more victims, the rather pathetic appeals of the needy bear eloquent witness to the inadequacy of the relief available. Usually they would provide evidence of revolutionary virtue as well as patriotism in order to render their case more convincing and their sacrifice more irrefutable. The wife of a butcher from the Section des Arcis in Paris, pleading for money to help raise her family while her husband was fighting for France, explained how she had taken in an abandoned baby which otherwise would have been committed to the care of the parish; now, she said bitterly, denied the money to which she was entitled, she had no choice but to deposit it at the *Enfants Trouvés*.[51] The widow of François Cigogne, a medical officer attached to the battalions of the Section de l'Observatoire, also petitioned the Convention for aid, pointing out that her husband had lost his life while tending wounded *sans-culottes* during the fighting in Paris on 10 August.[52] And *citoyenne* Petitjean, who had two sons serving in the Revolutionary armies, could reasonably ask for help on the grounds that she had not only lost her husband in battle but had herself been wounded while serving the Republic in its struggle with the rebels in the Vendée. Those petitions, and many others like them, conceal very real suffering, which the limited resources of the Convention were not always able to compensate.

Wives and children left at home while husbands fought in the Republican armies suffered just as much hardship, even in many cases when the authorities had already agreed to pay a monthly sum to maintain them. Such broken promises could at times lead to angry altercations between soldiers and their local councils, whom they were wont to accuse of treachery and deception. A good instance is that of the troops sent to Cassel by the Section des Lombards in Paris, who by the early summer of 1793 were complaining loudly that their families were being left to starve while they sacrificed themselves for France. The soldiers pointed out, quite fairly, that only patriotism had led them, as married men, to leave for the frontiers, while bachelors and others without commitments skulked at home rather than serve France.

Patriotism, however, must be supported and encouraged by the reassurance that their dependants would be cared for, and the section had agreed to pay a monthly grant of fifteen livres to wives and 7 livres 10 sous to each child. But the men claimed that this grant had not been paid during the two months following their departure, and they were threatening to return home to Paris, with all the humiliation this would incur for the section. To make matters worse, they themselves had received neither uniforms nor the promised daily allowance. 'Citoyens', they concluded with withering scorn, 'remplissez vos engagements comme nous remplissons les nôtres.'[53] Unhappily, Lombards was not a wealthy section: the unpalatable truth was that this was a commitment which simply could not be fulfilled.

If practical difficulties thwarted the good intentions of the Revolutionary authorities in the field of pensions and compensation, what of the welfare of the troops themselves? Like any army in time of war, the Revolutionary soldiers were in some respects highly privileged citizens. They were generally fed more adequately than other sections of the population, as food stocks were requisitioned for them and carts and barges forced to carry grain and other foods to the war zones on the frontiers. Despite complaints about the lack of uniforms and the shortage of weaponry, by 1793 and 1794 government controls were largely effective in ensuring that such essential supplies were delivered: a whole new bureaucracy came into being with the sole purpose of confirming that deliveries were prompt and transport unimpeded. That is not to say, of course, that French troops never suffered from scurvy or food shortages, or that they were at all times decently clothed and billeted. Especially after the lifting of economic terror at Thermidor, there were reports of severe instances of suffering and malnutrition. But, given the quality of communications and the efficacy of the eighteenth-century state machine, the Revolution did go further in the direction of producing a modern, well-maintained army out of the raw recruits of the *levée en masse* than most contemporaries would have dared to expect.

The regular complaints of the soldiery reflect a basic truth which the Revolutionary bureaucracy would have preferred to ignore, yet one which is quite fundamental to the entire history of Revolutionary conscription – that these new, raw recruits were serving only with the greatest reluctance and were looking for any excuse to escape from military discipline and from the ardours of army life. Without a modern civilian or military police the Revolutionary armies were unable to prevent widespread evasion, and if on the one hand we are impressed by the scope of reform in this period and the imposition of universal service, it is only reasonable to reflect also on the natural concomitant to conscription, a high rate of deceit and avoidance. The new liberalism which the Revolution showed towards it soldiers encouraged abuse, and the military command was continually complaining that the general laxity of control and the inadequate level of policing were undermining their authority and seriously sapping the strength of the armies in the field. Money was paid out and passports issued by military commanders who were totally unable to supervise their use. The signing-on bounties paid to volunteers in the earlier years of the war were open to the grossest forms of abuse, especially since half the money, along with the expenses needed for the journey, had to be paid in advance. It was an invitation to fraud. The *procureur-syndic* in Roanne was one of many officials worried by the number of highly unpromising recruits who presented themselves for service, asked to leave at once for the frontiers, and never arrived at their units.[54] Jean-François Vergoin, from Saint-Loup in the Lyonnais, was just such a man: having collected his money, he made a brief detour by Tarare to bid farewell to his parents, but he claimed that he was robbed on the way and was therefore unable to continue on his journey.[55] As in so many cases, there was little that overworked officials could do to verify his story. For new recruits were expected to make their own way to join their battalions, and this often involved long and hazardous journeys through wild, unpoliced countryside, the ardours and temptations of which could easily undermine their already shaky resolve. When their allowance was spent, usually on drink in the inns they passed on the first few days of their journey, such men were almost always reduced to begging and petty crime. So were wounded soldiers walking back from the front, armed with the valuable certificate that would gain them admission to hospital. Indeed, soldiers trudging backwards and forwards across the French countryside came to be regarded by the local population as an additional scourge on their lives, adding yet another dimension to the everyday violence of the French rural community. Even determined attempts by the French military authorities to force their men to keep to agreed, policed routes proved abortive and never succeeded in setting at rest the anxieties of local people.[56]

As the demands of the recruiting-officer became ever more grasping, the rate of desertion predictably soared, until under the Directory it was one of the major social problems which the government had to face. It was a damagingly widespread response in large areas of France, particularly in rural departments where service was especially resented, and one which did much to undermine the morale of those men still in uniform. The exact rate of desertion is very difficult to quantify – itself a symptom of the lack of control exercised by the military authorities – but it increased very markedly after 1793: for the ordinary peasant's son, without an exemption and without the money needed to buy a replacement, desertion was often the only way of avoiding the unsought ardours of army life. And it was unbelievably easy to desert, to fail to join one's regiment, to slip off home for the harvest, or, if that were impossible, to take refuge in the protective hills around one's native village. In Year III, the 5th Battalion of the Rhône-et-Loire, recruited from the countryside around Lyon, reported that eighty of its number had gone missing; but the officer in charge was careful to add that most of the conscripts might merely have gone home for the winter months, with every intention of returning for the new campaign season in the spring.[57] Others were less optimistic. Of 71 soldiers dispatched from Aurillac to Saint-Flour in the spring of 1793, the product of the *levée-en-masse*, only 19 were still there by mid-August: the others, the Saint-Flour authorities suggested with just a tinge of contempt, had doubtless returned home in the meantime.[58] By Year VII and Year VIII whole armies were disappearing, to the increasing consternation of generals in the field. Of men conscripted in the Creuse in Year VIII, very few bothered to join their battalions – a mere three hundred out of 1,314 called to arms.[59] In the same year another remote rural department of the centre, the Haute-Loire, reported with some alarm that out of 1,400 men in the first auxiliary battalion 1,087 had already deserted, and that in all some six thousand deserters were at liberty in that one department.[60] From all over the country the same pattern was evident: only six out of 333 troops from the Ardèche in Year VIII ever reached their regiment in Dijon;[61] in the Landes in Year VII, out of 1,200 men, only 60 were left in uniform after a single day of service.[62] Desertion was far from being a last desperate resort; in many areas of France it had come close to being the norm for those unfortunate enough to be enlisted.

What should desertion have reached such endemic proportions, not only in the more predictably remote areas of the Massif Central and the southwest, but even in departments like the Bas-Rhin and the Pas-de-Calais, near to the very frontiers which French armies were being forced to defend?[63] It was a question of near-obsessive interest to the military leadership, and again and again the same answers are provided. It was admitted that morale in the armies was not always of the highest order, that discipline could be harsh and commanders insensitive. From the Basses-Alpes came the allegation that their conscripts were often treated with the greatest inhumanity in the military *dépôts*, that they were sworn at and threatened, deprived of every basic comfort, made to sleep among the most insanitary conditions, and refused even water unless they had money with which to bribe their officers; in short, 'on nous a rapporté que des esclaves trouveraient moins de rigueur chez un peuple barbare.'[64] The Haute-Garonne, too, complained about the condition in which its sons were returning after a spell of military service. Even though the army was inclined to blame desertion on *malveillants* and their pernicious propaganda, the Department pointed out, it was the bad treatment the men received from the army, the total deprivation they suffered and their poor physical shape when they returned to their villages which made the propaganda so damagingly effective.[65] And if officers treated them badly once they reached their allotted battalions, military drivers had already, in many cases, introduced them in the course of their journey to the standards of cruelty they might expect when they got to their destination. These drivers were responsible for feeding as well as transporting their charges, and their cupidity and self-interest were often remarked on: new recruits passing through several departments of the southeast, for instance, complained that they were almost totally starved, or supplied with food so bad in quality as to be unfit for human consumption.[66] As the war effort grew more intensive and the rate of desertion spiralled alarmingly, the authorities came increasingly to point to the sheer awfulness of the journey as a major incitement to desert. Was it pure accident, they asked, that so many conscripts slipped away during the second night of their long march to the front?[67]

The boredom of war, the discomfort of service, the callous treatment by their superiors, all these were factors in inducing men to desert, but they are far from providing the whole explanation. The army tried to point the finger of accusation at royalist agents and anti-military propaganda from royalists, Vendeans and other miscreants but, apart from a few insubstantial allegations in areas like the Calvados,[68] there is little reason to believe that such men had more than the most marginal influence. Indeed, in one department – the Eure – the authorities could note with some pride that the local campaign against *chouannerie* had actually created a degree of peasant enthusiasm and that the number of deserters had been markedly reduced.[69] What did have greater effect in various areas was the power of more general rumour – that military service was a disguised form of butchery, that all the other conscripts had already left the army with impunity, that local people were ready to offer shelter and protection. This helps explain the rather uneven pattern of desertion, whereby in entire villages not a single recruit would turn up and recruiting-officers met with sullen resentment. In the Seine-Inférieure pamphlets were distributed urging recruits to resist the draft;[70] In the Basses-Pyrénées rumour spread like wildfire, encouraging young men to stay on their farms and alleging that the local authorities gave their blessing;[71] and in the Hérault news of serious reverses in the Italian campaign, passing rapidly by word of mouth from village to village, caused recruitment to dry up alarmingly in Year VIII.[72] The natural reluctance of young men to uproot themselves from the community was there to be played upon, and it was an excellent means of sowing dissension for any group opposed to the policies of those currently in power.

Of contemporary comment on desertion the most percipient was that which recognized that the decision to desert was usually a highly personal one, influenced by more deep-seated fears and aspirations than simply a distaste for military discipline or a single reading of a broadsheet. The Revolutionary authorities were always too ready to find political reasons for everyday behaviour, especially among a peasantry whom they inadequately understood and for whom they lacked any great sympathy. The Vendean peasant who did not rush to the defence of France was too easily dismissed as a royalist or a traitor; he might, like Guérin from Soullans, have had quite different personal reasons, choosing to retire into the *bocage* in order to enjoy the affections of his mistress who had enticed him to do so, and only emerging from his clandestine retreat in order to get married in Year IV.[73] Some observers, notably the new prefects of the Napoleonic period, were sufficiently well versed in the ways of the countryside to attempt to explain their low recruitment figures by reference to local mentalities. They recognized that there was no tradition of military service in many rural communities, that they were deeply attached to the soil and to the vicissitudes of the rural calendar, that they had – in the words of the prefect of the Landes – an 'aversion insurmontable' for military service away from their own *pays*.[74] Asking men to march across half of Europe in defence of something as impersonal, as dauntingly unfamiliar as the nation, or France, was as doomed to failure as the efforts of Prince Charles Edward Stuart in 1745, from the moment he marched his army of peasants away from their native Highland glens. There were other irritants in rural areas, like the extent of undernourishment and stunted growth, or the fact that the men were quite visibly needed if the harvest was to be completed.[75] There was bitter resentment of the rumour that the more wealthy of their fellow-citizens were buying replacements to fight in their stead. Local bureaucrats and councillors were frequently to the fore in claiming exemptions,[76] and the prefect of Lot-et-Garonne was not alone in pointing to this as a source of murmuring and sullenness amongst the population.[77] Talking in the café of an evening or listening to villagers returned from the front, the peasant could find a host of individual reasons why he or his son should not serve, and the degree of their antagonism to military service is well illustrated by the sums they were prepared to pay under the Empire to avoid call-up. But at root what we are witnessing, throughout wide tracts of rural France, is something much broader than economic self-interest or social resentment. The peasant's lack of military experience was a reflection of a wider aversion to soldiering; and the changes in the status of the troops carefully brought about by revolutionary legislation did little or nothing to alter the deeply-ingrained prejudices of the French countryside.

If the peasant had clear reasons for avoiding military service, he also enjoyed ample opportunity. It was not just, as has been seen, that hospital passes abounded and officers had little means of ensuring that those conscripted ever reached their battalions, though these were significant contributory elements. Just as vital was the complaisant attitude of the community at large to a form of behaviour which few Frenchmen really regarded as criminal. In rural districts especially there was little or no stigma attached to desertion, and the returning conscript would expect to be greeted warmly by his fellow-villagers and to be able with the very minimum of disruption to resume his accepted role in the agricultural economy. In normal circumstances there was no fear of harassment from the local authorities or the local population: when, in Year VI, troops were sent to the little village of Cayeux in Picardy to hunt for deserters, they were given instructions to find no fewer than forty-five men, all believed to be in hiding there.[78] Many simply returned to the family holding, but there were also employers, often in those marginal or itinerant trades which blended so easily into the forest, who were more than happy to engage a deserter from the *pays*. In the Yonne there were reports that stonemasons were regularly taking on young deserters as journeymen in their workshops and quarries;[79] and at Saint-Igny-de-Vers (Saône-et-Loire) some fifty new woodcutters were hired in Year VI in one of the most impenetrable of forest areas, men who came from surrounding hamlets and who, it was reported, formed 'un rassemblement armé dans la forêt'.[80] There was very little that a hard-pressed military official could do to interfere in the long-established traditions of rural France. Deserters could find employment with the teams of timbermen floating logs down to Paris from departments like the Nièvre.[81] They could escape detection by slipping across departmental boundaries, even, in the farthest Pyrenees, crossing the frontier into Spain to elude capture: peasants, labourers and smugglers had used that border for generations and they knew intimately every pass and hiding-place along its length.[82] Desertion, in short, did not necessarily mean, at least in the 1790s, years of misery and fear, years spent on the run in constant danger of exposure and punishment. For many it meant a return to the assured tenor of rural life, protected by the farmers for whom they worked.[83] There are even instances, too frequent to constitute glaring exceptions, of groups of deserters seen openly at village dances, *bals champêtres*, making advances to the local girls and carousing in the local inns.[84] Life as a deserter did not of necessity involve great hardship.

The deserters were assisted by the open connivance of large numbers of mayors and local councillors, who lived in those small, intimate communities of rural France and who reflected very accurately their mentalities and their prejudices. Indeed, they could not afford to antagonize their fellow-citizens, and it is clear that the majority of mayors felt that bond of loyalty to be much stronger than any that bound them to the government in Paris. From department after department the same complaints were voiced, most heatedly by the military authorities who remained hypersensitive to the charge that desertion was really their responsibility and sought to show how little assistance they ever received from their civilian counterparts. In the Pas-de-Calais it was being claimed as late as Year XII that deserters were joining bands led by Jacobin activists and that local mayors were openly assisting them.[85] And in the southwest the general in charge in Bordeaux was equally insistent that the blame for high desertion figures in that region must lie squarely with the civil authority, on account of their 'inconceivable indulgence' towards deserters and the 'protection presque ouverte' which they extended to them.[86] Some allegations were more specific. Commune after commune, in widely-scattered departments, simply failed to submit the lists of conscripts which they were obliged to do by law, an omission which effectively prevented the military from being able to distinguish who was and was not a deserter from their ranks.[87] Mayors were alternately accused of stupidity and deception. In the Rhône, where few mayors from the more remote communes bothered to submit returns, it was not long before the prefect was attributing this to 'le peu d'intelligence de la plupart des membres des conseils muncipaux'.[88] The townsman's contempt for the country bumpkin was never far away. But such a dismissive representation of mayors' behaviour is both mistaken and naive: not even the Minister was likely to be deceived. For there is ample evidence that the failure to make returns was only one facet of a wider act of non-cooperation on this question. In the Gironde it is no accident that the fifty communes which failed to comply in Year VI were not all isolated settlements in the *bocage*: they included large towns like Bourg, Blaye, Cadillac, La Réole, Sainte-Foy, and Pauillac, besides the three *municipalités* of Bordeaux itself.[89] Elsewhere mayors were induced by threats of violence and disorder to refuse the information which Paris demanded. The prefect of Haute-Garonne was to admit that by the Napoleonic period the parents and relatives of deserters formed a powerful pressure-group which threatened vengeance against collaborationist local officials.[90] And in a remote department like Lozère the files of the Ministry of Justice show a number of instances of mayors helping deserters still more directly, by altering certificates, forging documents, even hiding them in their own homes.[91] In many parts of France deserters could with confidence look to their local *élus* for active help in avoiding discovery and arrest.

The connivance of local officials was, however, only one of several sources of help available to conscripts should their liberty be threatened. Parents, relatives, other young men of the village would rally round a deserter who was arrested or in danger of arrest, and open violence was often shown to *gendarmes* and soldiers engaged in this work. Cases where prisoners were freed by such a display of mob violence are legion in the 1790s, and often the hapless *gendarmes* had little choice but to free their captives and run, accompanied by the massed insults of the assembled villagers. Some of these *attroupements* were largely family affairs – like one in the village of Courlon in the Yonne in Year VII, where a captured deserter was freed by his brother and various of the womenfolk in his family, who all offered resistance to the *gendarmes*.[92] Elsewhere it was the young of the village, many of them *insoumis* in their own right and frequently armed, who challenged the arresting officers – such was the case in various villages of the Ariège, where it is clear that the young men of the area identified very strongly with those of their number who had been condemned to serve in the armies.[93] The violence of such encounters, though it risks being exaggerated by young policemen returning empty-handed from their missions, is not in doubt. There are numerous reports of troops being stoned and fired on by angry civilians, of prisoners being freed from gaols as well as on the open road, and occasional instances of *gendarmes* being killed while trying to round up deserters.[94] The conscript almost always enjoyed the support of his village, and on frequent occasions the village could be depended upon to come to his aid.

A rich variety of frauds and criminal activities also helped ensure that the bulk of deserters from the Revolutionary armies remained at liberty. Public officials, un-accustomed to the weight of responsibility placed on them by Revolutionary legislation, were particularly prone to take bribes or accept favours in return for a small act of charitable partiality. *Officiers de santé* were especially suspect in the eyes of the military, as scores of seemingly able-bodied men continued to escape their clutches by producing a blandly-written medical certificate. Some were to be con-victed of trafficking in exemptions and *congés*; others contented themselves with helping the conscript to produce the symptoms of illness by prescribing drugs for them.[95] In one hospital in the Creuse, it was alleged, patients developed the cunning ruse of taking medicines which would, for short periods, create a high level of fever and difficulty in breathing.[96] In the Landes potential conscripts appeared with medical statements certifying that they suffered from epilepsy and were therefore unfit for service.[97] In the military hospital at Amiens passes were so easy to obtain that the authorities were convinced that money was changing hands, and they listened eagerly to informers who alleged that *congés* could be procured 'au prix de l'or'.[98] But there, so often, was the rub: medicine remained a closed, mysterious area of competence, and usually there were only strong suspicions of fraud rather than firm evidence. Occasionally real proof of swindling came to light, but it *was* occasional and tended to involve middlemen rather than the doctors themselves – like the case of a forgery racket in Mende, where false hospital passes were produced for sale on the street corner and sold at high prices to desperate conscripts and their gullible relatives.[99] Just such a forgery, picked up on a deserter near Agen in Year XIII, had cost him and his family a princely 120 francs from an unscrupulous *embaucheuse*. The trade in false papers was as likely to be swindling the needy and vulnerable as it was to be genuinely helping the hapless conscript. Indeed, so widespread did it become that there were Jacobin deputies who favoured the ending of the entire system of *congés* precisely in order to root out its abuse.[100]

But of course fraud was not confined to the area of medicine. Throughout most of the 1790s the conscription laws were helpfully specific: from 1793 onwards it was not every Frenchman who was liable to serve, but every able-bodied Frenchman without family ties, over eighteen and not in a reserved occupation.[101] This provided every would-be draft-dodger with a plethora of useful loopholes and local officialdom with a Pandora's box of temptation and corruption. If *officiers de santé* could make personal gain from the issue of medical certificates, so military administrators might hope for favours in their turn when they handed out precious *feuilles de route* to their more reluctant soldiers.[102] And the mayor and his *secrétaire de la mairie*, often the village schoolmaster supplementing his meagre stipend through clerical work in the town hall, could find their new tasks of maintaining the *état civil* a surprisingly interesting and even lucrative activity. The range of options open was astonishingly wide, and almost always when a fraud was committed by a conscript or his family some secretarial assistance was required. The general lack of order in many of the communal registers did, of course, play its part, but it can hardly explain frauds like the falsifying of birth certificates, much favoured in the upland villages of the Tarn in Year VII;[103] nor can it be cited to excuse mayors who allowed their quotas to be filled by men under the stipulated height,[104] by youngsters under eighteen who were ineligible for service,[105] or by the designation of citizens who had died or left the parish and could not be traced.[106] Rural departments with high mortality rates lent themselves to frauds of this kind, with older brothers using the passports of younger, dead children to conceal their age, or parents sending along younger boys to the *scrutin* in the knowledge that their stature would ensure them an exemption.[107] In communes where such practices were widespread the government was not entirely wrong to suspect the local officials of, at best, serious non-cooperation in the war efforts, and, more probably, some form of graft and corruption.

Word of those ruses that were likely to bear fruit spread rapidly from village to village, and the pressure on local *élus* was often intense. Conscripts knew, for instance, in Year IV that a sworn statement by ten of their fellow-soldiers testifying to their incapacity to serve would be enough to excuse their service, and coins changed hands over eagerly-proferred drinks as convenient deals were amicably concluded.[108] They understood, too, later in the Revolution, that the *jury de révision* before which their appeal would be heard would probably be most reluctant to send them off to the front, being composed of local men whose interests interlocked conveniently with those of their own families. To the unconcealed dismay of the military, such juries were notoriously lax in granting exemptions, particularly, it was alleged, to young men with whom they had family ties. Weak on bureaucracy and in dire need of volunteers to service its many local functions, the Revolutionary government was to discover only gradually that volunteers could serve their own interests, too. In Libourne in Year VII the *commissaire* of the Directory felt moved to suspend the local jury on the grounds of suspicion, so repeated were the rumours of backstage deals and plots to defraud the government.[109] Elsewhere the government could merely resort to angry protests when juries solemnly released the majority of those appearing before them: only occasionally, as in the case of the Canton of Murviel (Hérault) in Year VII, did they respond with firm action, and then only when provoked by a jury that had taken none of the sixty conscripts sent before it. In that instance the official enquiry did timidly suggest that the jury had erred in the direction of leniency and might have been influenced by the opinions of the young men's parents.[110] But such action was rare, and the *classes de l'an VII, de l'an VIII, de l'an IX* were justified in regarding the majority of juries as a soft touch whom they could hope with some confidence to sway.

Two escape-holes more than all others seemed obvious to the conscripts of the 1790s, however, anxious to remain on their farms whatever the cost. If they lacked the money to buy themselves out and had the misfortune to be presided over by an incorruptible local officialdom, they could still avoid service, for much of the period, by ceasing to be single or ceasing to be able-bodied. The second of these may seem rather drastic, yet a rash of cut fingers and bleeding noses seemed to afflict France every time a requisition was ordered, and medical certificates and inspections by local committees bore witness to a thousand self-inflicted wounds. Two kinds of injury, it was well known, rendered the soldier unfit for active service, and despite the pain both were widely used. Cutting off the index-finger of the right hand made it impossible to pull the trigger of a musket, and extracting the upper front teeth prevented the conscript from reloading in the heat of battle.[111] Both forms of injury were prevalent throughout these years – even, significantly, in the Vosges, the only department in Year VII which still claimed to be experiencing no problems with recruitment[112] – with conscripts describing the most farflung accidents in their attempts to convince the authorities. The monotonous regularity of these injuries, sometimes messily and painfully executed, clearly angered the local recruiting-officers, but there was little they could do. Men already in uniform knew that a carefully-timed sabre blow could be relied upon to gain a satisfying respite from army life; and the peasant's son from Brittany or the Franche-Comté could always turn to the limited if rather bloodcurdling resources of the domestic armoury – many a wound in Year III or Year IV was inflicted by means of a scythe or a shotgun, a pitchfork or a humble kitchen knife.[113] Painful and unsophisticated it may have been, but the tradition of self-mutilation was established with conscription and would last long into the nineteenth century, for as long as the sons of the peasantry remained liable to military call-up.

As it was single men who were automatically called up for the army, the more cunning among the peasantry might easily be tempted to seek the other escape-hatch, that of a timely marriage. Not that I should wish to be accused of casting any shadow of doubt on the inherently romantic spirit that was abroad in the French countryside in the springtime – spring, after all, has other associations than those of military recruitment. But it is nevertheless a fact that it was in the spring of such years as 1793, 1795, 1808, and 1810 that some of the largest recruiting drives were conducted, in preparation for the new campaign season and in order to replace the deserters from the previous season's fighting. And I am not alone in displaying a certain cynicism with regard to the happy couples queuing up to be wed in the shadow of a new conscription law: it was shared by such as the prefect of the Somme, who in 1807 and 1808 was to be found bemoaning the 'manoeuvres matrimoniales' in his area.[114] A glance at the *état civil* of one little village in Picardy, Maucourt, for the spring of 1808 goes far to confirm these suspicions. The village and its environs produced such rare matches as that of Siméon Leroy, a farmworker aged 21, marrying Cathérine Merlu, who was a sprightly 72; a conscript of 20 marrying a woman of 74; a man of 21 choosing a bride aged 77; and another conscript who, at 23, married a woman aged 87. It is a trend that was paralleled all over France; indeed, the Revolutionary laws facilitating divorce could almost be said to have encouraged such weddings. Cathérine Merlu, for instance, was something like a professional wife for village boys threatened by the draft: in 1795 she had married another conscript, who had duly divorced her, as he was entitled to do, after the danger of military service had passed. Only on the second occasion did she fall foul of authority, since the recruitment law of 1808, foreseeing exactly this circumstance, insisted that anyone claiming exemption on the grounds of marriage must have been married for at least three months before the promulgation of the law. Rather than condemn poor Siméon to the battalions, the couple persuaded the village officials at Maucourt, the mayor and his *secrétaire de la mairie*, to falsify the marriage records, an offence which led to all four of them spending a few months in prison. The court records leave us in no doubt that they all knew exactly what they were doing, and that they enjoyed the sympathetic support of most of their fellow-villagers. Their offence, after all, was inspired by fellow-feeling and neighbourliness in a community united by its dislike of soldiering. Elsewhere the marriage market could be big business for the local councillors, and in those cases punishments were more severe. At the beginning of Year VII in Gap, for instance, no fewer than nine members of the local council were involved in forging marriage certificates and making false entries in the *état civil*, the ringleaders antedating as many as seven marriages each in return for cash payments from grateful local families.[115]

Such frauds were as widespread and successful as they were precisely because the bureaucracy of the Revolution was so weak and its legislative ambition so boundless. In an area like conscription which was widely detested by the bulk of the population, it is clear that the writ of the government could not run with anything approaching the efficiency of a modern government. Desertion, we have seen, was a virtually automatic concomitant of compulsory military service in such a society, and there was only a limited amount of policing that could be undertaken, at least until Napoleon's reforms went some way to provide France with a modern, efficient police force. Throughout the 1790s there were constant complaints from the military and civil authorities alike, that they lacked the manpower to round up deserters, that cavalry were needed for the job, that their gross undermanning made the law a virtual dead letter.[116] But this was only half the problem. For even where local authorities made a serious effort to root out deserters, the risk was always worth taking. Technically, anyone deserting after 1793 could face a death sentence, but the practice throughout France was very different. The death penalty, even at the height of the Terror, was reserved for those who crossed to the enemy and fought against France: in the Pas-de-Calais, for example, all 122 death sentences were either for that offence (including a number of men caught wearing British uniforms) or for taking up arms for the *chouans* of the west against the Revolution.[117] For the rest, for those who simply slunk off home or failed to turn up to their unit, it was only in the Year II that any serious attempt was made to bring them to book. Thereafter, in many cases, the most severe punishment meted out was the issuing of a simple statement, publicized throughout the locality, that the man in question had behaved shamefully.[118] But since the majority of the villagers would tacitly agree with what he had done, there was in fact no shame attached to the offence. This was, in the final analysis, the principal difficulty faced by legislators and tribunals alike: a law can only be satisfactorily enforced if it corresponds with the basic beliefs of the community for which it is designed, and the Revolution's laws on desertion were never able to command that degree of support.

Even the one wholehearted attempt by the Revolutionary authorities to bring deserters to book – the Directory's scheme to force them to return home by billeting garrisons on their families – ran into difficulties precisely in this area of public opinion. The plan appeared quite sound on paper: the deserters, on seeing their families forced to house and feed Republican soldiers until such time as they returned from their hiding-places, would be overwhelmed by feelings of guilt and filial devotion and would end their defiance of the conscription laws. The sheer inconvenience of having noisy, often drunk and dissolute troops billeted on a village would unite the villagers in demanding that the young *insoumis* return to the colours. It would be universally understood that obedience to the law was, after all, in everyone's interests. Or such was the theory. Soon government officials were to realize that rural resistance ran much deeper, that the sympathy of local people lay squarely with the deserters. In Year VIII the prefect of the Gers reported that he could get the law enforced, but only if he were backed by a unit of at least one hundred men.[119] Elsewhere there might be benefits in the short term, as recruits emerged from hiding to relieve their parents of the burden of the *garnisaires*; but within days they would take to the hills again, almost challenging the garrison to return.[120] Or the parents might evolve their own methods of resistance to a government measure which most condemned as tyrannical. In the Tarn, garrisons had to be withdrawn from some villages as the local people refused to give them anything to eat; cumbersome provisions trains would have been required to save the government's face.[121] Recalcitrance, moreover, could take even more damaging forms, for in many areas the most immediate impact of the *garnisaires* was not to reimpose order but to swell the numbers of brigands and outlaws living rough in the forests outside the communes, as entire families left their cottages and joined their sons and brothers on the run. In the Lot there was even talk of the policy causing a second level of desertion among the local community,[122] and authorities in the poorer agricultural areas of the country were right to worry that farms would be left abandoned and the rural economy would be made to suffer.[123]

Such widespread resistance to military service shows the degree of distrust and hatred of the army that ran through much of rural French society. It does not, of course, alter the fact that for the majority of those called to arms the Revolution did mean a long, energy-draining period of service on the frontiers, a period of service that would often stretch on into the Napoleonic years. And in the eyes of the men who did serve, desertion on such a massive scale merely added to their sense of grievance, to their awareness that the system of conscription was really far from universal and that they were suffering so that others could evade their responsibilities. Many were the Frenchmen who, forced to complete their military service and spend the best years of their lives in uniform, looked back on their experience of the Revolutionary and Napoleonic Wars with ill-concealed loathing and bitterness. Like François Bellardie, the Auvergnat hero of Martial Chaulanges' emotive novel of peasant life in the Massif Central, they could not forgive the pressures applied by the civil authorities to make them fulfil their service, or – under the Empire – forget the threats of damnation held over the heads of *insouciants* by bishops and priests who would refuse absolution and even the last rites to deserters. François had, like so many others, lost all chance of building up a modest prosperity for himself and his family, sacrificed all possibility of consolidating his *métairie*, and seen his youthful vigour wastefully drained out of him in the service of France. And why? Putting into words what many of his fellow-peasants believed, he harboured few doubts:

> Six ou sept ans de jeunesse perdus! . . . Et tout ça parce que nous avions eu mauvaise chance au tirage et qu'il nous avait manqué trois mille francs pour payer un remplaçant.[124]

Therein lay the bitter disillusionment of François and his generation – in the fact that the price of salvation, of freedom, of being his own master, was clearly recognized and lay tantalizingly outside his youthful grasp. He was quick to blame this for all his subsequent failures and disappointments:

> Depuis l'âge de dix-huit ans je n'ai jamais été mon maître. Et tout ça parce qu'il n'y avait pas 3,000 francs à la maison. . . . Les riches restent chez eux, mais toi, bon pour partir à l'armée! Là-bas plier, toujours plier.[125]

Notes to chapter 8

1. This image is common to much established Revolutionary historiography. For a refined version of it, see A. Soboul, *L'armée nationale sous la Révolution, 1789–94*.
2. Among the most interesting studies of the impact of the Revolution and its egalitarian philosophies on the French army are A. Soboul, *Les soldats de l'an II*; J.-P. Bertaud, *La Révolution armée: Les soldats-citoyens de la Révolution Française*; J.-P. Bertaud (editor), *Valmy: la démocratie en armes* and S. F. Scott, *The response of the royal army to the French Revolution*.
3. J.-P. Bertaud, *op. cit.*, annexes, pp. 289 ff.
4. L. de Cardénal, *Recrutement de l'armée en Périgord pendant la période révolutionnaire, 1789–1800*, pp. 134–6.
5. G. Lewis, *Life in Revolutionary France*, p. 154.
6. A.D. Bouches-du-Rhône, L2010, letter of 5 June 1793 to Section 21 of Marseille.
7. A.D. Rhône, 1L769, letter from Louis Deroire, 13 *thermidor* II.

8. S. F. Scott, 'The line army in the French Revolution'.

9. A.D. Seine, VD* 1633, Section de la Rue Beaubourg (de la Réunion), recruiting list for 1793.

10. G. Sangnier, *La désertion dans la Pas-de-Calais de 1792 à 1802*, p. 47.

11. J. G. Gallaher, '*Recruitment in the District of Poitiers, 1793*', pp. 252–5.

12. M. Giraud, *Levées d'hommes et acheteurs de biens nationaux dans la Sarthe en 1793*, p. 53.

13. A.D. Cantal, L248, report on recruitment in Marcolès, 13 March 1793.

14. A.D. Cantal, L248, report from Laroquebrou, 13 March 1793.

15. A.D. Bouches-du-Rhône, L736, text of the law of 7 February 1792.

16. A.D. Rhône, 1L769, *Exemptions de la réquisition*.

17. R. Legrand, *Le recrutement des armées et les désertions, 1791–1815*, p. 15.

18. B. Schnapper, *Le remplacement militaire en France*, p. 16.

19. Quoted in J.-P. Bertaud, 'Voies nouvelles pour l'histoire de la Révolution', p. 80n.

20. A.D. Rhône, 1L216, letter of 29 *germinal* II from the commune of Millery (Rhône).

21. B. Schnapper, *op. cit.*, p. 18.

22. J.-P. Bertaud (editor), *Valmy: la démocratie en armes*, p. 197.

23. A.D. Bouches-du-Rhône, L1171, requisition list for Ceyreste, April 1793.

24. A.D. Rhône, 1L740. *Listes de volontaires, levée de 1792*, District de Lyon-campagnes. The list contains 243 names with occupations, and in 241 cases the age of the volunteers is also supplied. The breakdown by age for these men is given in table 5.

Table 5

Age	Number of recruits	Age	Number of recruits
17	1	27	6
18	61	28	8
19	23	29	1
20	23	30	6
21	22	31	2
22	25	32	2
23	11	33	1
24	10	34	1
25	18	35	0
26	14	36 and over	6

25. A.D. Bouches-du-Rhône, L1171, recruitment lists for March and April 1793 for the city of Marseille.

26. A.D. Cantal, L252, *Recrutement des 300,000*, correspondence of the commune of Saint-Martin-sous-Vigouroux.

27. A.D. Cantal, L251, deliberation of the District of Saint-Flour, 7 March 1793.

28. A.D. Cantal, L250, petition to the District of Murat from the commune of Saint-Bonnet.

29. A.D. Cantal, L252, correspondence between the commune of Saint-Martin-sous-Vigouroux and the District of Saint-Flour, 1793.

30. A.D. Cantal, L253, petition from Pierre Charbonnel and Pierre Bonhomme of Arpajon to the District of Aurillac.

31. A.D. Cantal, L253, petition from ten citizens of the Canton of Junhac, 31 March 1793.
32. A.D. Cantal, L253, petition from commune of La Besserette, 31 March 1793.
33. A.D. Cantal, L202, correspondence between the commune of Saint-Etienne-de-Maurs and the District of Aurillac, 1792.
34. A.D. Cantal, L253, letter from Ruat in Saint-Flour to the District of Saint-Flour, 7 May 1793.
35. G. Vallée, *La conscription dans le département de la Charente, 1798–1807*, p. 15.
36. L. de Cardénal, *op. cit.*, p. 204.
37. *ibid.*, p. 170.
38. I. Woloch, *The French veteran from the Revolution to the Restoration*. For the remarks that follow on Revolutionary policy on veterans' pensions and on reforms to the Hôtel des Invalides, I have drawn heavily on Professor Woloch's researches.
39. *ibid.*, p. 81.
40. *ibid.*, p. 89.
41. *ibid.*, pp. 83–4.
42. A. Cochin and M. de Boüard, *Précis des principales opérations du gouvernement révolutionnaire*, pp. 156–9.
43. I. Woloch, *op. cit.*, pp. 18–28.
44. *ibid.*, pp. 67–73.
45. *ibid.*, p. 159.
46. *ibid.*, p. 100.
47. *ibid.*, p. 183.
48. *ibid.*, p. 91.
49. A.D. Rhône, 1L768, *Etat des dépenses relatives à la levée des réquisitionnaires*. A typical breakdown of such expenditure is shown in table 6 – the costs of equipping one Pierre Germain, a soldier from Villefranche, who left to join the Armée du Rhin on 10 April 1793.

Table 6

	livres	sols	deniers
Suit, jacket, with two pairs of trousers	138	5	3
Small items of equipment	35	15	8
Shoes, hats, spats	45	12	6
Shirts (3), pairs of stockings (2)	42	0	0
Guns and holsters	17	0	0
	278	13	5
Also pay of 20 sous to sign on and 5 sous per day thereafter	12	0	0
TOTAL:	290	13	5

50. A.D. Bouches-du-Rhône, L2010, subscription from the *Amis de la Constitution* for the armies of the Republic, March 1792.

51. Arch. Préfecture de Police de Paris, A^A59, report of the *commissaires de police* of the Section des Arcis, 14 June 1793.
52. This and the cases that follow are drawn from petitions to the *Comité des secours publics* from widows of soldiers killed in action. These are to be found in A.N., F^152818, *Secours publics: affaires concernant les militaires.*
53. A.D. Seine, VD*890, Section des Lombards, *Adresse des citoyens soldats du Bataillon des Lombards au camp sous Cassel*, May 1793.
54. A.D. Rhône, 1L738, letter from *procureur-syndic* of the District of Roanne, 22 February 1792.
55. A.D. Rhône, 1L738, letter from the District of Lyon-campagnes, 5 March 1792.
56. A.D. Bouches-du-Rhône, L862, District of Aix, *Mendicité, 1790-an II*. The problem of enforcing fixed routes for soldiers is discussed in minutes of 7 January 1792 and 20 June 1792.
57. A.D. Rhône, 1L743, letter from an officer of the military police, 5th Battalion of the Rhône-et-Loire, to the District of Lyon-campagnes, 28 *floréal* III.
58. A.D. Cantal, L255, letter from the *vice-procureur-syndic* in Saint-Flour to the municipal council in Aurillac, 16 August 1793.
59. A.N., F^9174, *Recrutement, correspondance générale – Creuse*, 'Tableau des conscrits de l'an VIII', 22 *vendémiaire* IX.
60. A.N., F^9308, *Désertion: série départementale (Elbe-Lot)*, Department of Haute-Loire, report of 23 *nivôse* VIII.
61. A.N., F^9156, Department of Ardèche, letter from Prefect to Minister of Interior, 10 *thermidor* VIII.
62. A.N., F^9199, Department of Landes, report on the *levée* of Year VII.
63. A.N., F^9239, reports of conscription problems in Bas-Rhin; F^9232, report of desertion rates in Year VIII for Department of Pas-de-Calais.
64. A.N., F^9301, Department of Basses-Alpes, letter to Minister of Interior, 9 *fructidor* VII.
65. A.N., F^9306, Department of Haute-Garonne, letter to Minister of Interior, 23 *ventôse* V.
66. A.N., F^9306, Department of Gard, report of 26 *germinal* VII.
67. A.N., F^9316, Department of Tarn, letter to Minister of Interior, 11 *prairial* VIII.
68. A.N., F^9302, *imprimé* of Department of Calvados, 5 *fructidor* VII.
69. A.N., F^9181, letter from the *commissaire du Directoire* in Eure, 2 *frimaire* VIII.
70. A.N., F^9248, letter from Department of Seine-Inférieure, 28 *thermidor* VII.
71. A.N., F^9236, letter from Department of Basses-Pyrénées to Minister of Interior, 18 *fructidor* V.
72. A.N., F^9190, letter from prefect of Hérault to Minister of Interior, 11 *thermidor* VIII.
73. A.N., F^9318, letter from *agent national* at Soullans (Vendée), 20 *thermidor* IV.
74. A.M., F^9199, report of prefect of Landes to Minister of Interior, 9 *thermidor* VIII.
75. A.N., F^9209, report of prefect of Lozère, 5 April 1806.
76. A.N., F^9225, report from Department of Nièvre, 12 September 1792.
77. A.N., F^9208, report of prefect of Lot-et-Garonne to Minister of Interior, 1 *fructidor* XIII.
78. R. Legrand, *op. cit.*, pp. 40–1.
79. A.N., F^9319, report from mayor of Coulours (Yonne), 6 *fructidor* IX.
80. A.N., F^9314, letter from *commissaire du Directoire* of Saône-et-Loire to Minister of Interior, 5e *jour complémentaire* VI.
81. A.N., F^9225, report from prefect of Nièvre to Minister of Interior, 9 *thermidor* VIII.
82. A.N., F^9237, report from Hautes-Pyrénées to Minister of Interior, 19 *brumaire* VI.

83. A.N., F⁹309, letter from *commissaire du Directoire* in the Lot-et-Garonne to Minister of War, 21 *prairial* VII.
84. A.N., BB¹⁸42, report from *gendarmes* at Marvejols, 4 *pluviôse* XII.
85. A.N., F⁹232, report of *général de brigade* at Arras, 2 *brumaire* XII.
86. A.N., F⁹306, report of Dufour, *général de division* at Bordeaux, 28 *pluviôse* IX.
87. Departments where councils are accused include Dordogne (F⁹176), Gironde (F⁹189), Creuse (F⁹174), Eure (F⁹181), and Pas-de-Calais (F⁹232).
88. A.N., F⁹241, prefect's report to Minister of Interior on Department of Rhône for Year XI.
89. A.N., F⁹189, report to Minister of Justice, 25 *prairial* VI.
90. A.N., BB¹⁸26, letter from prefect of Haute-Garonne, 22 December 1807.
91. A.N., BB¹⁸42, *Ministère de la Justice, Division Criminelle*, reports on criminal cases arising out of conscription offences in Lozère, an VII–1814.
92. A.N., F⁹319, report from Courlon (Yonne), 10 *ventôse* VII.
93. A.N., F⁹301, report to Minister of Interior from Vicdessos (Ariège), 10 *ventôse* IV.
94. Various cases are cited in A.N., F⁹301–319, especially F⁹306, 308, 309, 310.
95. A.N., BB¹⁸53, cases reported from Pas-de-Calais and Nord, 1807–8.
96. A.N., F⁹315, letter from deputies from Creuse to Minister of Interior, 18 *nivôse* IV.
97. A.N.,,, F⁹199, minute of Department of Landes, 29 *prairial* VII.
98. A.N., F⁹316, report of *commissaire du Directoire* in Somme, 21 *floréal* VII.
99. A.N., F⁹286, report from Agen, dated 5 *thermidor* XIII.
100. A.N., F⁹286, letter from *commissaire* in Molières (Lot), 3 *ventôse* IV.
101. E. Deprez, *Les volontaires nationaux* gives details of all Revolutionary conscription legislation.
102. A.N., F⁹286, cases from Year IV to Year IX.
103. A.N., F⁹316, letter from *juge de paix* of the Canton of Lautrec (Tarn), 9 *brumaire* VII.
104. A.N., F⁹190, letter from prefect of Hérault to Minister of Interior, 4 *pluviôse* XI.
105. A.N., F⁹237, letter from *commissaire du Directoire* in Hautes-Pyrénées to Minister of War, 11 *ventôse* IV.
106. A.N., F⁹190, letter from prefect of Hérault, *op. cit.*, 4 *pluviôse* XI.
107. A.N., F⁹286, case, for instance, of Pierre Gaillat from Cernay (Haut-Rhin), 15 *thermidor* VIII.
108. A.N., F⁹286, letter from *commissaire du Directoire* in Chinon to Minister of Interior, 12 *nivôse* IV.
109. A.N., F⁹189, report from *commissaire du Directoire* in Gironde, 5ᵉ *j.c.*, an VII.
110. A.N., F⁹286, denunciation of jury in Murviel (Hérault), 7 *pluviôse* VII.
111. There are numerous isolated instances, e.g. A.N., F⁹176, *compte rendu* of prefect of Dordogne, 3 May 1809; or A.N. F⁹286, report of *commissaire* of directory in Saône-et-Loire, 11 *prairial* VII.
112. A.N., F⁹260, reports of two different *commissaires du Directoire* in the Vosges, 9 *prairial* VII and 15 *brumaire* VII.
113. R. Legrand, *op. cit.*, p. 19; G. Lewis, *Life in Revolutionary France*, p. 152.
114. R. Legrand, *op. cit.*, pp. 53ff. The cases cited here are drawn from Legrand's analysis of the Department of the Somme.
115. A.N., F⁹286, letter from *accusateur-public* at Gap (Hautes-Alpes), 9 *prairial* VII.
116. A.N., F⁹308, report from Department of Jura, 16 *pluviôse* IX.
117. G. Sangnier, *op. cit.*, pp. 89–90.

118. R. Legrand, *op. cit.*, p. 22.
119. A.N., F⁹306, report from prefect of Gers, 6 *fructidor* VIII.
120. A.N., F⁹316, report from *commissaire du Directoire* in Somme, 21 *floréal* VII.
121. A.N., F⁹316, decree on deserters, 21 *prairial* VII.
122. A.N., F⁹207, minute of Department of Lot, 29 *prairial* VII.
123. A.N., F⁹165, report from prefect of Cantal, 8 *thermidor* VIII.
124. M. Chaulanges, *Les mauvais numéros*, p. 188.
125. *ibid.*, p. 150.

9 Conclusion

The establishment of some sort of *bilan*, of a balance-sheet of the successes and failures of Revolutionary policy towards the poor, must be approached with some delicacy. The legislative achievement, were that to be taken at its face value, was unquestionably impressive, both in the reforms that were introduced and the pensions voted. The reports and the day-to-day proceedings of the *Comité de Mendicité* reflected the heady optimism of an enlightened age, as the deputies set about solving social problems by uniform, legislative methods. If we were to judge the Revolution's achievement by the yardstick of its intentions and its decrees, then we should be entitled to take a vicarious pride in the new humanitarian concern and to proclaim the Revolution's policies as a major contribution to human progress in this most neglected of fields. But this book has not been about laws and intentions so much as about results and practical accomplishments, about the actual impact of these well-intentioned decrees on the lives of the poor and on the welfare of the institutions that cared for them. Only too frequently the text of a law proved a poor guide to achievement, since there was often a yawning gulf between expectation and realization and since the enthusiasms of 1790 and 1791 could be cruelly dashed by the frightful winter of *Nonante-cinq* which drove so many desperate, starving people to the verge of suicide. Given the misery of the Thermidorian and Directorial period in particular, it is even tempting to sympathize, momentarily at least, with Léon Lallemand and his brand of counter-revolutionary social history and to condemn the French Revolution as having been one unmitigated disaster for the poor.[1] The Enlightened, humanitarian approach already appeared outmoded and unrealistic, as the poor struggled to stay alive and hospitals were reduced to the most demeaning expedients if they were to stay open. The dream of the Physiocrats and of La Rochefoucauld-Liancourt seemed to many to have turned into a chilling nightmare.

It is certainly the case that the poor of the later 1790s felt no better for the political rights and privileges which they had gained from the Revolution. Never had so many measures been passed in the name of the people and supposedly in their interests; yet for the poor these reforms had brought little direct benefit. Often what they had gained took the form of civil rights, the ending of privileges once enjoyed by others, paper benefits in law only which had little effect on their highly marginal existence. The right to vote, the privilege of citizenship, the doctrine of *égalité*, all these had little impact on people too poor, too insecure to understand their implications. Even the great social reforms in the countryside scarcely benefited the poorest members of the rural community. Of course, seigneurial power was abolished, and with it the feudal exactions of the Ancien Regime; but what replaced it was a new system of social and economic obligation, firmly rooted in the cash nexus and in the relationship between a new breed of capitalist farmers and the labourers they employed.[2] Tolls, *octrois*, internal trade barriers were, it is true, abolished, and the poor doubtless gained some fleeting advantage from their suppression. But their lives under the Revolution hardly lived up to their exaggerated expectations during the early months of 1789 and 1790, amidst the bonfires and festivities that had heralded the installation of the National Assembly and the fall of feudalism. The much-vaunted sales of *biens nationaux* did little to ease the lot of the poor, since in most areas only those with substantial property holdings could hope to make any profit from them.[3] Taxes, contrary to their hopes on the morning after the storming of the Bastille, still had to be paid, and soon there were extra demands upon government coffers, like the waging of war and the cost of internal administration. The *maximum* brought short-term advantages to the rural poor as well as to their urban counterparts, but these advantages were soon dissipated, and after *thermidor* the subsistence farmer and landless labourer alike were again faced with rapid and pitiless rates of inflation that threatened to topple their fragile domestic economy. In a whole range of ways the poor could be excused for thinking by the end of the decade that the Revolution they had lived through was not their revolution at all but one devoted to the interests of others, of the *bourgeois*, of the towns, of Paris, of people who had little knowledge or understanding of their plight.

The Revolution, moreover, expected so much of them. As we have seen, it was to the poorer sections of society, the least vocal elements, least able to leap to the defence of their own interests, that the politicians turned to fill the battalions in the army. The effect on the peasant economy was predictably serious: yields fell and smallholdings became uneconomic when they were left without the strongest arms to shoulder the bulk of the work, and the ranks of the rural poor became still more swollen. For many poor families the sacrifice demanded was far greater than that of fighting for France: they were also called upon to renounce their cherished dream of achieving a degree of self-sufficiency. But if that was the greatest demand made on the poor, it was far from being the only one. The Revolution was a highly political period which judged people by political standards and expected from them a certain level of political conformity and commitment. Especially after 1793 everything risked acquiring political overtones, and any deviation from the Revolutionary orthodoxy brought with it the possibility of denunciation, surveillance, and, in more extreme cases, criminal proceedings. For the politically aware this presented dangers enough, but for the mass of the poor, kept abreast of events by gossip in the village inn or by the last orator to deliver a harangue on their street corner, the dangers were more pervasive and much more insidious. Working people might expect to be treated with a degree of leniency by Revolutionary courts, which were ready to be persuaded that they had been misled by men more educated than themselves; but that cannot hide the fact that very large numbers of those tried and convicted came from the ranks of the poor and politically illiterate.[4] It was so very easy to make a grave, even fatal error of judgement. The unemployed worker who tried to earn a few sous by selling newspapers on the bridges over the Seine could find himself in trouble for peddling the wares of the wrong political faction. The embittered farm labourer, facing starvation at the end of the agricultural year, risked treason charges for interfering with military requisitions if he attacked a corn convoy or stole from a grain barge. Or the Paris building-worker who, while drinking away his tribulations in his local *cabaret* – one of the simple pleasures of life which remained during the Revolution – absent-mindedly criticized the regime or lamented the recent increases in food prices, might easily find himself arraigned for the heinous crime of *aristocratie*. In the Vendée and in areas of federalist revolt there was the even more perilous possibility that a poor man might be lured by money or by personal loyalty into carrying arms against the Republic, a charge which often incurred an automatic death penalty in Year II. The danger of conviction was always present: of fourteen thousand victims of the Terror studied by Donald Greer, 28 per cent were peasants and 31 per cent urban workers – a very high proportion for a Revolution which purported to speak in the name of ordinary Frenchmen.[5] This is especially so when it is recalled that for many of them, the whole realm of political discussion lay outside their normal range of concern, with the result that they were not equipped to cope with the political issues that confronted them during the Revolutionary years.

If the effects of general Revolutionary change and of the new liberal policies did little to improve the lot of the poor, what judgement can be passed on the more specifically social measures directed at exterminating poverty? The pattern that has emerged in each of the specific fields examined – hospital provision, pensions and *assistance à domicile*, public workshops, and the provision for *enfants trouvés* – is remarkably consistent and allows certain general observations to be made. First and foremost, there was little that was truly novel in the solutions which the Revolution proposed. The *Comité de Mendicité* and its successors drew heavily on the experience of the previous twenty or thirty years, on the reform proposals of the Physiocrats and the papers read to learned societies by enlightened hospital administrators in the localities. In many respects Revolutionary change was no more than a continuation of previous reforms, just as Revolutionary attitudes to the poor were solidly based on eighteenth-century ideas. Indeed, the problems of hospitals and *dépôts de mendicité* in the Revolutionary years were in most cases problems that already loomed large in the last years of the Ancien Regime. In spite of all the rhetoric, the change instituted after 1789 in most fields of social provision hardly merits the term 'revolutionary' at all. The one great advance made lay in the attitude of government, in its willingness to listen to reform proposals and its preparedness to adopt ambitious welfare schemes. The reaction of Louis XV's governments had always been faltering and piecemeal, responding to individual crises rather than relishing major change. Private and religious charity had proved inadequate to the needs of the people long before 1789, yet royal governments had shown no willingness to make good that inadequacy. It was the Revolutionary administrations, from the National Assembly to the Jacobin Convention of Year II, that had first tackled the problem openly, accepting wider-ranging responsibilities which their predecessors had shirked. Their concept of *bienfaisance* as the right of those of the citizenry who fell below the poverty line was a tribute to their rationalism and their humanitarian approach. Their plans for an integrated system of public welfare, of different kinds dependent on the nature of the need and spread equitably across the area of France, were both ambitious and highly imaginative.

By 1795 it was obvious that these plans lay in ruins, but the ideal espoused by the Revolution should not be belittled. The labours of the *Comité* were not ignored, and imaginative innovation was rewarded. The early pension schemes did try to reflect those areas where need was greatest and, in the *Grand Livre de Bienfaisance* especially, there was a deliberate attempt to balance the cities and the countryside, the poor who could be treated at home and those who could only be cared for in hospital. And the block grant system, whatever its later deficiencies, had the inestimable advantage of distributing cash to those hospitals and those areas of France where it was most required. The researches of the *Comité* were a much more accurate gauge of need than the chance siting of a monastery or the placing of a fifteenth-century *fonds charitable*. The governments of 1793 and Year II had more leverage for coaxing information about hardship or storm damage from local authorities than did governments of the Ancien Regime. And in the early years of the Revolution, before the money ran out and other priorities became too insistent to be denied, the cash grants to hospitals and local councils did seem to be providing a standard of care to the old and the sick and a level of pension to the deserving poor that far surpassed the product of the random charities and legacies of the eighteenth century. But then came the turning-point. Under the Convention funds dried up, grants trickled through months late, and the dependence on the state – the dependence so sharply defined by the law of 23 *brumaire* II – turned from a source of potential strength to one of debilitating weakness. The Jacobins continued to believe in this form of state welfare, but they failed to finance it. With the arrival in power of the Thermidorians and the progressive dismantling of the Jacobin state, the political will was not there and the idea of a state-funded welfare system was doomed to failure. The Directory years were marked, as we have seen, by the gradual return of responsibility to individual hospitals, to local sources of finance, to self-sufficiency. With the reimposition of the *octroi*, the last vestige of central government responsibility was effectively removed, and the local treasurers, bewildered by the rapid changes which they had experienced, had no option but to try to rebuild their shattered finances. On this basis the hospitals slowly recovered; but many pension schemes, *ateliers*, and all aspects of *assistance à domicile* were condemned to contraction and frequently to rapid extinction. Under the Consulate and the Empire the tone of government policy on *assistance* was again pragmatic and undoctrinaire; the grandiose ideas of the early 1790s were not revived.

So why did the Jacobin ideal, the welfare state of La Rochefoucauld-Liancourt and his committee, fail to answer the demands placed upon it? The laissez-faire economics of the Thermidorians may have buried it, but its inadequacies were already exposed before the overthrow of Robespierre. Nor can the war be offered as a total explanation of these inadequacies. Already in 1790 and 1791 the fiscal shortcomings of the new regime were becoming apparent. Tax revenues, so essential to the success of these projects, fell away as the rich emigrated and the peasantry were engulfed by the confused euphoria engendered by the abolition of feudal dues. The forced sales of *biens nationaux*, the seizure of church lands, the issue of paper currency, all in essence flowed from the country's rather meagre tax base and from the understandable reluctance of the banking community and of foreign money lenders to risk their assets by lending to such uncertain debtors. Exceptional exactions on the wealthy were no substitute for a steady, dependable income and a healthy economic infrastructure; forced loans and patriotic donations could not compensate for poor harvests and lost production, whether through the loss of essential manpower to the armies, the economic distortion caused by the war, or the political troubles in large tracts of the French countryside. The stark truth is that the Revolutionaries never succeeded in stimulating the economy to produce the level of wealth required if their ambitious social dreams were to be realized.

Finance was not, however, the only barrier to effective action in the field of poor relief: the Revolution had also to overcome the deficiencies inherent in the method of aid which it chose to adopt. For virtually all change was to be achieved through legislation, by decrees issued at the centre and imposed equitably throughout the entire country. As we have seen again and again in connection with individual projects, local bodies were consulted only when information was required to establish the degree of suffering and to gauge the level of intervention which that suffering necessitated. Local authorities and charitable bodies were not expected to participate in the moulding of policy any more than hospital administrators were encouraged to show initiative in assessing the cases that appeared before them. Theirs was to be a purely executive role: decisions and policies must, in the sacred name of *égalité*, be adopted in Paris, not left to local people in Privas or Perpignan. Revolutionary governments believed unflinchingly in the universal power of the law, and they used it as an instrument of social policy on a heroic scale. Legislation freed the peasantry from seigneurial privilege and seigneurial jurisdiction; laws were introduced to raise, feed, and equip a conscript army; still further laws were required to fix maximum food prices, requisition the buildings needed for hospitals and for the billeting of troops, organize public workshops for the destitute, supply pensions to the indigent and to the dependants of soldiers, and generally intervene in the harsh economics of the free market in order to help the needy and the impoverished. Through legislation a succession of governments sought to persuade the French public that charity was a rather unworthy, patronizing concept that had been buried along with the other evils of the Ancien Regime, to be replaced by *bienfaisance*, a national duty to come to the help of those unfortunates incapable of making ends meet. Painstakingly the requisite committee of the Convention would assemble massive reports and collect local statistics to enable it to achieve its aim of solving the social ills of France by means of the statute-book. Yet the legislation which resulted, of necessity universalist in conception, took little account of local circumstances and particular needs. The same panacea was applied to the hospitals of central Paris as to the *hospices* of small country towns like Brioude and Issoire, which had to cater for all the casualties of the farming year in the mountainous Auvergne. The legislative solution could be crude and insensitive, ignoring local protests and brushing aside the views of local officials in the name of progress and of equal opportunity for all. It was a shortcoming that was always implicit in a republic dominated by the legal profession.

Starved of finance and largely deaf to local circumstance, a legislative approach to poor relief could never be wholly satisfactory, and the ideals of the Revolutionaries were never matched by their practical achievements. For one thing, the degree of income redistribution obtained by tax changes, by the abolition of feudal dues, and by the sale of *biens nationaux* was very limited, at least as far as the poorer peasantry were concerned.[6] For them the relief of misery was dependent upon the success of new pension schemes and of legislation on hospitals. But that legislation was often confused and ill-directed. As we have seen on several different occasions, the social goals of relieving poverty could so easily clash with more general political aims, and in such cases it was usually the poor and infirm who were sacrificed. Thus the abolition of feudal dues had the unforseen effect of destroying the economic base of many of the country's charitable institutions, just as the anti-clerical decrees of the early months of the Revolution led to an acute crisis in the staffing of the hospitals. On the frontiers, the demands and the casualties of war were placing extra strains on the hospital service at precisely the moment when the government's financial embarrassments ensured that they were deprived of funds and lacking in even the barest necessities. Like all government, that of the 1790s was a question of competing priorities, and the old, the sick, and the feeble-minded lost out to more pressing demands – to trade controls and the *maximum*, to the purging of suspects and the implementation of Revolutionary government, to dechristianization and requisition, above all to winning the war. These all cost money, money for which the social budget had to compete; and it has to be admitted that the *vieillard* and the *pauvre malade* could never constitute a very effective pressure-group. They lost out not because of any failure of will, at least during the Jacobin period, but because they ceased to be one of the most urgent problems facing a severely-harassed government.

Above all, they lost out because of the shortcomings of Revolutionary bureaucracy. A legislative solution to the problems of poverty implied an ability to enforce that legislation, to achieve the equality in fact which was promised in the government's decrees. It assumed the administrative trappings of a modern state, a habit of national legislation and a steady bureaucratic rhythm which were unknown in the eighteenth century and which were impossible to conjure up in the political turmoil of the Revolutionary decade. Even at the height of the Terror the Jacobins could not attain their centralist ambitions, for there was no infrastructure on which to build. Tribunals composed of politically-reliable citizens were no substitute for an established system of courts, handing down justice on the basis of a widely-respected legal tradition. Regard for the law cannot be permanently imbued by the sight of a *guillotine ambulante* rolling on to the village square, or by the knowledge that one's neighbours are being encouraged to denounce any infraction of the Revolutionary canons. Nor could the bands of enthusiasts who made up the *armées révolutionnaires* really substitute for a police force – yet France had no regular police before 1795 and certainly no tradition of methodical policing until well into the nineteenth century. The departments, districts and municipalities did their job well, passing down decrees to local level and publishing decisions which affected the lives of their citizens. Clubs and sections helped to spread political awareness to people not previously involved in the practice of politics. In short, great strides forward were made in these years, but among the poor, the illiterate, and in remote rural areas, the impact of central government legislation was often quite minimal. For the politicians in Paris to believe that they could solve the problems of such people by means of laws and administrative orders was an act of gross self-deception.

It was not only the administrative framework of a modern bureaucracy that was missing in Revolutionary France; it was also the habit of communication, the common legal traditions, the common language and customs which play such an important part in the development of national unity. The Revolutionaries might preach the cause of the nation-state and boast of the creation of *la nation une et indivisible*. But the oft-repeated slogans and the constant reliance on the sacred trappings of nationhood must be seen less as evidence that national spirit was already formed than as symptoms of a deep-seated insecurity, as an expression of passionate hope that a dream was in the process of being fulfilled. Of course the Revolution did much, and the Revolutionary Wars even more, to foster a spirit of patriotism: ten years of exhortation and indoctrination could not fail to leave their imprint on the French people. They did not, however, succeed in their declared goal, that of changing the essential focus of a largely peasant population from the purely local to the national stage. The recent work of such historians as Jean Vidalenc, Eugen Weber, and Theodore Zeldin can leave little doubt that even as late as 1870 this process remained far from complete. France in the mid-nineteenth century was still far from being the streamlined, modernized nation-state of which the Revolutionary leaders had dreamed. Paris might boast a highly-centralized administrative machine of the sort for which the Jacobins had craved, but France remained a country of vivid contrasts, fragmented and localized in outlook and still rooted in the time-honoured traditions or rural society. Peasants throughout the south and west were still intensely provincial in their mentality until well into the Third Republic, identifying more strongly with Brittany or Languedoc or Poitou than ever they did with the amorphous, distant entity that was France.[7] In many areas French was a foreign language to the bulk of the population, who spoke nothing but dialect and whose parochial mentality was further intensified by the prevalence of local legend and folk memory: in the west between Honfleur and les Sables-d'Olonne, tales of the *chouans* of the 1790s were still haunting the popular imagination a century after the Revolution was over.[8] Contact with other areas was strictly limited, since people in peasant villages travelled beyond the boundary of their own commune only when economic necessity drove them to do so. Anyone from beyond a radius of ten or fifteen miles was still regarded with suspicion as a 'foreigner', an outsider who did not share in the very private affairs of the village community in the Corrèze or the Haute-Loire; and those representatives of the state, of the alien world of the government and its law, who entered their lives were likely to be viewed with intense hostility, as an unwelcome intrusion into their self-contained world.[9] It was no accident that military service was so widely resented in the Revolutionary years, or that deputies-on-mission were wont to be given a rough reception in the more remote hamlets of the Auvergne. For the Revolution was trying, by the use of sometimes draconian measures, to force a modern and often sophisticated legislative framework on a rural society where ignorance was widespread and national feeling in its infancy. It was an impossible goal. Indeed, it is astonishing that so much was achieved in such un-promising conditions.

Notes to chapter 9

1. L. Lallemand, *La Révolution et les pauvres*.
2. A. Soboul, *Problèmes paysans de la Révolution, 1789–1848*, pp. 15–17.
3. P. Bois, *Les paysans de l'Ouest*, pp. 331–44; G. Lefebvre, *Les paysans du Nord*, pp. 406–7; M. Marion, *La vente des biens nationaux pendant la Révolution, passim*.
4. M. Glover, *Collection complète des jugements rendus par la Commission Révolutionnaire établie à Lyon par les Représentants-du-peuple en 1793–1794*.
5. D. Greer, *The incidence of the Terror during the French Revolution*, p. 97.
6. G. Lefebvre, *Les paysans du Nord*, p. 407; the same effect is noted by most local studies of the peasantry during the Revolutionary period.
7. T. Zeldin, *France, 1848–1945*: II, *Intellect, taste and anxiety*, chapter 2, pp. 29–85.
8. J. Vidalenc, *Le peuple des compagnes*, pp. 46ff.
9. E. Weber, *Peasants into Frenchmen: the modernisation of rural France, 1870–1914*, pp. 45–51.

Bibliography

PRIMARY SOURCES

A Manuscript

Documents used for this study were drawn primarily from the Revolutionary series of the *Archives Nationales* in Paris and from a selection of departmental and municipal archives in the provinces. Limited use was also made of the *Archives de la Préfecture de Police* in Paris, the *Archives de l'Assistance Publique*, the Chamber of Commerce archive in La Rochelle, and the archive of the Hôtel-Dieu in Lyon, which, unlike many hospital archives, is still kept independently by the Hôtel-Dieu.

I   ARCHIVES DÉPARTEMENTALES (A.D.)

Bouches-du-Rhône

C1733	Administration des hôpitaux, 1763–84
L451	Hôpitaux militaires (période révolutionnaire)
L494	Hôpitaux, Comité de Bienfaisance
L736	Recrutement des volontaires, 1792
L785	Hôpitaux militaires, an II–an III
L856	Hôpitaux et maisons de charité, 1790–an IV
L858	Hôpitaux et maisons de charité, District d'Aix
L862	Mendicité, District d'Aix, 1790–an IV
L863	Ateliers de charité, District d'Aix, 1790–an IV
L868	Secours: tableaux de distributions individuelles
L1062	Police des personnes logées en chambres garnies
L1171	Recrutement, 1793: tableaux de jeunes gens
L1240	Hôpitaux et hospices de Marseille, 1792–an IV
L1241	Hospices du District de Marseille: comptabilité
L1242	Oeuvres de charité supprimées, District de Marseille
L1244	Livre de Bienfaisance, District de Marseille
L2009	Sections de Marseille: Comité de Bienfaisance
L2010	Sections de Marseille: souscriptions et dons patriotiques

Cantal

L161	Etats de population des districts par cantons et communes, soumis au Comité de Mendicité, 1790
L202	Listes des volontaires de 1792

L248	Recrutement pour la levée des 300,000 hommes, District d'Aurillac
L250	Levée des 300,000, District de Murat
L251	Levée des 300,000, District de Saint-Flour
L252	Levée des 300,000, Commune de Saint-Martin-sous-Vigouroux
L253	Pétitions au sujet du recrutement des 300,000
L255	Levée des 300,000: déserteurs
L322	Travaux publics, 1792–3

Charente-Inférieure

C219, 220	Dépôt de Mendicité de La Rochelle: personnel des détenus, 1789

Cher

C36	Dépôts de Mendicité, 1766–88
C37	Bureau de Charité de Châteauroux: mémoires
C1340	Mendicité, bureaux de charité, 1768–88
C1341	Dépôt de Mendicité de Bourges, 1784
C1476	Fonds de charité: bureaux et ateliers, 1781–90
L497	Ateliers de charité: rapports des ingénieurs, emploi des fonds, 1790–an IV
L565	Dépôt de Mendicité, correspondance

Haute-Garonne

L4065	Etablissements de bienfaisance, 1790–an VIII
L4066	Etablissements de bienfaisance et hôpitaux civils de Toulouse, 1791–an III
L4068	Hospice de la Grave à Toulouse, 1790–an IV

Gironde

4L7	Procès-verbaux des séances extraordinaires du Conseil-général du District de Bordeaux, 1792–3
4L133	District de Bordeaux, hôpitaux, ateliers de charité, mendicité
4L134	Dépôt de Mendicité de Bordeaux
5L56	District de Bazas, hôpitaux, secours
6L53	District de Bourg, hôpitaux, secours
7L97	District de Cadillac, hôpitaux, secours
8L70	District de La Réole, hôpitaux, secours
8L71	District de La Réole, secours aux indigents
9L64	District de Lesparre, hôpitaux
10L101	District de Libourne, hôpitaux, secours
11L27–31	Bordeaux Intra-muros, hôpitaux, dépôts de mendicité, bureaux de bienfaisance, an IV–an VIII
12L3	Procès-verbaux et correspondance de la Section Simoneau
12L18	Société des Amis de la Liberté et de l'Egalité de Bordeaux, correspondance générale, 1793–an II
12L28	Club National de Bordeaux, secours moraux et matériels, 1790–an III

Isère

L61	Département de l'Isère, procès-verbaux de l'adminstration, 1793–an II

Jura

L861	Hôpitaux, hospices, assistance aux indigents, 1789–an V

Loire

840L	Ateliers de charité, District de Saint-Etienne
842L	Ateliers révolutionnaires, Saint-Etienne, an II–an III
843L	Assistance: hôpitaux et mendicité, 1790–an VI
844L	Hospices, assistance, Districts de Montbrison, Roanne et Saint-Etienne
845bisL	Décret de Javogues sur l'hôpital de Montbrison, 23 pluviôse II
846L	Soumissions pour l'acquisition des biens des établissements hospitaliers, an III

Bas-Rhin

1L1592	Enfants assistés et abandonnés: instructions et correspondance générale, 1790–an VII
1L1593	Hospice des Enfants-Trouvés de Strasbourg, administration et comptabilité, 1791–3
1L1594	Hospice des Enfants-Trouvés de Strasbourg, administration et comptabilité, an II–an VII
1L1595	Enfants assistés: Hospice des Enfants Naturels de la Patrie à Stephansfeld

Rhône

C6	Administration de la Police, 1739–89
C162	Hôpitaux de Lyon, 1672–1786
C163	Hôtel-Dieu de Lyon, correspondance, 1775–89
C164	Hospice de la Charité, correspondance, 1768–89
C175	Dépôt de Mendicité (La Quarantaine), 1773–85
1L216	Levée des jeunes gens de la Première Réquisition
1L217	Guerre et affaires militaires – déserteurs
1L221	Hôpitaux militaires, 1793–an III
1L257	Hôpitaux, vendémiaire – prairial II
1L520	Industrie et travail, circulaires et correspondance générale, 1791–an VIII
1L522	Industries textiles
1L738	Volontaires, correspondance, 1791–3
1L739	Feuilles d'engagement, listes des volontaires, District de Lyon-ville
1L740	Listes des volontaires, District de Lyon-campagnes
1L743	Volontaires, déserteurs
1L768	Etat des dépenses relatives à la levée des réquisitionnaires

1L769	Exemptions de la réquisition
1L901	Hôpitaux militaires, instructions et circulaires, 1793–an V
1L903	Hôpitaux militaires, traitement des malades, 1791–an VIII
1L988	Siège de Lyon: pertes et suites du siège
1L989	Siège de Lyon: indemnités, déclarations des pertes, correspondance diverse, an II–an VII
1L990	Siège de Lyon: rôles de valuation des pertes
1L991	Indemnités arrêtées par la municipalité rebelle
1L1137	Hôpital Général de la Charité, rapport, 1790
1L1139	Enfants abandonnés, correspondance, 1790–93
1L1142	Hôtel-Dieu de Lyon, mémoires et rapports
1L1144	Hôtel-Dieu: gestion, demandes de secours, régie et vente des terrains aux Brotteaux
1L1145	Hôtel-Dieu de Lyon, comptabilité, 1790–an II
1L1146	Commission des Hospices de Lyon, an V–an VII
1L1150	Hospice Général des Malades de Lyon: gestion, demandes de secours
1L1162	Assistance aux aliénés: L'Hospice de Fontaines, 1790–an VIII
1L1163	Aveugles, an IV–an VII
1L1167	Hospice des Pauvres Passants à la Guillotière, 1791
1L1170	Ateliers de charité, 1790–an IV
1L1174	Bureau de Bienfaisance: distribution de pain aux indigents, an IV–an VIII
1L1176	Caisse des Indigents, gestion
1L1177	Salle des spectacles, perception d'un décime par franc sur les billets
1L1178	Grand Théâtre de Lyon, revenus des pauvres
1L1226	Dépôt de Mendicité de Lyon, personnel, an II–an VIII
1L1228	Dépôt de Mendicité, régime intérieur, an VI–an VII
1L1229	Dépôt de Mendicité, gestion, correspondance, 1790–an VII
1L1230	Dépôt de Mendicité, comptabilité, 1790–an III
2L96	Police générale, vols et brigandages, 1791–an III
2L130	District de Lyon-ville, hôpitaux militaires, 1792–an III
2L154	District de Lyon-ville, assistance publique, 1791–an III
31L23	Section de la Concorde, pièces annexes
31L96	Section de la Rue Juiverie, enregistrement des indemnités de pain, an II
31L160	Section de la Rue Thomassin, enregistrement des indemnités, an II
3L143	District de Lyon-campagnes, affaires militaires, 1792–an III
3L179	District de Lyon-campagnes, assistance publique, secours et récompenses, 1793–an III

Seine

VD*948	Section du Mail, registre de correspondance
VD*969	Section du Mail, journal du Comité Civil
VD*890	Section des Lombards, registre de correspondance
VD*982	Section des Piques, registre des enrôlements des conscrits, 1793
VD*1633	Section de la Rue Beaubourg, registre
VD*1661	Section du Temple, registre

VD*1662   Section du Temple, correspondance
VD*1715   Section des Tuileries, registre des enrôlements pour la levée des
                 300,000 hommes, 1793
4AZ269ter   Dons et acquisitions: Sections de Paris

Seine-Inférieure

C2111   Procès-verbal des séances de l'Assemblée Provinciale de la Généralité
                 de Rouen, 1787
C2121   Mémoires sur l'administration et la mendicité, 1786–9
C2173   Correspondance sur le commerce, le secours, les indemnités, le bien
                 public
C2284   Assistance publique, extinction de la mendicité, Intendance de
                 Rouen, 1723–86
L321   Police générale: mendicité, secours, passeports, 1790–93
L1365   Dépôt de Mendicité, affaires générales, 1790–an IV
L1366–1368   Dépôt de Mendicité, correspondance, 1790–an IV
L1369   Dépôt de Mendicité, registres, 1790–91
L1371   Dépôt de Mendicité, registres, an II
L1376   Dépôt de Mendicité, quatrième registre d'entrées et de sorties
L2620   District de Rouen, secours publics
L2622   Secours publics, mémoire concernant les pauvres des paroisses de la
                 ville de Rouen, 1790

Haute-Vienne

L316   Recrutement, déserteurs
L373   Assistance: Hôpital Général de Limoges
L375   Hôpital Militaire de Limoges
L377   Hôpital des Enfants Trouvés
L382   Dépôt de Mendicité de Limoges

2   ARCHIVES HOSPITALIÈRES

Archives de l'Assistance Publique à Paris

NS72   Documents sur les congrégations hospitalières

Archives de l'Hôtel-Dieu de Lyon

E.HD.18   Registre des extraits des délibérations du Bureau de l'Hôtel-Dieu,
                 1778–91
E.HD.1613   Hospitalisation des militaires, états et correspondance, 1790–1802
E.HD.1618   Hôtel-Dieu, administration, période révolutionnaire
E.HD.1694,
  1722, 1750,
  1777, 1805,   Recettes des droits d'entrées sur les vins, 1790
  1816, 1843,
  1870, 1894

| F.HD.227 | Hôtel-Dieu, registre des entrées, 1793 |
| G.HD.67 | Hôtel-Dieu, Journal d'envoi des enfants de l'hôpital, 1787–91 |

3   ARCHIVES MUNICIPALES (ARCH. MUN.)

Aurillac

| sans côte | Tableau des patriotes indigens, dressé conformément à la loi du 13 ventôse II |

Bazas

| BB2 | Registre des délibérations de l'Hôtel de Ville de Bazas, 1765–90 |

Bordeaux

H40	Hôpitaux militaires, congés, prisonniers
L66–68	Pièces comptables (Finances de la commune): secours aux indigents, 1793, et répartition des sommes entre les sections
Q1	Hospices de bienfaisance et des Incurables, 1790–an III
Q4, 5	Hospices de Sainte-Croix, des Incurables, et des Femmes Enceintes, an IV–an VIII
Q6	Hôpitaux et hospices, 1790–an III
Q7	Hôpitaux et hospices, an IV–an VIII
Q8	Hôpital Saint-André, 1789–an IV
Q10	Hôpital des Enfants Trouvés, 1789–an VII
Q14	Bureaux de charité des paroisses, 1791–an III
Q17	Ecole des Sourds et Muets, 1790–an VIII
Q18	Droit des pauvres, 1791–an VIII

Le Havre

F²7	Commerce et industrie, renseignements statistiques, 1793–an VI
F²8	Les ouvriers du Havre pendant la Révolution
F²9	Commerce avec les colonies
Q1	Bureau de Bienfaisance, administration
Q3	Demandes et obtention de secours
Q4	Bureau de Bienfaisance, comptabilité
Q9	Secours aux indigents, 1793–an IV
Q10	Secours aux indigents, an II–an VI
Q12	Ateliers de charité, 1789–91
Q15	Hôpital Général, administration, 1792–an VII
Q17	Hôpital Général, personnel congréganiste, 1792–an II
Q27	Hôpital Général, biens et revenus, 1790–an VII

Marseille

Q³1   Hôpitaux de Marseille, 1790–93
Q³2   Hôpitaux de Marseille, an II–an IV
Q³3   Hôpitaux de Marseille, an IV–an VI
Q³14   Hôtel-Dieu (Saint-Esprit), délibérations et correspondance,
               1792–an V
Q³17   Enfants abandonnés, 1792–1813

Saint-Etienne

3Q249   Assistance et prévoyance: hospices, budgets et comptes, an VIII–1895

Strasbourg

Division III,   Enfants trouvés de Strasbourg: admissions, 1790–96
  Archives
Hospitalières,
  liasse 78

Toulouse

3Q1   Hôtel-Dieu Saint-Jacques, 1790–an VIII
3Q2   Hôpitaux de Toulouse, an II–an VIII
3Q5   Hôpitaux de Toulouse, administration, an V: plaintes et dénonciations

4   ARCHIVES DE LA CHAMBRE DE COMMERCE DE LA ROCHELLE

Carton 1, dossier 15 Charité et secours, 1786–1790

5   ARCHIVES DE LA PRÉFECTURE DE POLICE DE PARIS

Aᴬ 59–62   Rapports des commissaires de police, Section des Arcis, 1793–an IV

6   ARCHIVES NATIONALES (A.N.)

Series F⁷ – Police Générale

F⁷3035   Mendicité et vagabondage

Series F⁹ – Affaires militaires

F⁹150–261   Recrutement général: correspondance par départements, 1791–1837
               (*for selected departments*)
F⁹286–7   Fraudes, an VI–1846
F⁹297–319   Désertion, 1792–1813, série départementale (*for selected departments*)

Series F^{15} – Hospices et secours

F^{15}101–4	Papiers provenant du Comité des Secours, 1777–an IX
F^{15}129–30	Hôpitaux, secours, mendicité, 1790–an XIII, série départementale
F^{15}138	Projets sur la mendicité et la bienfaisance, 1775–1808
F^{15}247	Département de Paris, arrêtés du Comité des Secours Publics, correspondance avec le maire de Paris, an III–an IV
F^{15}249–60	Hospices: administration, biens, secours, 1791–an IV (série départementale)
F^{15}261–76	Hospices: administration, biens, secours, enfants trouvés, 1790–an VII (série départementale)
F^{15}277–304	Hospices: administration, biens, secours, enfants trouvés, an IV–an V (série départementale)
F^{15}305–33	Hospices: administration, biens, secours, enfants trouvés, an VI (série départementale)
F^{15}334–70	Hospices: administration, biens, secours, enfants trouvés, an VII (série départementale)
F^{15}371–82	Hospices: administration, biens, secours, enfants trouvés, an VIII (série départementale)
F^{15}383–93	Hospices: administration, biens, secours, enfants trouvés, an IX (série départementale)
F^{15}429–35	Dépôts de mendicité, enfants trouvés, monts de piété, 1781–an XIII (série départementale)
F^{15}436	Revenus des hôpitaux avant la Révolution (série départementale)
F^{15}440	Dépenses des nourrices, orphelins et enfants trouvés, an IV–an VIII
F^{15}441	Secours publics: filles-mères et secours individuels, an III–an VIII
F^{15}444	Monts de piété, assistance, rapports et pétitions, an II–1822
F^{15}1861	Hôpitaux de Paris, rapports et correspondance sur la mendicité, 1760–an IV
F^{15}1862	Bienfaisance et mendicité, correspondance et pétitions aux ministères, 1791–an V
F^{15}1863	Bienfaisance et mendicité, correspondance, an V–1815
F^{15}2653	Comité des Secours Publics, arrêtés, an III–an IV
F^{15}2790	Dépôts de mendicité, 1780–an VIII
F^{15}2811	Police des moeurs et de la mendicité, 1785–an III
F^{15}2818	Secours publics: affaires concernant les militaires blessés
F^{15}2820	Commission des Secours Publics, pétitions et rapports, an III–an IV
F^{15}2868	Droit des pauvres, octroi de Paris, 1789–an VI
F^{15}2869	Secours aux familles des militaires et aux indigents, an III–an IV
F^{15}3336	Commission des Secours Publics, correspondance et pétitions, an II–an IV
F^{15}3567	Filature des Recollets, rapports, états, correspondance, 1790–an II
F^{15}3575	Filature des Jacobins de Paris, rapports, états, correspondance, 1790–an II
F^{15}3576	Manufacture Sainte-Geneviève, rapports, correspondance
F^{15}3578	Ateliers de filature, correspondance, 1790–an II

Series F^{16} – Prisons

F^{16}936	Mémoires sur la mendicité, 1789–91
F^{16}937	Mémoires sur la mendicité, 1791–1810
F^{16}966–968	Tableaux de population et de mendicité, série départementale, 1790–an IV

Series AJ^2 – Fonds Privés: Maison Nationale des Aliénés à Charenton

AJ^{2}59	Rapports, 1791
AJ^{2}60	Actes constitutifs
AJ^{2}87	Administration

Series BB^{18} – Correspondance générale de la Division Criminelle

BB^{18}1	Délits relatifs à la conscription – Ain
BB^{18}26	Délits relatifs à la conscription – Haute-Garonne
BB^{18}42	Délits relatifs à la conscription – Lozère
BB^{18}53	Délits relatifs à la conscription – Nord

Series D^{xxvii} – Comité des Secours

There is only one *carton* in this series, of correspondence.

7 BIBLIOTHÈQUE NATIONALE (B.N.)

Series N.A.F. (Nouvelles Acquisitions Françaises)

N.A.F. 2654	Section du Mont-Blanc, travaux publics

B Printed Sources

1 ARCHIVES NATIONALES (A.N.)

Series AD – Imprimés

AD.I^{88}	Imprimés sur le vagabondage et la mendicité
AD.VI^{63}	Imprimés sur les hôpitaux militaires
AD.XIV^6	Bienfaisance et assistance
AD.XIV^7	Hôpitaux civils, 1789–1815
AD.XIV^8	Hôpitaux civils, 1789–1815: série locale et départementale
AD.XIV^9	Mendicité et mendiants, nourrices, monts de piété, 1789–1815
AD.XIV^{10}	Secours publics en général, 1789–1815
AD.XIV^{11}	Secours et indemnités, 1789–1815
AD.XIV^{12}	Appendice: sociétés de charité

2   OTHER PRINTED SOURCES

Le Moniteur.

Ballainvilliers, Bernard de, *Mémoire sur le Languedoc – hôpitaux* (Montpellier, 1788).

Bloch, C. and Tuetey, A. (editors), *Procès-verbaux et rapports du Comité de Mendicité de la Constituante* (Paris, 1911).

DuPont de Nemours, P. S., *Idées sur les secours à donner aux pauvres malades dans une grande ville* (Paris, 1786).

Gorjy, J.-C., *Mémoire sur les dépôts de mendicité* (Paris, 1789).

Le Trosne, G., *Mémoire sur les vagabonds et sur les mendiants* (Paris, 1764).

Markov, W. and Soboul, A. (editors), *Die Sansculotten von Paris* (East Berlin, 1957).

Montlinot, M., *Discours sur . . . quels sont les moyens de détruire la mendicité dans la ville de Soissons* (Lille, 1779).

Montlinot, M., *Etat actuel du dépôt de Soissons* (Soissons, 1789).

Montlinot, M., *Observations sur les enfants trouvés de la généralité de Soissons* (Paris, 1790).

Necker, J., *De l'administration des finances de la France* (Paris, 1784).

Smith, J. P. de, *Des ateliers de secours établis à Paris et aux environs* (Paris, 1791)

Tenon, J., *Mémoires sur les hôpitaux de Paris* (Paris, 1788).

Tenon, J., *Réflexions en faveur des pauvres citoyens malades* (Paris, 1791).

Tuetey, A. (editor), *L'assistance publique à Paris pendant la Révolution*, 4 vols, especially III, *Les hôpitaux et hospices, 1791–an IV* (Paris, 1897).

Watteville, A. de, *Législation charitable de 1790 à 1863*, 3 volumes (Paris, 1863).

Young, A., *Travels in France* (Cambridge, 1929).

SECONDARY SOURCES

For reasons of space I have deliberately confined this bibliography to major works on the subject and local studies of eighteenth-century poverty and the Revolutionary response to it. Books and articles to which reference is made in footnotes are listed. I have used one abbreviation, *AHRF* for *Annales Historiques de la Révolution Française*. For a more comprehensive bibliography of the pre-Revolutionary period, see the secondary works cited in Olwen Hufton's *The poor of eighteenth-century France.*

Accarias, L., *L'assistance publique sous la Révolution dans le département du Puy-de-Dôme* (Savenay, 1933).

Adams, T. M., *An approach to the problem of beggary in eighteenth-century France – the dépôts de mendicité* (unpublished Ph.D thesis, University of Michigan, Ann Arbor, 1972).

Adams, T. M., 'Moeurs et hygiène publique au dix-huitième siècle: quelques aspects des dépôts de mendicité', *Annales de la Démographie Historique* (1975).

Adher, J., *Recueil de documents sur l'assistance publique dans le District de Toulouse de 1789 à 1800* (Toulouse, 1918).

Barrière, P., 'Les Académies et la vie intellectuelle dans la société méridionale au dix-huitième siècle', *Annales du Midi 62* (1950).

Bellande, B., *L'ancien Hôpital Général d'Issoire* (Clermont-Ferrand, 1961).

Bertaud, J.-P., *La Révolution armée: les soldats-citoyens et la Révolution Française* (Paris, 1979).

Bertaud, J.-P., *Valmy – la démocratie en armes* (Paris, 1970).

Bertaud, J.-P., 'Voies nouvelles pour l'histoire de la Révolution Française – histoire militaire', *AHRF* 219 (1975).

Bézard, Y., *L'assistance à Versailles sous l'Ancien Régime et pendant la Révolution* (Versailles, 1924).

Bien, D., 'The army in the French Enlightenment', *Past and Present* 85 (1979).

Bloch, C., *L'assistance et l'Etat en France à la veille de la Révolution* (Paris, 1908).

Bloch, C., *Inventaire sommaire des volumes de la collection Joly de Fleury concernant l'assistance et la mendicité* (Paris, 1908).

Bois, P., *Les paysans de l'ouest* (Paris, 1962).

Bolotte, M., *Les hôpitaux et l'assistance dans la province de Bourgogne au dernier siècle de l'Ancien Régime* (Dijon, 1968).

Bouchard, G., *Le village immobile: Sennely-en-Sologne au dix-huitième siècle* (Paris, 1972).

Bouchet, M., *L'assistance publique en France pendant la Révolution* (Paris, 1908).

Boussoulade, J., *Moniales et hospitalières dans la tourmente révolutionnaire* (Paris, 1962).

Buchalet, F., *L'assistance publique à Toulouse au dix-huitième siècle* (Toulouse, 1904).

Cameron, I., 'The police of eighteenth-century France', *European Studies Review* (1977).

Cardénal, L. de, *Recrutement de l'armée en Périgord pendant la période révolutionnaire, 1789–1800* (Périgueux, 1911).

Chaulanges, M., *Les mauvais numéros* (Paris, 1971).

Castan, Y., *Honnêteté et relations sociales en Languedoc, 1715–1780* (Paris, 1974).

Chotard, H., 'L'assistance publique en Auvergne au dix-huitième siècle', *Revue d'Auvergne* (1896–9).

Cobb, R. C., *Death in Paris, 1795–1801* (Oxford, 1978).

Cobb, R. C., *Paris and its provinces, 1792–1802* (Oxford, 1975).

Cobb, R. C., *The police and the people: French popular protest, 1789–1820* (Oxford, 1970).

Cobb, R. C., *Reactions to the French Revolution* (Oxford, 1972).

Cobb, R. C., *A second identity: essays on France and French history* (Oxford, 1969).

Cobb, R. C., *A sense of place* (London, 1975).

Cobb, R. C., *Terreur et subsistances, 1793–1795* (Paris, 1965).

Cochin, A. and Boüard, M., *Précis des principales opérations du gouvernement révolutionnaire* (Paris, 1936).

Coiffier, J., *L'assistance publique dans la généralité de Riom au dix-huitième siècle* (Clermont-Ferrand, 1905).

Corvisier, A., *L'armée française de la fin du XVIIe. siècle au ministère de Choiseul*, 2 vols (Paris, 1964).

Crépillon, P., 'Un *gibier des prévôts*: mendiants et vagabonds au dix-huitième siècle entre la Vire et la Dives', *Annales de Normandie* 17 (1967).

Cros-Mayrevieille, G., *L'assistance publique et privée en Languedoc* (Montpellier, 1914).

Delaspre, S., 'L'émigration temporaire en Basse-Auvergne au dix-huitième siècle jusqu'à la veille de la Révolution', *Revue d'Auvergne* 68 (1954).

Deprez, E., *Les volontaires nationaux, 1791–1793* (Paris, 1906).

Desgranges, H., *Hospitaliers d'autrefois: l'Hôpital Général de Paris, 1656–1790* (Paris, 1952).

Dreyfus, F., *L'assistance sous la Législative et la Convention, 1791–1795* (Paris, 1905).

Dreyfus, F., *La Rochefoucauld-Liancourt, un philanthrope d'autrefois* (Paris, 1903).

Dreyfus, F., 'Note sur les ateliers charitables de filature, de 1789 à 1795', *Revue philanthropique* (1904).

Fairchilds, C. C., *Poverty and charity in Aix-en-Provence, 1640–1789* (Baltimore, 1976).

Forrest, A., 'The condition of the poor in Revolutionary Bordeaux', *Past and Present* 59 (1973).

Forrest, A., 'La Révolution et les hôpitaux dans le département de la Gironde', *Annales du Midi* 86 (1974).

Forrest, A., *Society and politics in Revolutionary Bordeaux* (Oxford, 1975).

Fortin, M., *La charité et l'assistance publique à Montbéliard sous l'Ancien Régime* (Besançon, 1933).

Fosseyeux, M., 'Les comités de bienfaisance de Paris sous la Révolution', *Annales révolutionnaires* 5 (1912).

Foucault, M., *The birth of the clinic* (London, 1973).

Foucault, M., *Discipline and punish: the birth of the prison* (London, 1977).

Furet, F., 'Pour une définition des classes inférieures à l'époque moderne', *Annales* (1963).

Gallaher, J. G., 'Recruitment in the District of Poitiers, 1793', *French Historical Studies* 3 (1963–4).

Garden, M., *Lyon et les Lyonnais au dix-huitième siècle* (Paris, 1970).

Gégot, J.-C., 'Etude par sondage de la criminalité dans le bailliage de Falaise', *Annales de Normandie* 16 (1966).

Giraud, M., *Levées d'hommes et acheteurs de biens nationaux dans la Sarthe en 1793* (Le Mans, 1920).

Glover, M., *Collection complète des jugements rendus par la Commission Révolutionnaire établie à Lyon par les représentants-du-peuple en 1793–1794* (Lyon, 1869).

Gontard, M., *L'enseignement primaire en France de la Révolution à la Loi Guizot, 1789–1833* (Lyon, 1959).

Goubert, P., and Denis, M. (editors), *1789: les Français ont la parole* (Paris, 1964).

Grange, H., *Les idées de Necker* (Paris, 1974).

Greer, D., *The incidence of the Terror during the French Revolution* (Cambridge, Mass., 1935).

Gutton, J.-P., *L'Etat et la mendicité dans la première moitié du dix-huitième siècle (Auvergne, Beaujolais, Forez, Lyonnais)* (Lyon, 1973).

Gutton, J.-P., 'Les mendiants dans la société parisienne au début du dix-huitième siècle', *Cahiers d'histoire* 13 (1968).

Gutton, J.-P., *La société et les pauvres: l'exemple de la généralité de Lyon, 1534–1789* (Paris, 1970).

Higgs, D., 'Le Dépôt de Mendicité de Toulouse, 1811–1818', *Annales du Midi* 86 (1974).

Higonnet, P., *Pont-de-Montvert: social structure and politics in a French village, 1700–1914* (Cambridge, Mass., 1971).

Hufton, O., *Bayeux in the late eighteenth century: a social study* (London, 1967).

Hufton, O., 'Begging, vagrancy, vagabondage and the law: an aspect of the problem of poverty in eighteenth-century France', *European Studies Review* (1972).

Hufton, O., 'The life of the very poor in the eighteenth century', in Cobban, A. (editor), *The eighteenth century* (London, 1969).

Hufton, O., *The poor of eighteenth-century France, 1750–1789* (Oxford, 1974).

Hufton, O., 'Women in Revolution, 1789–1796', *Past and Present* 53 (1971).

Imbert, J., *Le droit hospitalier de la Révolution et de l'Empire* (Paris, 1954).

Imbert, J., *Les hôpitaux en France* (Paris, 1966).

Jeorger, M., 'La structure hospitalière de la France sous l'Ancien Régime', *Annales* (1977).

Jones, C., 'The Bon Pasteur and the repression of prostitution in Montpellier, 1691–1793', *History Workshop* (1979).

Jones, C., *Poverty, vagrancy and society in the Montpellier region, 1740–1815* (unpublished Oxford D Phil thesis, 1978).

Jones, C., *Social aspects of the treatment of madness in the Paris region, 1789–1800* (unpublished Oxford BA thesis, 1972).

Jones, C., 'The welfare of the French foot-soldier from Richelieu to Napoleon', *History* 65 (1980).

Kaplow, J., *Elbeuf during the Revolutionary period* (Baltimore, 1964).

Kaplow, J., *The names of Kings: the Parisian labouring poor in the eighteenth century* (New York, 1972).

Kaplow, J., 'Sur la population flottante de Paris à la fin de l'Ancien Régime', *AHRF* (1967).

Labrousse, E., *La crise de l'économie française à la fin de l'Ancien Régime et au début de la Révolution* (Paris, 1944).

Labrousse, E., *Esquisse du mouvement des prix et des revenus en France au dix-huitième siècle* (Paris, 1933).

Lallemand, L., *Histoire des enfants abandonnés et délaissés* (Paris, 1885).

Lallemand, L., *La Révolution et les pauvres* (Paris, 1898).

Lebrun, F., *Les hommes et la mort en Anjou aux dix-septième et dix-huitième siècles* (Paris, 1971).

Lefebvre, G., *La Grande Peur* (Paris, 1932).

Lefebvre, G., *Les paysans du Nord pendant la Révolution Française* (Lille, 1924).

Legrand, R., *Le recrutement des armées et les désertions, 1791–1815* (Abbéville, 1957).

Le Roux, C., *Le vagabondage et la mendicité à Paris et dans le département de la Seine* (Paris, 1907).

Lewis, G., *Life in Revolutionary France* (London, 1972).

Loupès, P., 'L'assistance paroissiale aux pauvres malades dans le diocèse de Bordeaux au dix-huitième siècle', *Annales du Midi* 84 (1972).

Loupès, P., 'Le clergé paroissial du diocèse de Bordeaux d'après la grande enquête de 1772', *Annales du Midi* 83 (1971).

Loupès, P., 'L'Hôpital Saint-André de Bordeaux au dix-huitième siècle', *Revue historique de Bordeaux et de la Gironde* (1972).

Lucas, C., *The structure of the Terror: the example of Javogues and the Loire* (Oxford, 1973).

MacAuliffe, L., *La Révolution et les hôpitaux de Paris* (Paris, 1901).

McCloy, S. T., *Government assistance in eighteenth-century France* (Durham, North Carolina, 1946).

McCloy, S. T., *The humanitarian movement in eighteenth-century France* (Kentucky, 1957).

McManners, J., *French ecclesiastical society under the Ancien Régime: a study of Angers in the eighteenth century* (Manchester, 1960).

McManners, J., *The French Revolution and the Church* (London, 1969).

Marion, M., *La vente des biens nationaux pendant la Révolution* (Paris, 1908).

Massé, P., 'Disette et mendicité en Poitou (18e–19e siècles)', *L'Actualité de l'Histoire* 27 (1959).

Mathiez, A., 'Notes sur l'importance du prolétariat en France à la veille de la Révolution', *AHRF* (1930).

Mathiez, A., *La vie chère et le mouvement social sous la Terreur*, 2 vols (Paris, 1973).

Mège, F., 'Notes et documents concernant l'histoire d'Auvergne: la Grande Peur', *Bulletin historique et scientifique de l'Auvergne* (1900).

Merle, L., *L'Hôpital du Saint-Esprit de Niort, 1665–1790* (Fontenay-le-Comte, 1966).

Mourlot, F., 'La question de la mendicité à la fin de l'Ancien Régime', *Bulletin historique et philologique* (1902).

Parturier, L., *L'assistance à Paris sous l'Ancien Régime et pendant la Révolution* (Paris, 1897).

Paultre, C., *De la répression de la mendicité et du vagabondage en France sous l'Ancien Régime* (Paris, 1906).

Poitrineau, A., 'Aspects de l'émigration temporaire et saisonnière en Auvergne à la fin du dix-huitième et au début du dix-neuvième siècle', *Revue d'histoire moderne et contemporaine* 9 (1962).

Poitrineau, A., *La vie rurale en Basse-Auvergne au dix-huitième siècle*, 2 vols (Aurillac, 1965).

Prentout, H., 'Les tableaux de 1790 en réponse à l'enquête du Comité de Mendicité', *Révolution Française* (1907).

Quétin, M., 'L'hôpital d'Aurillac de 1649 à la Révolution', *Revue de la Haute-Auvergne* 39 (1964–5).

Saint-Jacob, P. de, *Les paysans de la Bourgogne du Nord au dernier siècle de l'Ancien Régime* (Dijon, 1960).

Sangnier, G., *La désertion dans le Pas-de-Calais de 1792 à 1802* (Blangermont, 1965).

Santi, L. de., Un épisode de l'histoire des maladies vénériennes au dix-huitième siècle', *Annales de dermatologie et de syphiligraphie* (1910).

Schnapper, B., *Le remplacement militaire en France: quelques aspects politiques, économiques, et sociaux du recrutement au dix-neuvième siècle* (Paris, 1968).

Scott, S., 'The regeneration of the line army during the French Revolution', *Journal of Modern History* (1970).

Scott, S., *The response of the royal army to the French Revolution* (Oxford, 1978).

Scott, S., 'Les soldats de l'armée de ligne en 1793', *AHRF* (1972).

Sée, H., 'Les conceptions économiques et sociales du Comité de Mendicité de la Constituante', *AHRF* (1926).

Sée, H., 'Statistique des pauvres de Rennes vers la fin de l'Ancien Régime, d'après les rôles de la capitation', *Annales de Bretagne* 41 (1934).

Sheppard, T. F., *Lourmarin in the eighteenth century: a study of a French village* (Baltimore, 1971).

Soboul. A., *L'armée nationale sous la Révolution (1789–1794)* (Paris, 1945).

Soboul, A., *Problèmes paysans de la Révolution Française* (Paris, 1976).

Soboul, A., *Les soldats de l'an II* (Paris, 1959).

Sol, E., 'Les bureaux de charité en Quercy à la fin de l'Ancien Régime', *Annales du Midi* 60 (1948).

Sussman, G. D., *Three histories of infant nursing in eighteenth-century France* (text of an unpublished paper read to the Fourth Berkshire Conference on the History of Women at Mount Holyoke College, 1978).

Sussman, G. D., *Wetnursing in the eighteenth century* (text of unpubished paper kindly lent by the author).

Tackett, T., *Priest and parish in eighteenth-century France* (Princeton, 1977).

Vallée, G., *La conscription dans le département de la Charente, 1798–1807* (Paris, 1936).

Vidalenc, J., *Le peuple des campagnes* (Paris, 1970).

Vovelle, M., 'De la mendicité au brigandage: les errants en Beauce sous la Révolution Française', 86th *Congrès National des Sociétés Savantes* (1962).

Vovelle, M., *Piété baroque et déchristianisation en Provence au dix-huitième siècle* (Paris, 1973).

Vovelle, M., 'Le prolétariat flottant à Marseille sous la Révolution', *Annales de la démographie historique* (1968).

Vovelle, M., *Religion et Révolution: la déchristianisation de l'an II* (Paris, 1976).

Weber, E., *Peasants into Frenchmen: the modernization of rural France* (London, 1977).

Woloch, I., *The French veteran from the Revolution to the Restoration* (Chapel Hill, 1979).

Zeldin, T., *France, 1848–1945*, 2 vols (Oxford, 1973, 1977).

Place Index

Names of departments appears in small capitals

Name and Subject Index